THE FOUR-LETTER COUNTRIES

THE ZANY ADVENTURES OF THE ALPHABET TRAVELLER

DAVID JENKINS

www.knowthescorebooks.com

KNOW THE SCORE BOOKS TRAVEL PUBLICATIONS

TITLE	Author	ISBN
DOING THE WAINWRIGHTS: 214 Fells, Four Seasons And A Caravan		
	Steve Larkin	978-1-905449-34-7

THE FOUR-LETTER COUNTRIES: The Zany Adventures Of The Alphabet Traveller
David Jenkins   978-1-905449-99-6

NEW BOOTS IN NEW ZEALAND:
Nine Great Waks, Three Islands And One Tramping Virgin
GIllian Orrell   1-905449-40-8

FORTHCOMING PUBLICATIONS

CULT HEROES	Author	ISBN
BLIND DAVE TAKES ON THE WORLD		
	David Heeley	978-1-984818-800-6

CHASING THE EIGHTIES: The Ultimate North American Roadtrip
Spencer Austin   978-1-984818-951-5

THE FROZEN DEAD GUY: And Other Interesting Americans
Amanda Jane Green   978-1-984818-950-8

THIS IS THE WAY TO AMARILLO: A Musical Odyssey Across The USA
George Miller   978-1-905449-98-9

THE
FOUR-LETTER
COUNTRIES

THE ZANY ADVENTURES
OF THE
ALPHABET TRAVELLER

DAVID JENKINS

www.knowthescorebooks.com

First published in the United Kingdom
by Know The Score Books Limited, 2008
Copyright David Jenkins, 2008

Know The Score Books Limited
118 Alcester Road, Studley, Warwickshire, B80 7NT
Tel: 01527 454482   Fax: 01527 452183
info@knowthescorebooks.com
www.knowthescorebooks.com

A CIP catalogue record is available for this book from the British Library
ISBN: 978-1-905449-99-6

Printed and bound in Great Britain
By Cromwell Press, Trowbridge, Wiltshire

Jacket design by Ellen McIntosh
Book design by Simon Lowe

Mixed Sources
Product group from well-managed
forests and other controlled sources
www.fsc.org Cert no. TT-COC-2082
© 1996 Forest Stewardship Council
FSC

Acknowledgements

Special thanks ...to the team in St Albans for all that hard work behind the scenes, the smiles and the cups of coffee, and for teaching me how to switch on the computer ...to the Jenkins family for the love, support, go-for-it spirit and wacky sense of humour that keeps us all so close together ...to Lizzie for her kindness, wisdom and unforgettable spaghetti bolognese, ...to Monique and the girls in Sydney for their wonderful and generous hospitality and ...to Katharine, a special lady whose contribution has been more than she will ever know.

And finally, to all the wonderful people I've met out there 'on the road'. Your faces, laughter, fun and friendship will be remembered long after the rest has been forgotten.

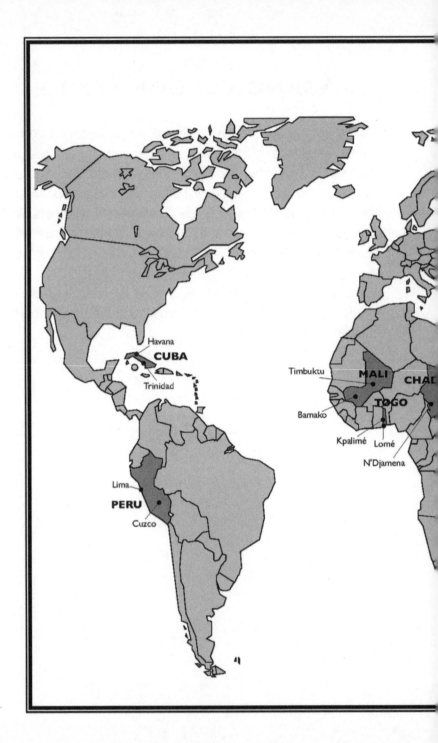

The FLC World

Tehran
Sulaimaniya
Erbil
IRAQ
IRAN
Shiraz
OMAN
Muscat
Khasab
LAOS
Luang Prabang
Vientiane
Abéché
FIJI
Nadi
Suva

Contents

In memory of my Dad, Ken Jenkins.

*Thank you for filling my life with
opportunities and for the belief that
most things are achievable.*

Introduction

It was 2.46 am; not a good time to be lying awake. Four hours of wriggling and kicking and filling my head with nonsense was taking its toll and the red digits glowing in the darkness only served to make things worse. I vowed not to look at the clock again and, to prove I meant business, curled myself up as small as possible, faced the opposite way and, as a final act of defiance, draped a sheet loosely over my head. All efforts were once again focused on an empty landscape. This time I was going to sleep.

"But before you do, Jenks. Just answer this." A mocking sort of whisper from an unknown voice.

"How many countries have only four letters in their name?"

"What?"

"You heard – not territories or regions or principalities. Just countries."

"Sod off and leave me in peace. I need to go to sleep."

"Come on … counting countries is just like counting sheep. Then, when you've got them all, you can sleep like a baby."

The bastard! Where he came from and why will always remain a mystery to me, but the voice knew I just wouldn't be able to resist the challenge there and then.

If this was going to be tackled, and clearly it was, it needed to be done quickly and methodically. I began to unfurl a world map in my head (was I really doing this in the dead of night?), picking out countries from South America on the left, scanning my way right over via Africa and Europe to Asia and finally island-hopping across the Pacific to the International Date Line. It took me a little while and I guessed it was now

The Four-Letter Countries

well after 3am. I had counted nine. The mystery voice didn't need to speak again. He already knew I would have to check it out.

The lights went on and I scurried across the landing to the front bedroom and the Collins World Atlas. Huddled over my desk, very cold and very naked, I did at least manage the consolation of a wry smile at the absurdity of this little game. Would a neighbour on a conventional pee-run spot the pathetic unclothed figure shivering under his lamp? No matter. Concentration at this stage was absolutely critical. I ran my finger through the list twice, I had to be sure, and in fact ... there were ten. Ten four-letter countries. Who the hell even thinks about Oman in the middle of a cold winter's night?

I jumped back into bed, my mind now well and truly up and running. What a fascinating collection of countries, tantalisingly spread across the Americas, Middle East, Africa, South East Asia and a Pacific archipelago to boot. Some tiny, some very large. Seven coastal and three landlocked, eight north of the equator, two south. Mountains, jungles, oceans, deserts. A breathtaking mix of languages and religions, cultures and customs. Oh my goodness, would I sleep at all tonight?

I wondered how many of the world's seven and a half billion people had actually been to all these countries and decided that the answer was not very many. A bit of a vague answer, I grant you, but probably the closest I would ever get. I looked at the clock, (yes, I cheated), it was past 3.30am. The mystery voice had slipped away, but a satisfying calm had taken its place. Somebody had to tackle this one. The seed had been well and truly planted.

OMAN

"The flying time to Muscat will be approximately 35 minutes." It was the lipsticked lady, the one that had attracted a better-than-usual audience for the safety demo.

Is that all? It was a relief to be sitting on the plane and a half-hour flight seemed scant reward for the two hours of escalators and security checks at Dubai's enormous space age airport. So the project was finally under way and how appropriate that the Sultanate of Oman, the very country that had eluded me a few months earlier in those hours of insomnia, would be the first port of call on the journey to the Four-Letter Countries (FLCs).

The aircraft was almost full, something I hadn't really expected. Why on earth would anybody go to Oman? It struck me as unlikely that other passengers would be in search of countries with small names, but I glanced around the cabin anyway, turning quickly to catch any shifty-looking characters taking notes. They all seemed innocent enough, reading papers and sipping orange juices, but I couldn't help wonder at the chances of recognising one of these faces in a canoe in Fiji or a jungle in a remote part of Togo further along my journey.

I was on my way and for the first time really analysing what a ludicrous caper this was. Although I'd done my best not to show it, the negative vibes from the boys back home had made something of an impact and my thoughts drifted back to the day I asked if any of them wanted to join me.

"Where?"

"Oman."

The Four-Letter Countries

"Is that one of those countries where there's no booze?"

"Yep."

"And you can't touch the women?"

"That's right."

"Not even at Christmas parties?"

"It's a Muslim country. They don't celebrate Christmas, their holy month is Ramadan. During Ramadan they don't eat, smoke, have sex or even drink water during daylight hours."

I half took the silence which greeted this information to be one of admiration for such abstinence in the pursuit of true faith.

"So – who's up for it?" I ventured.

"It sounds great fun but unfortunately I can't make it", came the most polite answer, a mock serious face soon giving way to an inane grin. Followed up by the more traditional, no-nonsense and totally expected response: "Piss Off Jenkins."

* * * * *

Oman is not a country I'd ever imagined myself going to. It's four-lettered-ness had, in truth, been its single attraction, but surely there had to be more to the Middle East than car bombs and hostages in orange overalls? Nice things? I'd thought about that long and hard, but really only managed to come up with houmous from Waitrose, served on pitta bread gently warmed in the toaster. At least it was a start.

The "Middle East", a confusing term, isn't it? Have you ever asked yourself where The East actually is? How it can possibly have a middle? What is it east of anyway? (Or don't you ask yourself questions like that for fear that people might think you're a bit nerdy?) Anyway, let me tell you about the Arabian Peninsula, a chunk of land that dangles down parallel to the top right hand corner of Africa. Have a look at it if you get the chance and you'll see that it's shaped like a wellington boot with the toe pointing to the right and raised off the ground. Most of the vertical part

Oman

is Saudi Arabia and then two countries take an almost equal share along the sole. The bit towards the heel is Yemen and the section that goes up to the toes is the Sultanate of Oman. All of which might sound a bit dull but as the story unfolds you will see that Oman's location is, or at least was, of considerable significance. But don't worry, I won't go into that just now …

* * * * *

The sky was completely clear, a perfect view of my first ever Sultanate four miles below except for the scratched window and the thoughtless positioning of a wing. Not the bare, red Aussie-outback landscape I'd imagined, but rugged grey mountains, a sheer, harsh expanse of rock, like lumps of coal with shiny chiselled edges. Only when we approached Muscat did the picture soften, the pink of the desert adding in another colour and that in turn broken by the occasional rectangles of cultivated fields; green postage stamps stuck randomly on a huge manila envelope.

The landing card offered all the usual questions, but written right to left, Arabic-style, across the page. All straightforward enough (well, straightbackward enough), but then came Purpose of Visit and that horrid flood of self-consciousness. Was I really to call this a holiday? Like it or not I was there, adrift in a sea of glistening polished marble, lining up in the Arrivals Hall, then face to face with an immigration officer and a rather unexpected beaming smile. His first day at the job perhaps, or was there something going on in that cubicle? He smiled throughout and the visa was issued quickly in an atmosphere of friendly silence, the rubber stamp thrice brought into play and my passport returned with a welcoming nod. There was no going back. This was it. FLC number 1. Towards the opaque sliding door, no idea what to expect beyond it, and yes, I did glance ever so quickly under his chair on my way past.

The airport is located on the road between Muscat, on the coast, and Nizwa, some hundred miles inland. My plan was to visit both at some stage and, depending on transport options from the airport, I figured heading straight off to Nizwa might not be a bad idea. Unfortunately the Tourist Information desk I'd counted on didn't exist (would an independent tourist come to Oman?), so I mingled with the mass of white-robed people in the busy terminal building and tried to work out what to do next.

The gentleman at the taxi desk suggested very confidently that bus timetable enquiries would be handled at the Avis counter and he could obviously tell from my face that I didn't believe a word of it. So he repeated his instructions, this time with even more conviction. He clearly knew something I didn't. It was – after all – my first time in his country, so off I went obediently in search of the familiar bright red booth. Wouldn't I feel a plonker asking the uniformed person with the We Try Harder badge when the next bus was due? My thoughts were cut short, it mattered not. The booth was empty, not a soul was there in sight, not even the consolation of a sign saying: "Actually, We Can't Be Arsed."

The spotless taxi zoomed along the spotless highway and dropped me onto a spotless pavement in a part of Muscat known as Ruwi. When the car pulled away, I stood there on the kerb for quite a few minutes, just looking around and admiring the neat lawns, fountains, and colourful flowers that seemed to be everywhere. It was midday, the sun was bright and warm and probably the reason there were hardly any people at all on the streets. It was all so calm, very calm, a sort of fairytale-like town, quite surreal. It felt so utterly peaceful, unthreatening, entirely harmless. I could even start to feel a grin coming on.

This was obviously the business part of town, though low-key to say the least. The first thing I spotted was a tour operator's office of sorts, so I decided to pop in for a chat to see what local information was available. And what a very friendly man he was. He explained at length the expeditions he ran all over the country and how I would be welcome and it was good I could understand German because he had German-speaking guides and they were cheaper than English speaking ones. (What would The Master Race make of that? I thought with a smile). We looked at the itineraries, talked more about prices and covered a substantial amount of detail in a short space of time. He worked hard to convince me and I have to admit some of the trips were really tempting. I moved the conversation along to booking, deposits, departure dates and that was the point at which he suddenly became very quiet. And then he broke the news that nothing would actually be happening for at least the next six weeks.

Until that moment I hadn't thought about Monty Python's cheese shop sketch for years. To be fair, the guy was far too nice to shoot, and anyway I was unarmed at the time, so I accepted his guidance on the best part of town to stay and with a shake of the hand bade him good day.

Back on the squeaky clean streets, the only action came from the orange and white taxis, drivers tapping on their horns to attract customers, so I headed to the old harbour area of Murtah for an agreed price of 1 Riyal. This seemed fair enough, (or should I say fare enough?) even though it hadn't really sunk in that this is one of the few currencies in the world that is stronger than sterling; a pound actually buys you three quarters of a Riyal, or 750 Baisa. Yes, believe it or not, the currency is divided into units of 1,000. Wacky, but perhaps not so wacky as the country I grew up in where a pound was divided into two hundred and forty pennies, written with a letter d. Remember those days we used to get four blackjacks from the penny tray – so how many blackjacks could you get for a Baisa? I think we're digressing.

I found a nice little hotel, dumped my bag and headed back onto the streets in search of some lunch. Here I was, a foreigner in Oman, the only person not wearing a white ankle-length shirt and a small brimless hat. It all felt very strange, though not in any way intimidating. It was easy and comfortable to wander around. The men were mostly sitting in groups taking shade under trees, or quietly drinking tea in front of their market stalls, occasionally smiling or nodding politely at the white-legged alien. The womenfolk, I soon realised, were nowhere to be seen.

The Four-Letter Countries

The only lunch option that presented itself was a crumbling building with the word 'restaurant' on the wall and a few tatty tables and chairs scattered outside that could have been left there for the binmen to take away. Not exactly Egon Ronay, but this was the start of a mighty four letter adventure and not the time to behave like a wimp.

"Hello Sir," said a man emerging from the doorway.

"Anything to … er … eat?" was the best I could come up with.

"Chicken Massala." The intonation didn't really tell me whether this was a statement or a question, whether this was the Special of the Day or – more likely – the only dish available. Ever.

"Er … yes that'll be great."

I pulled up a chair and surveyed the scruffy expanse of wasteland, a far cry from the polished marble and flowers of a few hours earlier. Dusty streets, thousands of men dressed in cool white outfits, the ubiquitous embroidered little hats or the occasional loosely-worn turban. Donkeys would not have looked out of place. But black wires dangling from the ears? Yes, almost everybody had at least one. What was all that about? Was this another quaint facet of Omani culture? It puzzled me for quite some time until I heard the cringe-making tune that answered the question. It was, of course, the Nokia mobile.

Within a minute of my sitting down, a bowl of brown liquid, with an island of bones in the middle, appeared before me and a plateful of hot freshly-baked chapatis duly deposited alongside. I stared down at the dark soupy stuff for just a few seconds, wondered rather crudely how long my body would succeed in holding on to it, and then tucked in. It was really quite tasty. The stack of chapatis disappeared with a lot of liquid still remaining, but seconds later a fresh supply arrived over my right shoulder. Then the liquid exhausted before the bread and before I could object over came the waiter again, this time with another cupful of hot curry soup. How would I break the cycle – would I have to keep going until chapatis and curry expired simultaneously? The only answer was to simply stop eating and, as no sweet trolley emerged from the kitchen, I paid my 600 Baisa and got back on to the street. The occasional bus-load of tourists went by, Germans, I presumed, with their cut-price guide, but yours truly seemed to be the only independent traveller in town. It was now getting really sticky and I envied the men their loose-fitting white costumes – known, believe it or not, as dishdashas. They really did look so cool and comfortable in the heat of the day. Have you ever been to a country where almost everybody wears the same clothes, a uniform that eradicates all form of class distinction? It's impossible to start to guess what anybody does for a living. And how do they cope with, say, a robbery or a murder enquiry? "The police are looking for a man with black hair and a black moustache wearing a white smock and a small hat. So far two million people have been questioned ..."

* * * * *

I sat on the harbour wall and looked around in all directions, still feeling that this was somehow part of an elaborate dream. I'd had absolutely no idea what to expect of Muscat, or Oman in general for that matter, but most certainly it was not this. Craning my neck and squinting into the bright sunlight, I followed the dramatic silhouette of the jagged mountains on three sides of the city, then back down towards sea level and the cream-coloured rectangular buildings pushing right up to the shores of the Indian Ocean. Deep blue skies, grey mountains and cream buildings, three colours as distinct and contrasting as a traffic light. The only break in the pattern of shape and colour came in the form of the towers of the numerous mosques, like multi-coloured tattooed penises pointing towards the sky. Little ones, big ones, green ones, blue ones. Some might even argue more graceful and elegant than the male organ itself.

It was still early afternoon and the shops and market had closed for their regular 1-4pm break. Despite being winter it was too hot to work, this was only February and from here on in the temperatures would rise every day until August. I decided to follow the example of the locals and retire to my room for a couple of hours.

All was peaceful save for a slight breeze forcing my window shutter to swing to and fro. A restful doze came easily, my mind just floating away and then ... so suddenly. Seemingly from nowhere, a horrendous sound filled the room. A grotesque moaning, a man in terrible pain, pleading for mercy. It got worse, louder, perhaps somebody had reversed a truck over his genitals? Then a long, steady, pitiful wailing. I darted across to the window to witness the tragedy that was unfolding and it was then that I realised. It was coming from right next door. The good citizens of Muscat were being called to prayer for the second of their five daily visits.

* * * * *

That first evening, having rested, showered and changed (ie. swapped T-shirts) I was feeling nicely relaxed, looking forward to the evening ahead though more than a little uncertain what to do next. "Well, what do Omanis do on a night out?" I asked myself brightly. "Probably nothing," I answered rather glumly. "Let's try the hotel staff, they had seemed very helpful at check in."

"Oh yes – there is a beautiful restaurant 2kms from here – the Al Inshirrah." Well, any place named after a former England centre-forward sounded good enough to me, so off I went to investigate. I had not the faintest idea what to expect (an already very familiar feeling), but suspected it would be a slightly glorified version of my lunchtime venue. Could I face another bowl of massala sauce, tasty though it had been?

The taxi dropped me outside a very splendid looking building and an immaculately dressed maitre d' stepped out to invite me into his exclusive candlelit restaurant. I pinched myself to be sure it was really happening and then realised that this unexpected leap from the sublime to the ridiculous was simply too much for me to handle. I hadn't travelled to Oman to sit in a poncy restaurant (at least not on my first day), so, like an embarrassed teenager walking into the Ladies toilet, I mumbled a few words, turned round and fled back towards the centre of town.

I did some more walking, had a schwarma (chicken wrapped in bread) at a street stall and concluded that a light supper was in any event far more healthy and sensible. And then off to bed nice and early to read my book, something that was to become a regular feature of my nights in the Sultanate of Oman. It occurred to me that if it wasn't for pubs and restaurants at home I would never see any of my mates, or more to the point, I wouldn't even have any mates. Was this a sad reflection of the way our society had become or merely a cultural difference? Wow! Had I already started talking to myself, making sweeping remarks and generalised statements after only a few days? Or was the enforced abstention from alcohol already having a positive effect, allowing my mind to explore concepts and theories that hitherto had been lying dormant in my brain? It seemed that this little break from excessive eating and drinking was going to do me the power of good and I went to sleep happy in the knowledge that my body was ridding itself of all impurities. How would the boys at home have coped with this transition?

In the days that followed I explored the different parts of Muscat, the highlight most definitely being the palace of Sultan Qaboos. He is the boss, the chap that pretty much runs Oman single handedly, the equivalent of King, Queen, Prime Minister, Foreign Minister, government, parliament … all rolled into one. If there are any laws that he doesn't like, no problem, he just changes them. A job for life is that of the Sultan, and he rarely gets pulled over for traffic offences.

I wandered round the outside of the enormous building, admired the fantastic gardens and found myself studying the face of the man in the overalls kneeling by the flower beds. It didn't seem to correspond to the photographs mounted on the walls of the country's shops and offices and I came to the disappointing conclusion that this was more likely to be an employee than the Sultan himself. But I continued to peer through the railings – the likes of you and I do not get within a few hundred yards of the front door – and marvelled at the extraordinary beauty of it all; an incredible residence far exceeding anything The Queen or even David Beckham could ever expect to own. Even in the unlikely event that one day they shack up together.

*　*　*　*　*

Eight Riyal was enough to get me a taxi all the way to Nizwa, about £12 to cover the same distance as London to Birmingham. And that was "Engaged", the local term meaning the cab was all for me, there would be no sharing. It seemed like a pretty good deal.

Oman is twenty percent larger in area than the United Kingdom, but the population is only about two and a half million, probably the same as the number of cars that appears on the M25 every morning. Which leads me nicely into the best statistic of all, my absolute favourite bit of Omani trivia. In 1970 – and that doesn't seem so long ago does it? – the whole of Oman only had 7 miles, repeat SEVEN MILES, of surfaced road. In fact, even now it only really has a couple of major roads, one from north to south through the middle of the country and one north to south along the coast. And that's it.

So we bombed along this sparkling new dual carriageway for the two hour drive up to Nizwa. The road cut its way between the mountains that I had seen from above on the plane and from a distance in Muscat. Now here I was, right in the middle of them. Mountains … If your mind is conjuring up images of undulating green carpets and the jingling of cow-bells please let me stop you right there. The Hajar Mountains of Oman's interior are a very different scene altogether: enormous, endless piles of cruel, harsh, grey stone, tons and tons and tons and tons of the stuff. It was like driving through a huge quarry, though every so often little villages would appear, small houses like white sugar cubes, a striking colour contrast in such an overwhelming sea of grey. Imagine opening your curtains every morning and seeing that huge expanse of rubble, wondering when it would start to slide and bury you alive.

My hotel was on the outskirts of Nizwa and strategically positioned between the said dual carriageway and a rather large slagheap. For the first time in my life I was actually pleased to be offered a room that had no window and I lay on my bed feeling a tad glum and wondering why guidebooks seemed to give Nizwa such glowing reports. Then it dawned on me that there was no point in wondering. I jumped in a mini-bus (a lower cost alternative to a taxi) and headed off to the town.

And indeed it was lovely. The dismal landscape on the outskirts gave no indication of the prettiness of this little place. Dominated by a huge fort – I'll come on to forts in a minute (that's set your pulse racing) – and the ever-present mosque, this really did feel like walking through history. Admittedly the souq (market) had been modernised into a kind of Omani shopping centre in readiness for the tourists dropping in, but it was all extremely tasteful and the character of the place had certainly not been lost.

I wandered for hours around the old town, initially from choice and then because I couldn't find my way out of the maze of narrow, dusty paths. The sandy-coloured dwellings beyond the walls all looked so old, so very humble and yet there was nothing to suggest squalor or anything other than a happy, orderly little community. The locals wandered by, chatting and smiling, children played in large groups, while teenagers split their groups into two and played volleyball. No screaming, no fighting, no crying, everybody seemingly very content with their simple lives.

I did finally escape from the labyrinth and returned to downtown Nizwa to assess the dining options. They were extremely limited, and rather less than enticing, but, as it turned out, it wasn't going to matter anyway. My priorities had quite suddenly been diverted by an unpleasant sensation in the lower abdomen and waves of pain were now flooding in every few minutes and forcing me to stop walking. Dinner had been cancelled, that was for sure, and as I stood in a shop doorway clutching my waist and baring my teeth my mind went back to the very first day and the bowl of Chicken Massala. My number was almost up, but for some perverse reason a little part of me found this ever so slightly amusing.

I wondered how long it would take to get to the nearest remotely usable public toilet and decided the answer was probably about four hours by plane. The plan for the evening had now changed dramatically and the only sensible course of action was to get back to the hotel as quickly as possible. Still thinking positively I grabbed some bread and cream cheese (*La Vache Qui Rit*, the smiling cow in his circular box) from a small grocery shop and with my little plastic bag jumped into the first mini-bus that was heading out of town.

By now the pains had become frequent and more intense. My fate was in the driver's hands and I soon realised, to my horror, that he was slowly touring the suburbs to recruit more passengers. Oh no, please no! Should I just bail out there and then? And then what? I might even be worse off. So I just stayed where I was, leaned forwards, stared at the floor, and clenched every part of the body that was in any way clench-able. Conversation, smiling, even eye contact was a distraction I simply couldn't afford. How long could I possibly hold on? Round and round and round we went to find more paying customers and each time that I thought we were heading back the vehicle slowed down once again, the horn was sounded and more people laden with bags pushed back the sliding doors and climbed aboard.

A deep gurgling sensation from below signaled that defeat was nigh and I wondered what the Omani reaction would be to a foreigner voiding his bowels in a crowded vehicle. Would they feel sorry for me or consider it the ultimate insult? Would they even think it was normal behaviour in foreign countries? All I could do was sit and wait, breathe very, very slowly, stare at the floor of the vehicle and ... just hang in there lad, hang in there.

After what seemed an eternity, we drew up at the hotel, some twenty-eight seconds ahead of the inevitable moment. By an incredible coincidence this was the same length of time that it took me to complete the penguin-like shuffle along the corridor and across the bedroom, including the twice-failed insertion of key into lock. At least I made it as far as the bathroom, though one more second in my favour would have made life so very much easier.

Lavatorial anecdotes are of course all part of travelling and I'm sure one day there'll be a book to embrace the finest stories. It could even be turned into a film ... and wouldn't that give an entirely different meaning to the term "motion pictures".

* * * * *

Omani towns and villages, as with everywhere else in the world, appear more basic and less altered by time the further inland you travel. Tourism has yet to make any real impression and consequently most places away from the handful of resorts have little in the way of accommodation. But what they lack in hostelries they more than make up for in forts, some, like the one at Nizwa, still in excellent condition. Normally I would start snoring at the mere mention of the word fort or castle, but even I enjoyed this one, particularly the fantastic views from the top over the town and the surrounding countryside.

According to my research more than five hundred forts were built on high ground all over Oman to protect towns and villages from rival communities and also, at strategic points along the coast, to keep dangerous foreigners out. It obviously did the trick – no other power was ever successful in completely taking over the country – though the Portuguese did try to stake a claim and they too built huge forts along the coastline near Muscat to fend off rival would-be colonisers. Take another look at the map and you will see why the Omani coast was of particular significance back in those seafaring days. With the mighty Persia to the north, India to the east and Africa to the west, all the ships with their precious cargo would regularly need to pass through these waters. The Omanis to their credit defended their country proudly and even built up their own little empire in the 19th century, colonising part of what is Kenya and Tanzania today.

All pretty fascinating stuff, but it was time for me to head back to Muscat and this time I would make for the beachside suburb of Qur, perhaps even visit an 'international' hotel and maybe even partake of a glass or two of shandy.

The taxi dropped me close to the Hotel Intercontinental, a building so large compared to my usual humble surroundings that it took ten minutes to find the front entrance. I wandered into the grandeur of the lobby and the first thing I saw was a scruffy unshaven man with shorts, sandals and a dusty little backpack. He was standing next to a group of business executives in suits with their elegant ladies, each sporting a fancy hair-do, outrageous make-up and the best part of a bottle of perfume. And then the solitary, bedraggled man turned his head a little to one side, and to my considerable embarrassment, I recognized it as my own face in the large gold-framed mirror.

I decided against the £170 a night Interconti (an abbreviation favoured by those who can afford their exorbitant room rates) and instead found a very pleasant family hotel nearby where £170 would cover the bills for a week. But I did shower, shave and put on my least crumpled clothes to go back later that day and occupy a stool in their plush cocktail bar. And what an exciting moment that was. Drooling at the sight of all the bottles, beautiful bottles I hadn't seen for over a week, I ordered a delicious cold beer and inevitably soon found myself in conversation with a fellow Brit. Neil was a telecommunications man from Essex, based in Oman, and his party piece was being able to describe every single bar in the country permitted to serve alcohol, together with a full listing of the food, drink and music on offer in each. Just when I thought he'd finished he then moved on to special menus according to days of the week, various theme nights in selected locations and his own recommendations according to mood and circumstances. It was clearly a subject close to his heart and it took us several cold beers and a few peanut refills to work through the list. I got the impression that Neil hadn't made it to many forts.

The Interconti also has its own English style pub, a typical overseas version where people stand around in freezing air-con and semi-darkness to play darts and watch soundless TV. No great surprise that I saw more Western people there than I had done in the whole of my time in Oman, but what I hadn't expected was to see local men dressed in dishdashas slugging back pints of Fosters. Not so many of them, granted, but it was interesting to see the liberal attitudes of a country where the rules of Islam are presented as a choice rather than an obligation.

The dry mouth and throbbing head of the following morning made the prospect of returning to the nightly routine of mint tea and book reading very appealing. Part of my therapy that morning was a long cobweb-clearing walk on the beach – a huge, delightful expanse of sea and sand, but most definitely not a Copacabana or even a Brighton. Despite the perfect weather it was almost completely deserted, just a few tourists paddling in the sea and some local teenage lads who'd come out to play football. I guess a religion that allows ladies to bare only their eyebrows on the streets is hardly likely to encourage them to get their jugs out on the beach.

* * * * *

There is something very unusual, perhaps even unique, about the geography of Oman. And that is because the extreme north of the country is completely cut off from the rest, a peninsula that can only be accessed by sea, or across land from the UAE. A bizarre situation indeed, rather like Cornwall being a part of Scotland. It's known as the Musandam Peninsula and is actually a lot nearer to Dubai than it is to Muscat. It was a temptation I just couldn't resist.

The Four-Letter Countries

After a night in Sharjah (the emirate next to Dubai) and re-acquaintance with the miseries of traffic, I got a cab to drop me at the Ras al Khaimah taxi stand, that's Khaimah with a very throaty Kh sound and much easier to say if you happen to be an Arab or a scouser. A fancy name for a cab rank you might think, but it refers to the northern city, and emirate of the same name, through which you have to pass to get up to the Omani border.

A share taxi is a civilised arrangement whereby four passengers split the cost and within twenty minutes of leaving the skyscraper city our car was whizzing along a dual carriageway with camels roaming around freely in the desert on both sides of the road. Quite a contrast. At R-A-K another taxi offered to take me to the Omani border for 15 Dirham (£2) engaged, then once under way he explained in perfect English that his English wasn't very good and that when he'd said one-five fifteen he'd actually meant to say five-oh 50. We settled on something in between – in response to his threat to turn the car round – and continued north through rubble country towards the familiar grey mass of mountains in the distance. The desert had gone now, ugliness had taken its place, so I passed the time studying Arabic numbers on car licence plates. It's easy to remember that 1 and 9 are like ours, a 0 is a 5, a diamond is a 0, a 7 is a 6 … and then I always seem to get mixed up. Perhaps the taxi driver had a point after all.

I'd expected a simple little frontier post with the usual hubbub of activity on either side of the border, but standing in that empty car park, my dodgy driver and a fat wad of Dirhams already heading south again, I found myself looking at something altogether very different. Not a soul in sight, just a series of modern tinted-glass buildings on a lonely coast road with a huge grey mountain on one side and the sea on the other. Where was everybody? There were no cars, no locals, no travellers, no staff, nobody at all except one man standing in the sunshine holding a little bag.

Again, it seemed I was watching a movie, waiting to see what would happen next. And then came a voice from nowhere, a uniformed man had emerged into the sunshine to direct me to a window in the wall.

He smiled, asked where my car was, smiled again at my answer. Then he realized I wasn't joking. The suggestion that I would take a taxi really brightened his day, though, to be fair, his laugh was more friendly than mocking. Another officer then appeared and looked equally bemused at my predicament, had a quick chat about me with his mate in Arabic, then dashed round the corner as though not wanting to play even a bit part in The Demise Of The Stranded Tourist.

It was all looking a bit grim, but just as the UAE departure stamps were getting hammered into my passport, Officer 2 poked his head out from around the corner. "You go with German?"

I don't recall producing any words, just a confused, blank stare.

"It's OK for you to go with German?"

Saying yes seemed a better answer than no, even if it was just a general question about the appeal of women with hairy armpits.

"Come."

Behind a wall was another lane hidden from view and a man sitting in a 4 Wheel Drive. Yousef was a German of Palestinian parents and whether he liked it or not had been told he was giving me a lift. And what a journey it was. Forty five minutes along an incredible coast road, the turquoise water almost reaching the car on our left side and the sheer vertical face of the grey rock to our right. It felt as though we had the country to ourselves, no sign at all of any other cars or people, just the winding road and the occasional village with a mosque at its centre. Once again that feeling of immense space and the familiar trio of colours: white buildings, grey mountains, blue sky.

Yousef dropped me at a surprisingly modern hotel on the entrance to Khasab, the only town of any note. It turned out to be a lovely place, perched on a slab of rock looking out across the sparkling water of the Strait of Hormuz, the grey mass of mountains to the right and the shoreline of Iran away in the distance. Where else in the world could you sit and have a beer in one FLC and look out across the ocean to another? A dream come true, well, apart from the price of the beer.

* * * * *

There is a premier league of diving sites around the planet and the Musandam Peninsula, by all accounts, is up there challenging for honours with the Maldives and a range of other exotic locations. The dive centre in the hotel was offering daily trips and so, I thought, 'why not go for it?' and I put myself down for snorkelling. Snorkelling, you pussy! OK, I know it's not the real thing, but the idea of engaging in a sport that punishes carelessness and stupidity with brain damage or even death is definitely not for people like me. Particularly when there are nine more FLCs still to visit.

Early the following morning, Andy (sensible lawyer from Hemel Hempstead with a tank) and me (Mr Bean figure with a little plastic tube) were transported across the choppy waters to a part of the bay designated as our first dive site. Once anchored, the boat bobbed about like a mad dog fighting to get off its leash so, as soon as my colleague disappeared from view, I donned my plastic and rubber attachments, leaned back over the side and reverse flopped into the briny.

Darkness, bubbles, daylight, disorientation. Oh shit the mask is off! Don't Panic! And the snorkel has come out of its thingy! Don't Panic Mr Mainwaring! Gulp, quick – grab it, wave approaching over head, splash, darkness, gulp, salt, stinging eyes, arms in air, tread water, assemble kit, another wave, splash, darkness, gulp, salt, mask on, snorkel in mouth, gulp, mask steamed up, bastard, stinging eyes, mask off, another fucking wave, gulp, fit of coughing, tread water, splash, mask on again, gulp ...

Snorkelling, I discovered some time ago, shares a lot in common with ski-ing. When conditions are fine, you feel comfortable, calm and relaxed, it's one of the greatest pleasures known to man. But when nature bites back with scratchy pistes or choppy seas then misery, in quite substantial measure, can very quickly set in. And worse still, there's not always an obvious escape. Ever tried to play a violin whilst driving along the motorway and having a burning cigarette dropped into your lap?

That day I persevered, got my mask on, went through the motions, drank several more gallons of sea water, and bobbed around for maybe half an hour. It wasn't the best, but it was a Monday morning and several million poor buggers would be on their way into London on the tube. Should I be moaning about snorkelling conditions?

What really fascinated me about that expedition was all the activity ON the water, particularly the incredibly fast speed boats that shot by every few minutes. Why were they there? What were they doing? The skipper explained – in his best Omani boatman English – and the story he told wasn't at all what I'd expected. They were Iranian smugglers no less, collecting goods from Khasab and delivering to Bandar-i-Abbas, a town on the south coast of their country a couple of hours away. An accepted part of life on this peninsula, confirmed Hemel Hempstead Andy knowledgably, though neither he nor the boatman could expand on this in any detail. Intriguing stuff. I resolved to find out more.

The port of Khasab was a constant buzz of energy and activity, quite clearly the heartbeat of this small, isolated community. The vessels moored up inside the harbour told the story of daily life: fishing boats, dhows, tankers, police boats … even an enormous cruise liner, they were all there. It was a great scene and I wandered around for ages, mingled with the men in sparkling white dishdashas and turbans, and watched them loading and unloading vessels from the trucks pulling up on the quayside. Some worked hard, others just lay in hammocks lashed up on the decks, enjoying the shade and staring up at the huge mass of grey mountains encircling the town. At the far end of the harbour, almost an exclusive mini-marina, I could see a series of pontoons where the speed-boats were tied up and yet there was no activity at all. This was, by all accounts, where the naughty stuff happened very early every morning. The smugglers' jetty. An adventure story if ever there was one.

The Four-Letter Countries

The town by contrast was an unremarkable sprawling sort of place, a series of souks (really just 1960s-style shopping arcades) built around car parks and a couple of important-looking roundabouts. The first thing I spotted was the word BOOKSHOP on a bright green overhead sign, translated from an impressive series of wavy lines that was obviously the Arabic equivalent. Just what I wanted, I owed a paperback to the Dutch guy from the Dive Centre, but would they have books in English?

Ping went the doorbell and a big smile greeted the white man. "Do you have any Eng…" If I actually added "lish books" it came out ever so slowly because it was immediately apparent that not a single book was there in any part of his emporium. He spoke no English, so the least I could do was give him my best book-reading charade which, though I say it myself, I'm rather good at. Another smile and a wave of his arm introduced me to a collection of stationery, followed by a shrugged apology for being bookless then a pointed finger towards the street, an indication that I might have better luck elsewhere.

According to the signs above the windows there are three bookshops in Khasab … and the third was most definitely the most informative. For it was here, amongst the now familiar items of stationery, that I finally elicited an official response on behalf of the booksellers of the town. "Aaagh, you mean READING books". The penny had finally dropped, or should I say seven Baisa. "Sorry sir, in Khasab we only sell WRITING books." Is anybody from Waterstone's reading this?

* * * * *

The Musandam Peninsula is a very sparsely-populated region with just a few small towns and villages dotted along its coast. On the west side the road to Khasab links these communities together, but transportation to the east coast is an altogether more tricky business. The only two land options are to drive along a track up and across the mountains or head back south to UAE and skirt around the southern base. Up and across the mountain pass. Wow, that sounded exciting. If only I had a car.

Well, as it turned out, 10 Riyal a day would get me a little Toyota, so I figured there was nothing to lose. To stoke me up further the guide-book suggested that the local insistence on using a 4WD to handle the terrain should be taken with a pinch of salt – a saloon car could do the job just as well. Say no more. The track cuts through the mountains and ultimately winds across as far as the east coast town of Dibba, a name that for some childish reason I'd really taken a shine to. I knew I wouldn't get that far, the military by all accounts had blocked the road anyway, but at least I'd get up high enough to see the views.

The signpost from Khasab pointed the way and within a few minutes of leaving the tarmac of the town I was churning up the red dust and heading towards the towering expanse of grey that dominated everything before me. The land of Bedouins, wolves, possibly even leopards. And now, a very tiny Toyota.

The signs at the roadside warned that the terrain ahead was difficult, the road was steep, only suitable vehicles should proceed. So this was it, the moment of truth. Man or mouse? Between you and I, I'd never felt quite so mousey, but now that I'd got this far surely just a small helping of courage was the order of the day.

The stony, gritty track soon began its journey uphill and for the first few hundred yards everything went swimmingly. I took it slowly, very slowly, not entirely because I'm a Sensible Old Hector but rather because the Toyota was stretched to the absolute limit. Round and up another hairpin bend we went, a little steeper this time, as was the drop off the left hand edge of the road. Second gear was now too high, we weren't moving, except perhaps for a little on-the-spot shudder, so down into first we went. It didn't exactly do the trick. A terrible screeching sound emerged from somewhere, and a lot of dust, a funny smell ... and the sensation of slowly moving backwards.

The Four-Letter Countries

That was the moment the first bead of sweat very noticeably sprung into life and trickled purposefully and at some pace in the direction of my right earlobe. 'Strange,' I recall thinking, 'that one should pick up on such detail when a more pressing issue like death is staring you squarely in the face.' I yanked the handbrake as it had never been yanked before or since and mercifully the little white useless bastard of a motor held its ground. A moment's respite, a chance to ponder, sweat, and do a little bit of swearing.

Pondering proved quite useful. It helped me to the conclusion that bringing the Toyota along this route was like entering a milk float into the Grand Prix and that the only sensible course of action was to go back down. Yes, that sounded good. Perhaps I should ponder more often, I pondered.

The only obstacles I could see to this most recently-hatched plan were the fact that the vehicle was on unstable ground, we were facing a steep gradient in the wrong direction and hovering several feet away from the edge of a spectacular gorge. It occurred to me, as I ran through a few more obscenities, that nothing in my three decades of driving had quite prepared me for this moment, certainly not the three-point turn on my driving test on a middle-class housing estate in Cheshire.

It will go down more as a memory than a highlight, but at least I managed to do the deed, despite a vehicle packed with local men and their family of goats weaving in front of my bonnet in mid-juggle. They looked on with curiosity and more than a hint of a scowl, no doubt thinking the Omani equivalent of "What a Dickhead." And that was just the goats.

* * * * *

It didn't take me long to get back to the flat terrain of Khasab, the small terminal of the airport almost the first building on the southern edge of the town. An airport, now there's an idea. I pulled up alongside the other four cars in the car park and yes, there were flights to Dubai and yes, there would be one at 4.30 on Friday afternoon. A problem solved, Iran Aseman Airlines, those giants of world aviation, would come to take me away in three days time. Sorted.

The Toyota then took me on a little tour of the town, little tours being pretty much the only type on offer in a town of maybe 10,000 dwellers. So was this it? Had I rented a motor just to scare myself shitless on a mountain pass and do a little loop around Khasab? Options were somewhat limited by the fact that there was only one road in this neck of the woods and I'd already been along it in both directions. Unless...

Unless I drove back across the border to the UAE, headed east round the foot of the mountains and crossed over to the other coast in a very civilised way. Why, I might even make it to Dibba! Yes, that was it, that would be my plan for the next day. And with that executive decision firmly in the bag, the dusty Toyota and I returned to base to charge our respective batteries.

The Golden Tulip was a bright, modern hotel with a lovely pool, just a pity Paddy the architect had placed it in the shadow of the building for the largest part of every day. There was also a "London Pub" (was this on Neil's list?), a predictably dark, icy little chamber seemingly aimed at tourists growing weary of the beautiful views and the lovely climate. Not the place to be in the late afternoon, or any time for that matter, so I opted for the veranda with a series of local publications plucked from the lobby, a collection that had intrigued me all week. *Dams of the Omani Environment* actually turned out to be a bit boring, as did *Seashells of Oman*, though the booklets on beaches, trees, mammals and turtles offered several unexpected moments of pleasure. But the one that really floated my boat was the magical *Butterflies of the Omani Environment*. In what other sphere of our magnificent planet would you find names like the Salmon Arab, Grass Jewel, Desert Orange, Pigmy Skipper, Pea Blue and Caper White? Absolutely bloody fantastic. Life had never felt so good.

The Four-Letter Countries

The drive early next morning took me back along the magnificent winding coast road to the border and eventually the empty dual carriageways of the UAE. Windows down, zipping along, sky as blue as ever, wide open spaces. This was what it was all about.

It was about 11 o'clock when I hit the outskirts of Dibba, a town rather bigger and more developed than I'd imagined. There seemed to be more roundabouts than in Milton Keynes and definitely more national flags flying than anywhere I could ever remember. The black, red and green colours of the Emirates dominated the town until a small sign a little further north, heading back towards the mountains, announced that we were on Omani soil once again.

No checkpoints, no border to speak of, but the longest beach you ever did see. I pulled off the road and directly onto the wonderful sweep of golden sand, not another vehicle or person in view in either direction. How long could a place this beautiful, less than a hundred miles from the traffic of Dubai, remain as deserted as this? I parked up and walked along the sea edge to the very top end of the beach, no other sign of life at all except a large flock of white birds that always took flight and landed further along as I got within a hundred metres. This really was something a bit special.

I lapped up the solitude and rolled around for a couple of hours in the lukewarm water then slowly headed back to the small dot in the distance that was the trusty Toyota (we were mates again). It was now after 1pm and viciously hot, shoulders were bright red and burning and it really was time to get off the beach. It seemed to take forever to get to the car and it was with a mixture of panic and relief and thoughts of mad dogs and Englishmen that I finally crawled inside, fired the engine up and, opening the windows in mid U-ey, swung the little fella back towards the road.

At that point there was no real plan other than to get the hell out of the searing heat. So please, if you will, try to picture my considerable disappointment when, upon completion of said U-turn, the little Japanese bastard opted to plummet head first into the sand. Bastard! Bastard, bastard, bastard.

Despite my advanced driving skills, the car definitely wasn't going any further forwards, nor was it going backwards. It was just making those horrible dying cat noises that were becoming an all too familiar part of life, wheels were whirring round and making smells, sand was flying in all directions as the machine buried itself deeper and deeper into the beach. Beads of sweat were back in no uncertain terms; this was worse than Christmas shopping. The bastard. The useless, worthless, little Toyota bastard.

I got out. I stared. I did some more sweating. And I looked around. And not one of the four actions seemed to greatly improve my predicament. Then, I might as well admit, I knelt down alongside one of the front wheels and started to scoop handfuls of powdery sand from beneath the submerged tyre. A gesture which, had I continued diligently and without breaks, might have resolved the problem after say, twenty seven thousand years.

Twenty seven thousand years of bare-hand digging is a lot of work to free a hire car and so I decided it would make a lot sense to stand up again. A good thing that I did because, to my astonishment, an oval-shaped young man on a motor bike was heading along the road towards me and within a few minutes there were two of us staring at the stricken vehicle. I looked at him pleadingly, he was after all my only contact with the real world, and he explained in Arabic the situation as he saw it. And then he left. To get his mates? To pray at the mosque? Or to just go and get himself a burger? I only knew one word of Arabic and that just wasn't enough to know if I was ever going to see him again.

Well ... he did come back ... maybe fifteen minutes later, but not before two older lads had appeared, as if by magic, with a truck and a rope. I couldn't believe my luck, where had they come from? Had my tubby friend been to find them? Suffice to say within minutes I was shaking all three hands in a delirious lost-the-plot sort of way, truly confirming my status as a foreign lunatic. And then I gave the cheeriest of simpleton waves and, with all the windows down, headed back towards the flag-bedecked roundabouts of the UAE.

The journey back to Khasab was memorable for all the right reasons: watching the sun setting over the The Arabian Gulf, the circle of fishermen mending nets on a silent beach, the elegant white mosques lighting up the small villages in the fading light. I stopped the car and sat in complete silence to savour those special moments, images of Oman that I'm pleased to say will live in my memory long after the mini-disasters have been forgotten.

* * * * *

The Musandam is all about those harsh grey mountains and the bright blue water that surrounds them, so the peninsula's most spectacular phenomenon shouldn't really come as a surprise. But in a way, it does. Because who ever heard of an Arabian fjord? Aren't they exclusive to Norway and New Zealand? Read on.

The Khor Ash Sham is seventeen kilometres long and I reckon a couple of kilometres across, a long narrow inlet of crystal clear water with sheer rock faces on either side. It is strikingly beautiful and all you need to do to get there is board a dhow in Khasab and sail just around the corner. What a privilege for me to spend my last day in this small piece of paradise, lying on a persian-carpeted deck, alternating viewing positions between sun and shade, occasionally standing up to watch the dolphins swimming alongside. Every few minutes these fantastic beasts would re-appear, side by side in twos and threes like torpedoes cutting through the water, leaping into the air every ten seconds or so to pose for the cameras. The dolphins really were great entertainment, though the inane behaviour of the tourists with their precious cameras perhaps more fascinating still.

Oman

We cruised ever so slowly passing several small communities on the shoreline, each with just a few simple houses and a mosque. What a place to live! No roads at all, they depend entirely on their own small boats to transport provisions and send their children to school on the mainland while fresh water is shipped in weekly on a government vessel. I noticed that there were a few electricity cables, though, and couldn't help but wonder what luxury this adds to their simple lives. They might even get *Match Of The Day* on a Saturday evening.

I went to bed a happy person that night with the warm satisfying glow of a man who'd spent his day at sea. It was my last night, the end of the road, or at least this bit of the road. Unless ... mmm. My plane wouldn't leave until the following afternoon and there was still one more thing I really wanted to check out. Could I be bothered getting up at 6 o'clock in the morning?

As it turned out I woke up before the alarm went off, even though the world was absolutely silent and the sky as black as coal. It was 05.35, perfect. If I was going to observe Iranian smugglers in action, this was my one and only chance.

The road to the port was beautifully lit by the moon and at 05.39 the only other living creature around was a fox crossing from one side to the other. He stopped and turned to look at me, pausing for quite some time, no doubt wondering – as I was – what the hell I was up to. Then he disappeared into the bush and I carried on down the hill.

There was a security post by the entrance to the port, but luckily for me the gate next to it was unlocked. I slipped in very quietly, half expecting a voice to come from behind, but nothing, not a sound. I'd done it, I was in the port and still there wasn't another person anywhere to be seen. After all these years, my first appearance in an Enid Blyton story!

Taking care not to trip over ropes, I moved gingerly in the direction of the smugglers wharf. Total darkness was in my favour, a level of cover that would have been the envy of your average daytime sleuth, I reflected rather smugly. Within minutes I was there, less than a hundred metres from their boats, a carefully chosen position where I could see without being seen. Then, as with all reconnaissance missions, it was just a question of waiting.

It was very dark, even slightly cool, the sky was only just changing colour away to the east. I looked around, it was now after 6am, and I was completely alone. Not a single person anywhere in the port. Was this because it was Friday, their holy day? Did Iranian smugglers adhere that closely to the Koran? Something needed to happen.

The port of Khasab is sheltered by a long jetty, at the end of which a flashing light guides all vessels into the bay. Everything that sails in and out needs to pass that way and I figured any person hiding in the rocks just below the lighthouse would witness the movement of every single craft. If I was to take this seriously, and creeping around in the dark at 6am was serious enough, then perhaps this was the place to make for.

It turned out to be a hell of a long way to the very end of the jetty and it was distinctly cool and breezy sitting there on the boulders, practically in the middle of the bay. I found a cracking little spot, though, where three huge rocks formed an armchair facing the sea and if you ever get involved in maritime intelligence in the Middle East this is definitely a place you should make for. The sun was finally starting to rise and, after what seemed an eternity, a fishing boat chugged by – but in truth a pretty poor return for twenty minutes huddled in a stony hideaway. Sitting on rocks makes your bum very cold, some even contend that it can give you piles, and my thoughts were now drifting in a negative direction. In fact, it was worse than that, the whole sorry mission seemed doomed.

Feeling gloomy now and a prize contender for the Anorak of the Year Award, I headed back to the port, to the bows of the dhows (that catchy little one cheered me up a bit) and then once again towards the wharf at the far end. Wait a minute! They were there ... smugglers ... in the speed boats ... they'd been there all along sleeping under blankets! I couldn't contain my excitement, it was time to throw caution to the wind.

Oman

Quite how an Iranian smuggler would react to a casual observer strutting about near his pontoon was very much unknown territory, but there was only one way to find out. I stood there quietly and watched as they stretched, yawned, and moved some of the boxes stacked up alongside. What was this contraband, I wondered? I'd heard all sorts of stories about the goods they bought and sold: cigarettes going out to Iran, goats being brought in to Oman! Each to their own, that's what I always say.

They were youngish guys, in their twenties, and they seemed totally unconcerned by my presence. Then, slowly but surely, more appeared from under blankets, clearly not in any hurry to get stuck into a hard day's smuggling. This would make a great photo I decided, but would that be pushing my luck? Well ... what was the worst that could happen when they were in boats and I was on land? Abusive threats, missiles, gunshots? Surely not.

I slid the camera from my bag ever so slowly, pointed it up towards the mountains in a don't-worry-about-me-I'm-just-an-innocent-tourist kind of way, then surreptitiously swung round and pressed the button somewhere vaguely in their direction. They didn't bat an eyelid. Perhaps they realised the photo was just a blur of sky and water. The exercise was then repeated several times, each swivel much slower, more daring and deliberate than the last, until the ridiculous charade fizzled out altogether. Still there was no reaction at all from my subjects, so I just stood there, large as life, and photographed the boats, the men and their cargo. And then finally, eventually, something did happen. One of them laughed and waved.

Five minutes later I was shaking hands with a group of the smiling stubbly-faced lads – real life smugglers – and they were soon competing to pose for the camera. Larking around with a tourist was clearly more interesting than loading boxes of shoes (shoes?) and one by one they came over to join in the fun. None could really speak English, but one guy did manage a few words and how they made an old man very happy. "Hello – we are from Iran."

The Four-Letter Countries

* * * * *

The plane left early and landed in Dubai at more or less the time we should have taken off. The trip was over and this was all too sudden, like a lovely film that unexpectedly comes to an end. Oman had become a good friend, perhaps surprisingly so, and her stunning landscape and gentle people had given me much more confidence and fuelled my enthusiasm to explore more of the four-letter unknown. I would always look back and think of her with great affection and, thanks to her hospitality, I really found myself looking forward to the next leg of this very long journey. Perhaps this whole thing wasn't such a ludicrous caper after all.

Togo

"Going anywhere nice this year?"

It was a question that Terry had been putting to customers over thirty five years of short back and sides. In that time Torquay had given way to Torremolinos, Turkey and more recently Thailand, but this answer was going to throw him and I can't deny I was savouring the moment. I delivered it with the nonchalance of a Margate or Majorca:

"Togo."

The hum of the electric clippers came to an abrupt stop and the three waiting customers peered up simultaneously over the *Daily Mirror*, last October's *National Geographic* and a *Reader's Digest* from 1992.

"Where?"

"I'm off to the Republic of Togo."

A Jesus (with lots of eeees), a little whistle then a nervous chuckle was about all he could muster.

"It's in West Africa," I felt obliged to add, suspecting an Aids joke would not be far away.

"Unusual choice," he offered politely. "What you gonna do there?"

To his credit it was a very fair question and I think he could see I was floundering for a sensible answer. Thankfully he didn't push it:

"Make sure you stock up on condoms anyway."

We all laughed, some more heartily than others, and the clippers hummed back to life.

* * * * *

The Four-Letter Countries

I walked eastwards across a rickety bridge that separates Ghana from Togo, Terry and his barber shop already a memory from another life. This was an obscure border post indeed, just a clearing in the dense forest where I'd been dropped by taxi from the Ghanaian town of Ho. Yes, once again taken to a border by taxi. Not exactly David Livingstone in search of the source of the Zambezi, but unless I legged it to the border (and I wasn't *that* keen), it really was the only way I could get there. Next time perhaps I'll take a porter along with a tray and a nice cool jug of Pimm's.

Until the World Cup of 2006 most people thought that Togo was a costume you wore at parties. But no, we are talking African nations, west side, the sticky outey bit. The bottom part of sticky outey, in other words with the Atlantic to the south rather than the west is where you find Ghana, and the very much larger Nigeria. But those two countries have two tiny ones wedged in between, one is Benin and the other is Togo. It's a little sausage-shaped country only 56 kms wide at the coast, but about ten times that from north to south. All in all it's about a quarter of the size of the UK, and of the FLCs only Fiji is smaller than poor little Togo.

There is something oddly satisfying about walking from one country to another, a sense of adventure so much more profound than simply stepping off a plane. I stopped on the bridge roughly half way across and despite the searing afternoon heat thoroughly relished my few minutes in no-man's-land. A chance to enjoy the silence, the greenery all around and the sight of a brightly dressed lady, large bottom in the air, scrubbing clothes against the grey rocks in the river below. But what nationality was she? Which of the two countries was she scrubbing in? Did she carry her passport tucked into her bowl of laundry?

I had been stamped out of Ghana, but would only be in Togo upon reaching the other side and was ready with passport in hand to show to the waiting authorities. The bridge was bashed up, but looked as though it would keep going for a few more years, which is considerably more than could be said for the sad, rusty vehicle strategically positioned on

Togo

the other side. It occupied the space that my imagination had earmarked for an immigration office and a decidedly shifty-looking character was gesturing that I clamber into this carcass of decaying metal. Glancing inside I could see that seven or so locals had followed his instructions to the letter and in true African style they sat patiently in the blazing midday heat waiting for a few more punters to climb on board. Oh no, surely I wasn't about to join them?

I looked at Togo beyond the Renault and all I saw was trees and a dusty track. Where the hell was I? Why was there nothing here except this man and a clapped out motor? Why did everybody ignore my questions? Where would he take me? What were my alternatives? At last, a question I could answer. And in I climbed.

The inside of the vehicle boasted very few accessories generally associated with motor transport. The dashboard had long since departed and the front section of the car was just a huge ball of wires dangling hopelessly beneath a steering wheel. There were no controls, no switches, no handles on the doors. Presumably there were some pedals, but I wouldn't have put money on it. The ceiling, like the seats, was slashed to ribbons as though a lunatic with a Stanley knife had been on a big night out and the resulting strips of vinyl dangled down ludicrously onto everybody's heads. The smell of petrol permeated the air so strongly, even above the rancid odour of sweating bodies, that the heat of the sun could surely have turned us into a fireball at any second. This was adventure, I told myself. This was what I was looking for. Who would trade this on a Saturday afternoon for sitting in front of the fire watching rugby on telly?

Just as I was contemplating an unofficial disembarkation, Car Man squeezed in one more customer then walked round and lifted the doors into position for take off. A group had gathered to push the vehicle from its resting place (groups do gather in Africa for events of this magnitude) and with an almighty lurch and a cloud of orange dust the engine spluttered to life. Against all the odds we were finally moving forwards into the forest, destination unknown but frankly already of little significance.

The Four-Letter Countries

The journey passed uneventfully for the next three minutes. In fact until we reached a rope suspended across the road at tennis net height, the point at which our leader slowed us to a stop, clambered from his battered wreck and walked round carefully lifting off the doors. I had already long since surrendered any hope of knowing what was happening, but this development definitely had me thinking the journey was over and that the pleasurable and oft underestimated act of breathing might soon be able to recommence. When my turn came, I disentangled those limbs that seemed to be mine and crawled out into the heat of the jungle, saying nothing, asking nothing, just waiting to see what might happen next.

My fellow passengers seemed completely unfazed by the interruption to service and we'd started shuffling silently along as a group when Car Man ushered me, the very odd man out, towards an abandoned house set in the trees. I had no choice, he was my boss. Or so I thought.

The old house had nothing inside its crumbling walls except rotten coconut shells, but it did have a veranda with a table on it, behind which sat a very fat unhappy man. He wore a white vest, the kind old people buy from M&S and wear under their shirts, which would have been marginally more acceptable had it not sported a brown stain the size of a football. He was now my new boss because Car Man had just whispered the dreaded word into my ear: Immigration. The official frontier that I had so fancifully expected to be located at the riverside was, in fact, this wobbly table, in a derelict house, in the jungle, manned by a slob in dirty underwear.

New Boss took one very long silent look at the pathetic, sweaty white boy standing there clutching his little leather pouch. His grotesque oversized head then moved ever so slightly in slow motion, fat upper lip curled in disgust as though he'd just found a dog turd on his dinner plate. I sat down in front of him so he could get a closer look and let him stare at me right between the eyes. Time seemed to stand still and I found myself waiting for the sound of his flabby throat being cleared and mentally bracing for a fresh bolus of phlegm directed towards the bridge of my nose. I had seriously screwed up his day, of that there was no doubt. Ten hours of delightful uninterrupted nose-picking had been well and truly shattered by my impertinent arrival.

I spoke in whispers and with a very big smile, as one does to a dog that looks poised to gnarl you to death, then filled in and handed over the immigration card. Letter by letter, line by line he inspected my work ever so slowly, like an examiner marking a paper or even an immigration officer seeking a bribe. Then quite suddenly, to quote my mad old wood-work teacher, "The balloon went up". He SLAMMED the card down in front of me, the impact rather too severe for his fragile desk, then jabbed his grubby finger at the line I'd left blank. Should I try to explain it was unanswered because I didn't yet know where I would be staying in Togo?

He was now breathing heavily and mumbling a lot, presumably the French for "Don't Fuck With Me, Son", so I figured the best option was to scribble down a hotel name plucked from the guidebook. A slight gamble: if the place had been demolished a year earlier and my luck was out I'd be taken behind the trees for immediate execution. But then nothing in Africa ever gets demolished, it just falls down slowly, and he stamped my passport with all the remaining hatred he could muster.

The good news was that my official welcome to Togo had not necessitated a dip into the wallet and for that I was thankful. The loss of five bucks would not have changed my life for ever, but being insulted *and* mugged before even being formally recognised as a visitor into the country would I think have rattled the old cage. Within an hour I had gone from smiley Ghanaian man in smart uniform to obnoxious Togolese Twat in soiled underwear. Things needed to pick up a bit.

I settled back into my regular spot in the Renault where my travel companions waited with complete indifference. One thing I had to get used to again was that in Africa doing nothing is not looked upon as a waste of time. In fact doing nothing is what is done a great deal of the time, so waiting around is just one of its many forms. Why is it that we

The Four-Letter Countries

Europeans are always in such a desperate hurry? I needed to become more African.

When pinned into the back of an airless vehicle containing nine people, the only form of entertainment on offer is to observe the different features, clothes and mannerisms of those with whom one is entwined. That most of my new friends were clad in jumpers and anoraks held my interest for a good part of the journey, until, that is, the streams of salty sweat running vertically south from my forehead denied me the use of my eyeballs. This was a real big blow, my only moveable parts and remaining simple pleasure snuffed out in one fell swoop. I was rather beginning to wish we would get there soon, wherever "there" might be.

It turned out to be a place called Kpalimé. If you want to say it out loud, though I cannot imagine any occasion when you would find this necessary, your starting point would be to ignore the k – as in knob (a person who goes on holiday to Togo). Good news though, the guidebook had described the town as one of Togo's gems. This piece of information, plus the fact that I had actually arrived somewhere, lifted my spirits a treat and I sat on a little wall in downtown Kpalimé feeling totally liberated.

Within seconds I was in conversation with one of a group of young moped riders looking for business. He seemed quite innocent, genuinely friendly, and I enjoyed the first opportunity to try to speak French, a language my car mates had not understood. (More on that later, it's good to save the exciting bits). As far as I could see, he was asking me to give him 100 francs to take me as a pillion passenger anywhere in the town of my choosing and I responded with the haggler's routine gasp of outrage. The poor guy smiled at me and actually looked bemused, even embarrassed, at my reaction. I then made the calculation and realised that at 1,000 CFA franc (Communauté francaise d'Afrique) to the pound it was 10p for a taxi to anywhere I wanted to go. Perhaps it wasn't such a bad deal after all.

Since long before the Euro was ever dreamt up West Africa has had a regional currency, the CFA, which is used in all the French speaking

Togo

countries. Central Africa also uses a CFA, which is the same value, but Central African CFAs are not interchangeable with West African ones. Soon another group of West African countries (mainly English speaking) will simplify things even further by forming a third currency which, at a later stage, they will seek to integrate with one or both of the aforementioned CFAs. Then they may all get aligned to the Euro (they were in the past linked to the French Franc) in which case they could be scrapped and the Euro itself used as the official currency of West Africa. If you didn't understand this paragraph you can either go back and read it again or shrug your shoulders and say, as so many have done before: "I couldn't give a toss about African currencies". It wouldn't make you a bad person.

I climbed on to the back of the bike and off we went in search of a hotel. Not being too familiar with moped etiquette I clung tightly to his slender waist, for dear life I think is the expression, and wondered whether that was what passengers normally did. Looking around me, this was obviously the main form of transport and I guessed the locals were probably not as paranoid about becoming a paraplegic as I had always been at the mere sight of a motorbike. This down to a successful bit of brainwashing by my mother who, shortly after breastfeeding was over, got to work on convincing me that just to sit astride one of these things was tantamount to sawing off both arms and legs and hurling them onto a bonfire (though hurling your arms in such circumstances is harder than you might think). And here I was, some forty years later, tearing through the streets of Kpalimé at speeds approaching 20mph.

As though that wasn't terrifying enough, the man at the controls insisted on turning to chat to me over his right shoulder. Not in French, as we had started out but, for reasons I couldn't fathom, in German. I guessed he was keen to demonstrate his linguistic skills and for me, being equally below average in both, it made no difference whatsoever.

When it comes to languages, Africans are a pretty impressive bunch: everybody speaks at least one tribal tongue while the more educated also speak the languages of their former colonists. And in case

53

you didn't study Togolese history at school here's a potted version. I promise to keep it brief: We start in the 15th century, an era when the Portuguese were sailing big ships around the world with a view to putting an empire together. The Great Portuguese Empire! The terms piss up and brewery had yet to be linked, but the boys from Lisbon decided after a brief visit that they would not be working their magic on this particular piece of Africa. Instead they would concentrate on transforming Angola, Guinea-Bissau and Mozambique into the economic powerhouses they are today.

The next European nation to show an interest was ... wait for it ... Denmark. Could it be that the Scandinavians had seen huge potential to expand their grip on the world pastries market? No doubt the Togolese men were drooling in anticipation, their expectant faces scanning the Atlantic horizon for ships packed to the gunwales with blonde nymphomaniacs and hampers of blue cheese and bacon. But it didn't happen, it wasn't the Danish who came to colonise. As bad luck would have it, it was the Germans that took over. In 1884 the country became known as German Togoland and the poor bewildered locals had only three options left open to them:

a) Live and work under German rule
b) Run away
c) Get shot

Not surprisingly the first option was deemed the least palatable of the three and most poor folk simply gathered their meagre possessions and ran like hell for the nearest border. In other parts of the world it would have been a daunting prospect, but this country was so narrow that before they had stopped for a breather they found themselves in neighbouring Gold Coast, a country run by nice chaps from Britain.

Those that hadn't been able to escape or mastermind their own executions spent the next thirty years under the Gerries, building railways and eating cabbage soaked in vinegar. So picture their joy when in 1914 both the British and French moved in and sent Fritz and his boys skulking back to the Fatherland. A great result for the Africans but the very idea of Britain and France co-operating on the running of a country, no matter how tiny, was, of course, unthinkable. So they divided it into two portions lengthways, Britain allowing France the larger slice in the hope of avoiding too much sulking and shrugging of shoulders. The smaller, western part was absorbed into the Gold Coast, later to become Ghana and the French section was to be known as Togo. And thus it remains to this day, though the country eventually achieved independence from France in 1960.

The newly-installed president was a chap called Olympio who came from the south of Togo. He didn't have much time for the folk from the north, so after three years of his antics the northern mob went south to Lomé to express their views. They killed him. That would teach him to be a racist. You don't mess with the Kabye tribe.

One Nicolas Grunitzky held the fort for the next four years and then they installed a good old northerner, name of Eyadema. He seemed to go down a lot better as he was a true Kabye and some 35 years later he was still in charge, the longest-standing African leader in power.

* * * * *

So, where was I? Ah yes, zooming through Kpalimé. We stopped in front of a simple hotel with a small bar and tables out front. It was clear that my new friend really wanted to have a chat, so I invited him to join me for a beer, a chance for him to practice his German and for me to show that I wasn't as tight-fisted as my earlier negotiating might have implied.

André explained that he had graduated from Lomé University (the only one in Togo) a few years earlier and that he could speak seven languages. So why was he a moped taxi driver? Because there were simply no jobs to be had in Togo. There was no enterprise, no companies, no investment, no money, no future. (And not many tourists either from what

I could see). I wondered whether he was painting a particularly bleak picture for my benefit, but no, this boy really seemed genuine. Most students in the country worked hard to get a degree, but in the knowledge that they would probably never find any employment. "Never", meaning "not in their entire lives." You didn't need to spend long in Togo to realise that the country was in a pretty sorry state and it had by all accounts got much worse in recent years. The international community had decided that President Eyadema was a nasty piece of work and so money that had hitherto been pumped into the country had now been completely withdrawn.

Having made me feel utterly depressed by his plight and that of his countrymen, André went back to his humble duties and I had a snooze, a shower and got myself ready for action. It was, after all, Saturday night. Darkness had brought relief from the baking heat and I decided to wander back down the road we had zoomed along a few hours earlier. But darkness also brought with it a new hazard, one for which I was not at all prepared. It was ... well ... dark. Very dark, as in having a black mask tied over your face. There was no moon or even stars in the sky and the streetlights weren't working. (How long had they been out? I later asked the question. About twelve years was the general consensus). And so I shuffled cautiously along the dusty road, the only illumination coming from passing vehicles and occasional candles from the roadside stalls. As the joke goes, what did the countries of Africa use for lighting before they relied on candles? The punchline? Electricity.

It was an odd experience. All I could see was the outline of palm trees set against a solid black mass and then suddenly, just a metre in front, the whites of the eyes of pedestrians walking towards me. There were lots of them, as there always are in Africa, and most offered a cheery 'Bon soir, Monsieur' as though everything was absolutely normal. Which, to them, it was.

After a few minutes I got used to the whole idea and came to the conclusion that the place looked a lot more pleasant in candlelight than it had in daylight. But to anybody who has spent time in African towns and cities that will not come as a big surprise. Please don't get me wrong, I love Africa and always feel I should spend more time there. It is unique in the true sense of the word. It feels different from anywhere else on the planet, but the beauty of the place does not lie in its towns and cities. It is the people, the culture, the tribal history and how they survive against the odds on the wide open savannah, in the jungles, alongside rivers (or even *on* the rivers), in the deserts. Then there's the incredible trees, the flowers, the animals, and the mountains. Beautiful birds. Africa is all about colour.

Except when it's pitch dark. The centre of town had a bit more lighting, but that was about all it had going for it. I trudged around the sad-looking place for an hour or so but it was hard to find much of interest amongst the run-down shops and stalls selling cheap clothes and fly-infested food. In truth I was happy to get back to my small hotel where I sat with a Flag beer and listened to the crickets while eating a fine dinner of Sea Bass Provencale and Banana Flambé. Sometimes travelling brings unexpected surprises just when you are starting to question your own sanity and this excellent meal was without doubt one of those golden moments.

* * * * *

In Africa I love six o'clock in the morning. The air is fresh and the sun is up, but it hasn't yet got to work in a serious way. All you have to do is pull your shorts on and walk out of the door.

I stepped out onto the street into a world that was so different from eight hours earlier. The bright blue sky and the morning sun were sitting on top of the trees, those spectacular forested mountains that loomed up behind the town, while right in front of me hundreds of people were already walking up and down the dusty road or riding their mopeds to look for work. I raised my hand as the next one approached, looked into the beaming smile of the rider and pointed towards the peaks.

The Four-Letter Countries

I was already getting to like this transport system and the thrill of the early morning breeze full in the face made me feel very happy indeed to be alive (long may "alive" continue, I couldn't help thinking). The end of the road was 15kms away at the top of the mountain, an area famed for its fantastic butterflies, and we had wound our way up there before you could say Jack Robinson. So I just had to settle for plain Jack.

My chauffeur then insisted on finding me a guide to lead me to see the butterflies. This wasn't because he had fallen in love with me, but so that he could engineer a commission for himself on the fee I was about to pay. He told the young lad that he must give me a 25% discount, then he charged me the equivalent sum for having negotiated the reduction on my behalf. On a different day I might have engaged in some verbal duelling but it was a lovely morning so I chose instead to admire his entrepreneurial spirit.

Pierre was 18 years-old, but looked a lot younger and he had lived all his life in the local village. He proudly showed me around and then took me to see the bamboo canopy structure on an open expanse of field that had served as his classroom in the years he was growing up. There were rows of old fashioned desks with inkwells and lids and a big blackboard with the teachings of the last lesson still unwiped. This took me aback, I found I was looking at a highly detailed scientific formula, not at all what I imagined would be served up to the young boys and girls of a humble mountain village.

He was an intelligent young man and delightful company. He spoke the local language of the Ewe (pronounced eevay) tribe as did his father, but his mother was a Kabye and so Pierre spoke her language too. He could also get by in Togo's other main African language, Mina. And at home they spoke French because this was the only language that his parents had in common! We walked and talked and scrambled up embankments and jumped across rivers and he pointed out all the fruits in the trees and the coffee beans and all sorts of things that I would never have noticed or been able to identify. I was loving every minute, but wringing wet from our exertions and when I ducked under a tree for a breather realised we were back where we had started. What about the butterflies? "On va maintenant," he replied, flashing that big African smile. He had just been showing me around.

The sun was starting to get hot, but thankfully our butterfly viewing spot was by a small stream under a canopy of trees. It was a lovely, tranquil place and a rare sight to see so many of these dainty creatures fluttering about in such a small area. I could have sat there all morning watching them come and go, had it not been for something of greater importance on the agenda. Time to go and eat.

We went for breakfast at the lodge where we watched the grey and pink lizards darting up the walls, sat and enjoyed the wonderful mountain landscape and talked about Pierre's ambitions and prospects. His dream was to become a professional footballer, his only hope of ever earning any money, but soon he would go to university just to delay the inevitability of a life without employment. Togo, and its people, he explained, had absolutely nothing to look forward to. He hoped things would one day get better but could not see any light at all at the end of the very long dark tunnel.

There was one more treat he wanted to share with me: The President's Palace which was up on the hill and just a few minutes' walk away. It looked impressive from a distance, but as we got closer it was evidently in a serious state of disrepair. An armed guard lay on his back on a wall by the entrance, knees in the air, cigarette in hand. Pierre went over to him and asked if the house was empty and if we could go inside. The answers were; yes it's empty, entry is forbidden, but yes you can go in if your friend gives me five bucks. A five dollar bribe to get into the President's house.

It was a very large country mansion and was worth going in for two reasons. The balconies offered fantastic 360 degree views of the surrounding mountains, on the west side looking across as far as the Lake Volta region of Ghana. The other memorable sight was the state of the interior of the so-called palace. It had the feel of an abandoned student house, everything inside was old and worn, dusty and damaged. A microcosm of the country itself. If this was how the President's residences were maintained, what hope was there for anything or anybody else?

It had been a thoroughly enjoyable morning and I was sorry to say *au revoir* to Pierre, who had been so much more than my butterfly guide. I only stayed one more day in the region after that, knowing that I'd already had the best of what Kpalimé and its environs had to offer. Next I decided to go for something completely different, a lake called Togo.

* * * * *

Lake Togo lies just to the east of Lomé, the (four-letter) capital, and so getting to it would inevitably mean having to go into the city and then coming out again the other side. I made for the bus compound in downtown Kpalimé, a frantic mass of humanity at 6am, and bought a ticket from a faceless person at a grill in the wall. Then I turned around, said the word Lomé to nobody in particular and found myself instantly thrust into a minibus full of people. This was luxury transport compared to how I had arrived, though the fact that not all the seats were actually attached to the floor of the vehicle was a matter of some slight concern.

Off we went without a fuss for the two-hour journey to Togo's biggest city. Discomfort was only minimal and everybody except me, and hopefully the driver, was asleep within minutes. I watched the villages flash by, the usual collection of mud huts, goats and chickens pecking in the dust, children waving, women hanging washing out to dry. The same sight that you see a million times throughout the mighty continent from Cairo to Cape Town. And then we had a puncture.

Everybody climbed out and stared at the driver, but he didn't have a spare tyre, so he just stared at the crumpled wheel. When it became clear that staring wasn't going to do the trick, all the people who had been sleeping started to talk at once, as though there had been a power cut and it had suddenly come back on. Arms were waved, opinions exchanged, controversy, discussion, a bit of anger, but only a bit. This was Africa. And because it was Africa another minibus pulled up behind us within a couple of minutes. Its driver had spotted that we had a problem and figured as his bus was only half full he could cope with everything and everybody that was on our poorly bus. So transfer we did and off we went. A non-stop journey to Lomé in the sense that we didn't collect or drop off any passengers along the way. But we did stop six times at roadblocks. On entering almost every village of more than ten people, the road was obstructed by a set of oil drums and a few officials monitoring the scene. The drill was that the bus stopped, everybody got out, walked 100 metres up the road and rejoined the bus again. Whether this was done for reasons of security or to generate a livelihood for the village vendors who cashed in on the passing trade was not entirely clear. Stretching legs was one thing, but repeating the process every fifteen minutes did start to become just a teeny bit annoying. At least there was plenty of time to say Jack Robinson.

We got to Lomé and I immediately grabbed a taxi away from the chaos of the bus station, agreeing a modest fee to be taken eastwards and lakewards. A chat with the taxi driver revealed that the country was falling apart, nobody could earn any money, there was no state revenue, no road repairs, no future, no nothing. It was already becoming a familiar tale. We crawled through the city traffic with the ocean to our right and were finally making some progress when my driver spotted a police checkpoint ahead. He slammed on his brakes and swung the car off the main road into a sidestreet and the next thing I knew we were bouncing across pot- holed wasteland, through endless piles of garbage and rubble and down a series of back alleyways. At first he seemed reluctant to reveal why we were going to such lengths to miss the roadblock, but then confided that the police would want documents and money and, surprise, surprise ... he didn't have either.

The Four-Letter Countries

The lake was big and imposing and gloriously serene (thankfully there isn't too much that man can do to destroy the beauty of an expanse of water) and I was dropped off at an establishment that had a dozen or so little thatched chalets on the beach. The word 'resort' had even been bandied about and the Italian people who had bought it had evidently seen its potential. No doubting it was a lovely spot, but the rooms were horrid and if the inmates of Parkhurst Prison were offered cells, beds and plumbing of that quality the Home Secretary would have another roof-top protest on his hands. I inspected a few of the chalets to verify that they were all equally unpleasant (there were no other guests of course) and then, to prove to you I am not a spoiled wimp, I checked in.

As well as very run-down accommodation and a very run-down restaurant, my new abode offered the use of a small boat complete with boatman. Whether this craft would be seaworthy I very much questioned, but I figured lakeworthiness would be less of a challenge and anyway my room was too disgusting to enter and the sun too hot to sit outside. What else was I going to do?

Across the other side of the lake and over to the left was a town known as Togoville and its claim to fame was that this was the place in which the Germans signed the documents to formalise their occupation over a hundred years earlier. They had called it Togostadt and made it their capital, but when the French took over they changed the name to Togoville and, to eradicate all things Kraut, decided that Lomé should be the centre of power instead. A fascinating bit of trivia indeed. Would a visit be equally as gripping? There was nowhere else to head for, so off we went, under sail.

* * * * *

Togoville was a dump. I stepped ashore from the tranquility of the little boat where a solitary figure at the water's edge, seemingly the only person in town, appointed himself as my guide and started to lead me through the ankle-deep garbage of the smelly streets. My instinct was to run back down the jetty and dive headlong on to the dinghy but I told myself to grow up and get a grip, the Pope had visited in 1985, so if it was good enough for him ...

Apparently it was the day after the market before and whoever was responsible for cleaning the place up had obviously not turned up for work. Whether this was my self-appointed leader trying to defend his pig sty of a town I will never know, but most certainly I won't be going back to check it out. He spoke good English and spewed forth facts and figures that went in one ear and came out the ... same ear. But there was something of interest there, something that very much dominates the lives of many in West Africa and beyond.

It is a kind of voodoo, or gris-gris as they call it, but its posh name is animism and around 70% of Togo's 5 million people follow this as their religion (the rest are Christian and Muslim). Contrary to popular western myth, voodoo isn't magic, it's a belief that attributes life or consciousness to natural objects and followers are convinced that these phenomena represent good and evil spirits which will determine their fate. They can exist in the form of mountains or rivers or animals or birds or anything really, it doesn't seem to matter. In Togoville the object of worship happens to be a large tree. Believers congregate around it and take presents to it and talk to it nicely and when special favours are required they sing to it and make wailing sounds and dance around its huge base. None of this was happening at the time of my visit unfortunately, there were just a few little gifts that had been left on the ground.

Throughout the world people do, and abstain from doing, all sorts of things in the name of spiritualism or religion. Some cut off women's genitals, some men mutilate their own, some denounce music as evil, some won't flush their toilets on Saturdays, some believe in adorning an orange with various bits and bobs at Christmas, while some sit in a box and confess their sins to a man who doesn't go out with women, and yes, some dance around trees. Oh, and some don't even eat bacon butties. Do they just eat the bread and the HP sauce? Make of it all what you will.

I was very glad indeed to climb back aboard my vessel and now I knew why the skipper had declined the option of the walk around town. The sail back took us longer since the wind was against us and for that I was extremely grateful – being on Lake Togo was very much more appealing than being adjacent to it. A day out on a boat, on a calm lake, in the tropical sun, delivers a lovely warm healthy glow to the face and that wonderful feeling of well-being. It cleanses the mind too and for a couple of blissful hours I gave not a single further thought to the squalid little hut on the far shore, my home for the evening.

And then I returned to it, stood in it, looked at it and contemplated the hours ahead. The sun would soon go down and then, without a shadow of a doubt, it would be dark. Would I then sit on my own in the dreary restaurant, or on my sagging bed with a broken spring sticking up through the middle or would I just sit on the beach and wait for it to come light again twelve hours later? None of the three options sounded terribly appealing, so I introduced another possibility. This was to get the proprietor to call me a taxi and have me transferred to a comfortable hotel in the centre of Lomé within the hour.

As though confirming my smart judgement, a strong wind suddenly appeared from nowhere. A storm was moving in and how pleased was I to be moving out. The resort manager (what else can we call him?) did one better than a cab and arranged for two Europeans who had dropped in for a beer to give me a lift back into town. Interesting guys too, one Polish, the other Norwegian, working in Africa for one of the many charity organisations. They talked knowledgeably about Togo and how it used to be a good place and how, like most of the rest of the sad continent, it was sliding downhill at a rate of knots.

The storm arrived within twenty minutes. The car windscreen wipers couldn't cope with the torrential tropical rain, neither could anything else, and the streets immediately turned into rivers, the flowing water picking up everything in its path. The lights of Lome, the ones that apparently sometimes worked, all went out at once and a sorry mass of drenched people waded through the filth in pitch darkness save for the beam of the car headlights and the increasing flashes of lightning overhead. As we drove, I decided to choose a very nice hotel.

Fifteen minutes later I was standing under a fantastic hot shower. An hour later I was eating steak au poivre and enjoying a nice glass of burgundy. Three hours later I was sleeping in a bed big enough for six people. Life just isn't fair is it? Who was it that famously said: "I've been rich and I've been poor. And being rich is better".

By next day all was calm, the sky had returned to its usual blanket of blue and I woke early to explore the capital city. I didn't know exactly where I'd been dropped the night before, but it turned out that I was right opposite what in other countries would be termed a beach. It was an area of sand that stretched a long way, but there was something decidedly gloomy and scruffy about it and it was not in the slightest bit tempting. I wondered if this was just my opinion, but noticed as the day went on that few people set foot anywhere near it.

I walked around Lomé for a long time and saw most of what there was to see ie. nothing. My biggest smile was reserved for the enormous sign identifying a smart-looking building as the American Cultural Centre. What went on in there I wondered? My mind drew a picture of the young boys and girls of Togo waddling around in absurd checked trousers, devouring buckets of tasteless food, cavorting with Ronald McDonald or Mickey Mouse and learning to speak at a volume guaranteed to drown out the world's noisiest helicopter.

The beauty of having a guidebook is that it does help you to find little-known highlights. This was certainly the case in Lomé where a daily market is held in a small street of an outer suburb, a special kind of market known to very few Lomerians, a word I just made up. I must have stopped at least ten taxi drivers before finding one that was able to take me to Le Marché des Feticheurs: the fetish market.

The Four-Letter Countries

I suspect you think a fetish is something to do with a man in leather whipping the bare buttocks of a lady in handcuffs. That indeed would make for an interesting market, but then all those taxi drivers would have heard of it wouldn't they? No, a fetish in West Africa is very different, it relates to something that we touched on a few minutes ago, an object thought to have mystical and magical powers and greatly sought after by those who need a helping hand. We have all heard that powdered rhino horn is supposed to help to make you ... er ... horny. Well, the Togolese have inherited beliefs that almost all parts of any kind of dead animal serve a special purpose for curing something. So where does the witch doctor go to get all his magic bits and pieces? Exactly, he goes along to the fetish market. So, after flagging down half the taxis in Lomé, so did I.

I had no idea what to expect. I suppose I had thought it would look market-like, which it didn't really, it was just a small bit of a street with about ten open stalls on either side. Upon each was piled a different family of skins and carcasses, an extensive selection that included dead rats, cats, bats, snakes, beetles, spiders, frogs, mice, birds, dogs ... even a horse's head that reminded me of Mr Ed. It actually had a big smile, maybe somebody had told him he was going to the Fetish Market.

There was every kind of creature you could possibly imagine and I suppose the skill of the witch doctor is to know what cures what. Income tax problems? What you need is the left paw of a dead mongoose. It was all quite organised in that each stall had a speciality, so when The Doc goes in search of a particular species of dead beast he doesn't have to push his trolley around the dusty road for too long. Which is no bad thing, what with the heat and the stench. It was fascinating in a ghoulish sort of way and I suppose an ideal opportunity to find that unusual gift for Terry next time he cut my hair. But sadly I didn't have space in my pack for a grinning decapitated horse.

Most cities in the world, even the really grotty ones, have a few pleasant streets with lots of trees and elegant buildings to house wealthy

Togo

industrialists and pampered diplomats. African ones are certainly no exception and it was no surprise to find a suburb in the north of Lomé with smart avenues and masses of bright red and purple bougainvillaea hanging over the high white walls. What a stark contrast this was to the centre of the city, where the general chaos had been made even worse by the rains of the night before, and the deathly stink of the fetish market from where I'd just landed.

The thought of swimming in a lovely big, clean pool had got the better of me during a moment of weakness at the dead locust stall, so I'd flagged down a taxi and asked to be taken to the British School. I'd read that their luxurious pool was open to the general public, or rather those that could afford the entrance fee; a worthless few coins to a tourist, but a week's wages to any local person with the good fortune to have a job at all.

Not surprisingly most of the sunbeds at poolside were empty, just a handful of people there who were lucky enough to have been born in another part of the world. I lay back and thought of Togo and reflected on the big nasty vicious circle into which it had been well and truly sucked. The bottom line is really quite simple: this country is broke so has no money to smarten itself up. What little money there is for public amenities is spent in the north of the country, where the president hails from, so few people ever see the benefit of that. Word gets round that Togo is a decaying mess and the tourists that once did consider the country the jewel of West Africa take their custom somewhere else. Sad, but I suppose if there is a positive side, Togo's loss must be somebody else's gain.

The next day I decided it was time to head back into Ghana which gives me the opportunity to drop in a delightful little quiz question. "In world geographical terms, what is unique about Lomé as a capital city?" I reckon this would be a challenge even for those nerdy pubgoers up and down the land that can run off the name of every US President in sequence and tell you the song that was at Number One in February

The Four-Letter Countries

1962. According to something I once read, and I'm more than happy for you to contest it, Lomé is the only capital city on the planet to be located on an international border.

It took me less than five minutes from the hotel to that unique crossing point, on the back of a moped of course, a mode of travel that I knew I was going to miss. It was the end of my short trip and I have to admit I wasn't sorry to be going back to Ghana, a country with so much more hope and optimism. Maybe one day I would return to Togo to spend some time in the north and see for myself how the President is spending his money, but with a good few FLCs still to get to, and a lot more countries besides, I suspect that may be quite a few years down the line.

PERU

The first time I ever set out to explore the slightly daunting continent of South America was in those carefree days of early life when being a back-packer was the nearest thing that some of us had to a full time occupation. It was a long time ago – 1986 to be precise – and the starting point for that big Latin adventure was Mexico City.

The journey south from there had started, in mind if not in body, shortly after 1pm, Sunday lunchtime, June 22nd. I remember it as though it was yesterday: the haze of cheap tequila, the flags, the horns, the deafening sound of 115,000 slightly deranged people. The enormity of the Aztec Stadium was like nothing else on the planet and the two goals in favour of Argentina like nothing else seen before or since in the history of Association football. A little man called Diego Maradona had scored them both in the space of four minutes, one with the help of God's hand, the other a work of pure genius: the Argies were through and England, once again, were left to contemplate a World Cup quarter-final exit. Never mind, it was only football. At least the Falkland Islands were still ours to enjoy. And so that was that. Gary Lineker and the crestfallen (1980s for gutted) lads boarded the plane for London and I boarded the bus, the first of several hundred, vaguely in the direction of Brazil.

This time it would be very different. I wasn't a backpacker anymore but a respectable, grown, fortysomething man with a serious objective in life – to travel to countries with four letters. This version of me would travel to Peru in a comfortable aeroplane and, so as to complete my South American circuit from two decades earlier, I would arrive from the south, via Argentina and Chile.

The Four-Letter Countries

* * * * *

Boca is a working class and somewhat intimidating suburb in the south of Buenos Aires, but I knew the journey to Peru would have to start there. It just felt right; for this was where Maradona had grown up, this was where he had taken the beautiful game to even more beautiful levels. Back in the days before he started eating all the pies.

I'd spent a few really pleasant days in BA, that elegant, sophisticated city, where the air was still a bit chilly in the morning hours and the trees still poised to reach full bloom. And finally it was Sunday, the big match, and I had a ticket. Boca Juniors v Estudiantes. La Bombonera, the chocolate box. A fantastic name for a football stadium don't you think?

The atmosphere was pure carnival: flags, drums, singing, dancing, and most of all, simultaneous jumping up and down on the spot. I felt a tad self-conscious, not obliging with any sort of a pogo movement, firm-footed and pan-faced throughout: Sven-Göran Eriksson at a rave. Freezing rain appeared from nowhere, well … from Antarctica actually, but only I seemed to care about being soaked to the skin. The party went on, this was Boca after all, where real fans don't just support the team till they die, they book themselves a plot in the Boca Players and Supporters' Cemetery. Oh and there was a match too, though at times it seemed largely irrelevant. Boca won, the mass of yellow shirts bounced up and down, the drum carried on beating but, alas, there was no Maradona.

The wild, youthful Jenkins had missed out on Chile, too, so I popped in to Santiago before heading north. The two-hour flight west from BA to the other side of the Andes was more like a pole vault really, an incredibly long flat run across the plains of Argentina followed by a very quick up and down over the snowy peaks. And there she was, Santiago, the Chilean capital, sitting quietly in a bowl, with those wonderful green and white-topped mountains looking down on the rooftops from all points of the compass.

Peru

The city itself, geographical setting aside, seemed quite unremarkable, but I enjoyed a few days in and around the capital and as with Argentina and Uruguay, Chile struck me as a surprisingly clean, orderly and well-disciplined kind of place. A sort of Latin American version of Scandinavia. Whatever happened to chaos, noise, pollution, misery? It just didn't seem right somehow. I knew it was time to head to Peru.

* * * * *

For once I had my pen ready, knew my flight number, had all my passport details to hand and was thoroughly prepared for the Peruvian immigration forms deposited onto my meal tray. I even had my reading specs, the true sign of the mature traveller, and decided to maximise the moment with a nerdish inspection of the customs regulations on the back. Always guaranteed to raise a smile. God forbid I might have even laughed out loud. The English was appalling, every few words a howler, but why? Why is it, in a world where billions of people speak and write in absolutely perfect, fluent English, that governments and companies and restaurants and so forth continue to have important documents and signs translated by a bunch of schoolkids with a pocket dictionary? But thank you Peru for easing me back in. And long may we continue to have restaurants where we can "come and gust and enjoy fine intercourse" and temples where "it is forbidden to enter women during menstruation".

A lot of international flights arrive into Lima late at night, but Peruvian immigration gets them through quite quickly. At least that was my observation in the glass-half-full moment immediately before I was invited to step forward. As I held my passport open in front of her, the lady tapped in whatever they tap into a computer in immigrations worldwide, then tapped again, and again, and then again. And then came a furrow upon the brow of officialdom, a flicking of pages, and finally a question.

"Do you have another passport?"

The Four-Letter Countries

It was then, and only then, that an image flashed through my mind: the first time I'd thought about it in nigh on twenty years. A hazy memory of a happy, smiling young Jenks and a fellow traveller, Swiss – Christoph, I think – being conveyed to the Bolivian border by young Peruvian lads pushing makeshift wheelbarrows. Bloody hell, now I remember. The Peruvian border post was closed for the night, but the Bolivian one up the road was open. So we did what any other young lads would have done. We said 'Bugger It' (and the Swiss-German equivalent), 'we're not hanging around here until morning.' So we entered Bolivia without ever getting stamped out of Peru.

"Pardon?"

"Do you have another passport other than this one?"

Keep it simple. Smile. Look a bit puzzled in a friendly sort of way.

"No."

It was a strange question and a half true answer. Did she mean another valid passport or was she referring to my drawer full of Black Beauties before purple Europlastic dominated the world? Was I about to be had up for two decades of tax evasion or conscripted into the Peruvian military?

"OK – no problem." Stamp. Stamp. And almost a smile.

I was tempted to ask what the story was, but it was a temptation I managed to resist. I was in, that was the most important thing, and it wasn't the time or place to start pushing my luck.

* * * * *

It's generally accepted that the most pleasant part of the city of Lima is the ocean-side suburb of Miraflores, so I got in a cab and said: "Miraflores, por favor." It has to be said that expectations were not great, this city had after all been described by one guidebook as: "the saddest place on Earth". (Bear in mind many guidebook writers have never been to Stockport or Lagos).

Peru

The Hotel Antigua Miraflores is a lovely old, colonial style property built around a courtyard with a fountain in the middle. The ceilings are high and the floors are tiled and the chairs are comfy and the books are plentiful and the paintings are fascinating and the internet is free and the food is great and I loved it all. It's one of those places that made you feel you were somewhere really different and that much of what the streets outside had to offer would likely be a disappointment by comparison.

Miraflores was actually OK. I wandered along the main commercial centre past the airline offices, companies and banks that had cut and run from downtown, the way Sandton has pulled away from the decay of Johannesburg. For the first time in my life I saw uniformed 'cambistas' (money-changers) on street corners, outwardly touting for dollars and proudly sporting their official cambista licence numbers. Whatever next – Dial-a-Joint, an official purveyor of spliffs? After the serenity of Salvador it was good to get back to some nice smoky exhausts and see people dangling precariously from minibuses in search of passengers. And three wheel bicycles with cages of food on the front and plenty of pointless hammering on car horns. Yes, oh yes, this was a bit more like it.

I was eager to see the sea, to get a first glance of the Pacific whilst wearing my FLC colours. This was, I had thought, the furthest west that our journey to the Magic Ten would take us, a special moment to ponder and savour. But I was wrong, I had fallen for this one before. What on earth is he on about, you might be forgiven for asking? You see, South America is not below North America, but diagonally across so to speak. The west side of the southern bit sits vertically below the EAST side of USA thus making Miami further west than Lima and New York even further west than Santiago. And yes, Havana and half of Cuba is the most westerly point on the FLC map. Got it?

I stared out to the Pacific Ocean and watched the huge waves come crashing in. There is always something compelling about the sea and this one is the Daddy of them all, not just a body of water, but a third of our entire planet, bigger by far than all the countries in the world put together. When this one goes wrong and El Nino arrives, the whole of mankind knows about it: sea levels rise in Peru, weather patterns change left, right and centre, and the whole global system goes, as it is known in scientific circles, tits up. I stared some more, fixated with the idea that I could float out to sea and quite possibly drift westwards for the best part of 10,000 miles without hitting land. If I was lucky, I might stumble ashore on an exotic Polynesian island dominated by topless, grass-skirted nubile females and if I wasn't, I'd probably hit the northern tip of Australia and be eaten by crocodiles. That's life, innit?

My gaze moved to the harsh cliffs and the deserted beach and a smile crossed my face as I thought of family holidays in Cornwall, cowering from the icy wind behind a piece of canvas on poles that my Dad bashed into the sand with a huge mallet. Did he really pack a mallet as part of our holiday gear? At least Newquay was rather prettier than Lima.

There were some nice flowers, as you would expect in a place called Look at the Flowers, as Miraflores translates, and also a few smart buildings scattered amongst the mix. But all in all it was pretty uninspiring stuff, a sort of drab seaside resort only people with failing health, no money or a desperate lack of imagination would seriously countenance. Anyway, I'd never thought of Peru as a tropical riviera.

But I had thought of Peru as a smallish, predominantly mountainous country on the west side of South America. You too? If so, sorry, but you only scored one out of three. It is in fact the second largest of the FLCs, amongst the top twenty countries in the world by area and two thirds of it is covered in rainforest. I won't bore you with more geography except to say that this unusual nation divides into three very distinct vertical slices – the coast, the mountains and the jungle – and my plan was to enjoy a little taste of all three.

There didn't seem a lot of point in staying any longer in Lima. I wouldn't describe the place as utterly toiletesque, but the two highlights for me were the home made food in the hotel and the departure lounge at the airport. The centre of the city was at best unappealing and the outskirts, viewed in daylight en route to the airport, nothing more than a depressing sprawl of urban misery. It was time to head for them there mountains.

* * * * *

It doesn't take very long to fly from the Pacific coast to the Andes, but the distance from west to east is of little importance. The big issue here is that Cuzco is more than two miles higher than Lima, a launch into orbit that equates to getting in a lift on the ground floor and stepping out an hour later on the 700th. Extensive research into the effects of sudden change in altitude would indicate that the body doesn't really take kindly to this and that once above 2,500m one needs to tread very carefully indeed. Failure to toe the line can be punished with any number of permutations from a menu that includes headaches, dizziness, loss of appetite, fatigue, pulmonary oedema, seizures, coma and death.

I stepped off the plane very cautiously in Cuzco, a mighty 3,500m above sea level, wondering if anybody had ever become delirious before collecting their bags from the carousel. This might not be my most westerly FLC experience, but it was definitely the furthest I'd be venturing above sea level – who knew what might happen? It had been a pleasant short flight and an unusual experience to have snowy mountains not only below the aircraft, but pretty much up alongside the windows!!

My memories of Cuzco from a former life were that of being very cold and having my bag slashed by one of the notorious gangs of old ladies who hovered around the tourist spots. The visitors in those days were largely backpackers like myself, but it soon became clear this time round that Peru was now very much a major tourist destination. I concentrated on walking slowly to adjust to the altitude, enjoying the clear sky and warm sunshine one minute and taking cover from the cold rain the next.

And what a beautiful place Cuzco is. An imposing square at its centre, a maze of sloping cobbly streets-cum-markets leading from it and the green of the mountains on all four sides, one bearing a huge 'Viva Peru' message carved just below its peak. This had been the home of the Incas, the core of their civilisation. For several hundred years they had dominated the continent, created buildings and towns and cities from nothing, brought their incredible architectural skills to the simple folk of the mountains. And they would, by all accounts, have continued to spread east towards the Amazon and Brazil had the Spanish not arrived and spoiled the party. That was in the 1500s, a brutal time in history when life was very much black and white: either they killed you, or you killed them. As it turned out it wasn't so much the wizardry of the Spanish warmongers that ultimately wiped out the 25 million or so Incas, but the nasty diseases they brought with them.

It was a joy to saunter along the narrow streets, between those walls of huge smooth rectangular boulders the clever Incas had built all that time ago. I had a very positive feeling about Cuzco this time round, there was no menace at all in the air, I would come back and stay a bit longer next week. Tomorrow, though, I would follow a guide up into the mountains, get some fresh air, enjoy the Andes, the longest mountain range in the world, and hopefully keep well clear of pulmonary oedema.

Urubamba is a neat little town that sits alongside a river of the same name, some 60 kms to the northwest of Cuzco. This is the heart of the Sacred Valley, an area of outstanding beauty that leads to the lost city of Machu Picchu and eventually snakes down towards the rainforest and the steamy heat of the Amazon basin. It had always baffled me how the flatter, western side of Peru and Chile could be so dry, even desert, when there is so much snow and rain in the mountains, but now the answer was right in front of me. Very little of it goes out towards the Pacific, it almost all ends up heading east and flowing out across Brazil and into the Atlantic way beyond.

To those of us who enjoy walking, cycling and having fun on the water, Urubamba is the place to be. I'd signed up for a few days of fresh air and fun and was out shortly after sun up the next morning along with a group of fellow booted individuals with white legs, funny hats and black Lowe Alpine backpacks. From a walker's standpoint, there was a hell of a lot to go at. The Incas were kind enough to develop an extensive network of over 30,000 kms of trails during their few hundred years of domination and thankfully only a small section of one of them has become commercialised in any way. The Inca Trail, as it has been marketed, is the 50kms or so leading into Machu Picchu and in the interest of preservation this is now restricted to ticket-holders only.

The walking pace above the Sacred Valley was cautiously slow to get us up to 4,000 metres above sea level. Even so, the thin air caused the heart and the head to pound simultaneously and at times it felt like running a middle distance sprint with a severe hangover. Strange the things some people do for fun isn't it? Everybody in the group had headaches at some point, some went a bit white and dizzy, one poor lady puked her way round the course for the best (or worst) part of two days. She took it all in her stride though, apparently, the same thing had happened to her in Nepal the year before. I didn't like to ask whether she was being sponsored for some sort of Vomathon for Comic Relief.

The bit I liked best was when we sat at the top in the sunshine, the hour of pleasure that makes walking seem like a sane thing to do. Thankfully we had porters to carry and prepare the lunch, two men, each with a llama, who had set out at 3am that morning for the five hour walk to our starting point. Their job was to lead us all day through the mountains, cook lunch, wash dishes and pack stuff away during our rest break and then they would make the five hour trip back home.

Life in the Andes is tough, a constant challenge for survival where the men have to squeeze every last drop from the land and their animals, llamas for the heavy work and the furrier alpacas for tasty meat and wool for clothing. Back down in the villages I watched the bowler-hatted ladies work tirelessly washing the wool, dying it all sorts of colours by mixing water with leaves and plants from the area then weaving the fabric for hours and hours on primitive hand looms. Day in, day out, year in, year out they sit there producing lengths of beautiful material, intricate designs, but for all their efforts they can generate little more than one metre a day. Do they get a better deal than the men? Which would you prefer: a) 17 hours walking in the mountains or b) 12 hours a day sitting with a hand loom strapped to your waist and a child hanging from your nipple? (You are allowed to alternate nipples).

If you think that sounds like hard going, what about those Incas? They would toil for years to turn the steep mountainsides into terraces, moving rocks and boulders the size of polar bears to create flat surfaces on which to build homes and grow crops. How did they do that? And then have the skill and presence of mind to smooth them all down with water and interlock them in such a clever way that earthquakes couldn't knock them over.

Their trails took us to Pisac and later to Ollantaytambo, to the remains of incredible Inca fortresses built on the sides of mountains, carefully planned to offer maximum defence to their citizens, always facing east/west to observe the rising and setting of the sun. That these people could create communities like this from nothing, with no technology, not even the wheel, did get me thinking. Will Barratt's cardboard homes still be standing in 500 years time?

The people of the mountains are not your typical Peruvians, just as merchant bankers from Vienna share little in common with the yodelling farmers of the western Tyrol. These simple country folk have their own traditions and spiritual beliefs, their clothes are heavy and brightly coloured, the roofs of their houses carry small messages to the Gods to ask for strength and fertility. They eat what they grow and it is actually here that one of the world's most important vegetables was first discovered. Yes folks, although it's the French who are famous for slicing them up and frying them, it was actually the Spanish who brought the magic spud to Europe.

Our second day in the mountains was quite different from the first. The terrain on the other side of the valley was flat and spongy underfoot, a wild and windswept landscape as exposed as the plains of Mongolia. The weather changed back and forth with frightening rapidity and when the hailstorm came how thankful were we to have a team of porters on hand to erect a large circular tent and prepare a bowl of spicy guacamole for lunch.

The rainy season in Peru is a predictable business and pretty much coincides with the winter months in Europe. The Peruvians also refer to this as their winter, despite the fact that it is their warmer season, and at this time the river levels rise considerably as the snow melts up on the peaks. Fortunately for me, the Rio Urubamba has enough water even at its lowest to make it raft-able year round and I wasn't about to miss the opportunity of being carted off downriver in a small rubber boat.

Six of us strapped on jackets and helmets and splashed our way through the rapids, not as rapid as they sometimes were by all accounts, but nonetheless it was great to be on the river with that inescapable view of the mountains. We got through the bumpy sections of white water without any dramas, but as it turned out that was by far the easiest part. Our skipper was determined we should have more fun, so once the "Yeehahs!" of celebration had subsided, he would have us turn the boat round, paddle like hell into the ongushing current and then ... "Attack!". He'd already told us what that meant and it was a pretty daunting little game. Myself and the guy straight across had to fling ourselves forward so that our bodies hung over the bow, while the others leapt on our backs to anchor us, and the boat, in position. The transference of weight ensured that the raft was held beautifully in place – slap bang in the centre of the rapid – though gallons of water eventually started to force it under and our two little weighted heads were for the most part half a metre below the surface. I must say it was a thoroughly invigorating experience, though, as I resurfaced from the torrent for a brief instant, it did cross my mind a few times that death was but moments away.

The Four-Letter Countries

* * * * *

Back in the wonderful dryness of the hotel room I started to realise that all was not quite as it should have been. The simple act of walking was causing a pain in a very delicate part of my anatomy and I wondered whether this was a direct result of my maniacal forward lunges into the teeth of the rapids. The next day I tried a bit of cycling, but the problem was getting very much worse and by the end of that afternoon there was a very definite swelling, er, down below. My mind turned to that bloke from Wiltshire, though I hadn't thought about it him for many years:

There was a young man from Devizes
Whose bollocks were two different sizes
One was so small it was no good at all
But the other was big and won prizes.

Within two days I knew I was looking at a potential prize-winner, an extremely ripe raspberry in colour, but very much grapefruit in circumference. This was new territory for me, and I can't say I liked it, but I would just have to take it like a man and look on the bright side of life. The first positive step I figured was to think of him as my mate and it seemed only right that such a magnificent gonad should be given a name. Alliteration is always essential in these matters and I tinkered with the obvious options: Graham, Gilbert, Godfrey … how about Gordon? Gordon the Gonad. That seemed to work quite well, but then … a sudden horrible moment of doubt. I have a good mate called Gordon, would he forever become synonymous with my enlarged scrotum? Oh, don't talk such bollocks.

I ordered asparagus soup from room service and raided my feeble little first-aid kit which, to my surprise and absolute delight, yielded some antibiotics that claimed to repair infections of the genitalia. It really did seem ironic that over the years I have been jabbed and filled with pills against malaria, cholera, typhoid, hepatitis of half the alphabet, yellow fever, and God knows what else and here I was looking at a testicle half the size of Greenland. Would these little white pills really work? Time would tell, but how much time? What else could I do? Should I take photos of me and Gordon to send to friends, or maybe draw a smiley face on him like Tom Hanks did with his volleyball in *Castaway?*

Gordon seemed at his happiest just lolling around on the bed, so I decided to tailor my evening's entertainment accordingly. The bedside lamp threw a very satisfying circle of light onto the side wall, so I spent quite a long time that evening engaged in the cultural activity of making a llama's head appear with the shadow of my hand. It took considerable patience to reach a standard I was happy with, though in truth it wasn't a patch on my Andy Capp. And you think travelling is just days on end of having fun don't you.

If you ever find yourself in Peru with a seriously inflamed gonad let me tell you that there are far worse places to be than Urubamba. Gordon and I spent a very pleasant time there drinking cappuccino in a café on the little square and it turned out to be a very special Sunday morning in the local calendar. It was the day of the year the children from all the local schools come in to town, in their very smart uniforms, to take part in the parades and to receive awards for their individual or collective achieve- ments. It seemed such a proud, happy and colourful occasion with the innocence of an era that in most parts of the world have long since passed and we felt really privileged to be there.

I liked Urubamba. As with everywhere in the Andes, the spectacular backdrop gave it an added dimension, but it was more than that. It was vibrant, colourful, the jacaranda trees were in bloom and overall the place had a pleasant cheery feel. The ladies in the town mostly dressed in their colourful skirts and ponchos and hats and I sat chatting to them at the juice bar in the huge indoor food market, a mind-boggling festival of freshly dug vegetables and recently-slaughtered animals. The vegetable section was rather the more pleasant of the two.

The Four-Letter Countries

* * * * *

Machu Picchu is far and away the most famous of all the Inca sites and rightly one of the biggest tourist attractions in the whole of South America. What a story this is: a lost city that was discovered less than a hundred years ago, high up on a peak, but so deeply bedded into the forest that it had been completely hidden to the world since the 16th century; real life Indiana Jones stuff.

Today the trees have gone and it stands there in all its glory, a setting of incredible beauty. The remnants of a city on top of a mountain, in the middle of a valley, surrounded by even bigger mountains. Like sitting on top of a traffic cone inside a large bucket, the views from Machu Picchu go round three hundred and sixty degrees. Well almost. The site can actually be reached from the mountains away to the east, the trail that brings the trekkers in, and this incredible vista is what greets them after five days of walking.

Gordon and I had to do it the easy way, so we took the train to Aguas Calientes, a pleasant mountain town that has a single railway track as its main street and the usual tourist mix of restaurants, hotels and internet cafes lining the platforms. This is the end of the line, a half-day journey that winds down through the Sacred Valley from Cuzco, and the point from which a battalion of small buses shuttles tourists up to the top of the mountain.

Walking and clambering, or should I say clanking, wasn't an option that day, but this suited me just fine. Once off the bus and through the entrance, it was easy to find a quiet spot and there was so much to simply sit and admire. I even penned a little verse, if you will allow:

Instead of viewing Inca walls
I'll just sit down and rest my balls,
Admire the river down below
And watch the tourists come and go.

Peru

The Japanese like rows of ants
With matching hats and matching pants,
Posing for cameras from every direction
The Japanese art of photo collection.

My patch of grass escapes the crowds,
To hear the birds and watch the clouds
On wooded mountains all around
Constant movement, gentle sound.

The Inca ruins, they can wait
For first, one ought to contemplate
Pure nature at its very best,
No better place one's balls to rest.

I went back again the next day, did some more sitting, then teetered gently along the terraces and around the walls, the former homes of perhaps 1,500 people. This was the city that the Spanish had never got their hands on and the reason it is still so well preserved today. Looking around, it was incredible to think that hundreds of years earlier each individual piece of rock had been carefully shaped and lifted into position to comply with the very strict Inca disciplines that blended the practicalities of shelter and defence with their respect for nature and the environment. The Sacred Rock was my favourite, a huge piece of stone the size of a small truck that occupied a gallery befitting a major work of art. This enormous slab had somehow been crafted and positioned such that its top edge formed a craggy line almost identical to the shape of the mountains in the distance way beyond. How on earth did they manage to do that?

The train back up to Cuzco, packed to the gunwales with charity walkers, seemed to take for ever, but then it is 1,000 metres higher than Machu Picchu. It seemed quite chilly back in the city and ever such a huge place after country life, but most importantly it was somewhere I could introduce Gordon to a doctor.

The man with the magic bag came round to the hotel and seemed suitably impressed with my new mate. He assured me it was not a case of Rafters Bollock, but an infection of the epidydimis, a bit of male tubing that, to the best of my knowledge, had not been invented in the days that I did biology O-level. (And though it's not remotely relevant I just have to tell you, without a word of a lie, that our biology teacher was called Mr Jermy). I took the injection like a man, thankful that my left buttock was deemed the best place for it, received a stash of anti-inflammatories and told to take complete rest. "Reposo, muy importante," he said several times, sensing his counsel might fall on deaf ears. And with that he shook my hand, took my dollars, and headed off to his next patient, completely oblivious that the weight of his large square case had caused it to swing round behind him and catch me in the nuts as I followed him to the door.

There were lots of things I'd wanted to do in Cuzco. Did I really have to waste a whole day convalescing? I supposed the doc knew best and, even though he probably wouldn't find out if I'd been dancing the Macarena into the early hours, I told myself in a very grown up way that it wasn't really the point. And anyway, I couldn't even dance the Macarena in the days when my scrotum was a thing of unparalleled beauty.

To rest was clearly the right thing to do, but resting, I figured, could take many forms. And so, feeling ever so naughty, I sneaked out onto the street, hailed a taxi (ever 'hailed' anything else?), and demanded to be taken to the main square. If I was going to do *reposo* it would at least be done with a measure of style.

I took up position on one of the eighty or so bright green benches in the Plaza de Armas, opting for one at the top end and facing down the slope. Sitting in a square had, in my previous life, generally been a pause between activities, but today this was my activity and so every decision surrounding it would take on a much greater level of importance: starting with bench selection. My game plan for the day was broadly to dedicate around an hour's staring to each of the four directions of the compass, enhancing viewing options by introducing new bench or benches as required. As I said earlier, resting can take many forms.

Looking around me on that lovely September morning it was mildly disconcerting to observe that, in fact, almost all the other seats were taken, albeit that few had multiple occupants. Competition was something I hadn't even considered and obviously would now have to be factored in. If it came to the crunch, would I be prepared to share a Peruvian form with a total stranger, risk him or her mistaking me for a sexual predator? No way, José. For a bloke with a diseased epidoodah this would be too ironic for words.

It is a lovely square with the backdrop of the Andes on all four sides and I didn't feel in any way that the day was being wasted. After all, what is more delightful than the sun on your back, the sight of orange and yellow and purple flowers in bloom and the sound of water cascading from a beautiful fountain. If I was going to behave like an old person, it would help me enormously to start thinking like one.

Most of the world's serious squares have at least one dominating building as its main feature. La Plaza de Armas actually has a couple. To my left was the strange-looking cathedral, more wide and solid than tall and pointy, almost like a fort, and straight ahead of me a huge and incredibly impressive church, La Iglesia de la Compania de Jesus. It is a little known fact that Jesus, sensing religion was about to take off in a big way, had the foresight to register a Peruvian company to invest in some prime worshipping real estate.

I looked around in all directions, not adhering to the original plan. Wow, how this place had changed since my first time in Peru when Cuzco seemed little more than just a country town. In those days all the local people wore clothes of the Andes and a handful of backpackers wandered the markets, getting their bags slashed by gangs of old ladies with razors. It was now truly a tourist destination, but a friendlier and safer place to be, evidently more developed and certainly more wealthy, but for me no less charming because of it. The market traders in the cobbled streets were still doing a great business with the tourists, competing fiercely to sell multi-coloured coats, sweaters, scarves and hats with earflaps and dangly cords while the square was full of posh, glass-fronted boutiques selling much the same thing, but boasting the finest baby alpaca wool and – always the tell-tale sign of a rip-off – charging in US dollars.

After a couple of hours and many, many 'No, gracias'-es to young boys selling postcards, the blue sky suddenly turned grey and the warmth of the sun had all but disappeared. It was incredible to think that Cuzco is a tropical city, on the same line of latitude as Darwin, where the heat drives people to mental breakdown and levels of alcohol abuse thought high even by Australian standards. In Peru, at this altitude of more than two miles above sea level, weather really is a very unpredictable business. Anyway it was time for lunch and looking around me there were plenty of restaurants to choose from, most with quaint wooden verandas looking out over the square, like a scene from a western movie. It was time to go for my second GP of the day.

There has to be good reason why Guinea Pig is the most prized delicacy of the Andes, why any groom wanting to impress his guests on the biggest day of his life would make sure that there were plenty to go round. Probably a whole animal per person if the budget would allow. It all seemed so utterly bizarre to me, why choose this pathetic little creature and is it generally served with a miniature plastic wheel? Anyway, when in Rome, have a pizza and when in Peru ... mmm ... probably a pizza wasn't such a bad idea.

Oh don't be a coward Jenkins, what's the worst that could happen? So I ordered up a *cuy*, as this local speciality is known, and within a few minutes the plate was set before me. On the left side three very pleasing slices of potato, on the right a brown crusty-skinned headless corpse somewhat akin to a very large cockroach. But perhaps slightly less appealing.

Peru

After an intense period of reflection, I gave the thing a flip and found myself staring into a tightly packed labyrinth of small bones, bits of fat and a range of other indecipherable substances. I reflected a little more, savoured my first cherished slice of potato and thought a bit more about pizza.

"You need to pick it up and really get in there."

Paul was from Norfolk and spoke with the experience of a man who had just finished 'pigging out' himself. He was enjoying the moment; probably rather more than he'd enjoyed his lunch, I couldn't help thinking.

Getting in there sounded as much fun as raiding a wasp's nest, but I did as I was instructed. Let me tell you now that I have never derived a millionth of a modicum of pleasure from consuming any sort of food that demands more than a basic fork to mouth transfer. Delicious the end product may be, but nothing thus far in my pampered world has ever justified the tedium of a pre-scoff dissection or the sheer indignity of wrestling with a greasy mass of innards.

In I went, no holding back. Bones, cartilage, tendons, gristle, more bones, fat, a bit of skin. And that was just on my chin. Oh, and about half a teaspoonful of reddish brown meat that tasted OK-ish. Then a big gulp of coke and some more lovely potato. Wow, I'd never realised potato could taste so good. Paul and I chatted about guinea pigs and came to a unanimous agreement that, dead or alive, these pointless little beasts would never again feature in any aspect of our lives. Then we watched the sky turn from grey to black and the tropical rain come tumbling down, in straight heavy lines, on the now deserted square. All those green seats were free at last – 'what an opportunity!' went through the mind of one sad old git.

* * * * *

Tropical countries to me mean palm trees, round the clock warmth, lots of sweating, the constant presence of bugs. Sometimes it's great and sometimes it's horrid, but, when you've done a few days of coats and hats in the eye of an equitorial downpour, it sounds just the ticket. And so it was time to head further east, towards the rainforest and the borders with Bolivia and Brazil, to a Peru that would have little in common with the country life of the Andes.

Bags packed and ready for off I was reading e-mail in the hotel reception when, to my great surprise, in walked the doc. Oh no, teacher had spotted me smoking behind the bike sheds! In fact he'd come to check me out for the last time, make sure I was OK, and slip a few more greenbacks into his sky rocket. A check-out check-out, so to speak. He looked around, spotted a door in the corner and by peering through its central window saw it was a small storage cupboard. That was to be his temporary surgery and a few seconds later he had me up against the shelves getting the full vertical inspection, shorts and undies around my ankles. Now I'm not sure how common this practice is in Peruvian hotel lobbies, but the face of the waiter that appeared at the window indicated to me that he rarely stumbled across such a sight in the course of storing his table cloths. He turned away and took his linen elsewhere, no doubt to a safe haven where he could share his 'two men in the cupboard' story.

Two more botty jabs and thirty dollars later I was on the plane to Puerto Maldonado, a shabby frontier town that had obviously grown too quickly for its own good. This was the most easterly of Peru's twenty four departementos, a region known as Madre de Dios because somebody once thought they had spotted God's mum there. (It turned out to be somebody else's Mum, but that wouldn't have made a very good name). A more aptly-titled place was my next destination, a settlement in the jungle that was first inhabited by migrant workers who came down from the mountains in search of a better life. The searing heat and malaria-carrying mosquitoes were not exactly what they'd bargained for and they could think of only one word to describe their new home. The Spanish for Hell is *Infierno* and the name has stuck to this day.

Peru

It took about an hour and a half on the bus, so that would be a three-hour round trip for the driver whose job it is to go to Hell and back every day. The assorted foreigners on board hadn't come to look at the shacks or the sad little rectangle of white crosses in the clearing, but to catch a boat up the Tambopata, a large C-shaped river that rises in Bolivia (at the bottom of the C), pops into Peru and then flows back across the border. The river was wider than I'd expected, perhaps 300 metres across, though why I should have had any preconceived ideas about a river I'd never heard of is in itself a fascinating point. Why do you expect a voice on the phone late on a Saturday night to be that of a tall, blonde person? I digress. It felt proper jungle, dense rainforest on both sides, and the three-hour trip up-river was the best way to spot the Howler monkeys in the trees, the turtles, caymans and capybaras (the world's largest rodent) on the banks and exotic species of birds darting across the river.

The birds were spectacular, the most graceful just quietly watching and waiting above the surface of the water, others squawking endlessly and circling in search of action. What a range of shapes and sizes and, above all, fantastic tropical colours. Most species I had never heard of, no surprises there, except for the kingfishers, parakeets and, king of them all, the macaws. Several times we saw them, both the blue/yellow and the red/green varieties, always flying in groups of their own colour and making that distinctive screech as they went.

Further upriver, and unfortunately far beyond the lodge to which we were heading, there was apparently a very strange phenomenon which I would love to have seen. A clay lick. Ever heard of one? The Tambopata Clay Lick is one of the biggest out of around 120 that have so far been discovered in the Amazon region. It's almost like a cliff on one side of the river upon which macaws, parrots and parakeets gather in huge numbers, shortly after daybreak every morning, and again around noon, to do some licking. The minerals in the clay serve as a huge indigestion tablet and help to neutralise the acids from their fruity diets, yet another of those bizarre quirks of nature that makes you wonder who first stumbled upon the idea.

The lodge was really a small jungle village made up of thatched cottages, a central dining area, a makeshift library, and a small bar. All this in an idyllic setting, one simply couldn't have wished for anything more. The main driving force behind it was, of course, to attract tourists, but it was very clear from our introductory meeting that everybody in that small community lived and worked there with pride and passion. Their mission was to explore and understand all that the rainforest had to offer, to ensure that it wasn't mistreated and to share their knowledge with those of us who would probably only get there one time in our lives.

I was shown to my cottage and had to resist the temptation to dive straight into the hammock that smiled from the balcony. The afternoon sun was dipping fast, the luxury of daylight would soon be replaced by torches and candles, but, as you know, a man's domestic duties must always come first. Darkness did indeed arrive quickly and with it a cacophony of the strangest sounds you could ever imagine. Though I hadn't realised it, the afternoon had been quiet, just the occasional screech of birds or monkeys, but suddenly it was all a very different story. Night-time was when the creatures of the jungle came out to play and suddenly an invisible world had burst into life. It was exciting, powerful and the sheer volume of it really took me by surprise. I decided to torch my way back down to the river, just to sit by the water's edge and listen.

The frogs stood out above all the rest. That unmistakable sound, every three seconds or so, like a creaking old bed with no change at all to the rhythm. And then the shrill, constant background whirr of the crickets that sounded like an alarm ringing somewhere away in the distance: just two of the many mysterious noises of the night. I sat there mesmerised, staring into the dark water, now partially lit by the glow of the moon. It was all so very calm. Then suddenly a splash – what was that? No way of knowing, just a few rings widening on the surface, then stillness, and then back to the now familiar noises.

Peru

The dinner was excellent and the "nature" walk that followed it another of the day's unexpected treats. Two guides with powerful lights led a small group of us tiptoeing into the darkness, pointing at bugs and whispering explanations as they scanned the trees and the forest floor. Nothing too exciting to be honest until ... "Step Back!" Bloody hell! She had a fat body and huge hairy legs. No, not a Russian discuss thrower, but the biggest tarantula you have ever seen after dinner on a Friday night. She didn't move, and, adhering to the quickly-hissed instructions, neither did we. This spider was the size of my hand and apparently if we got too close (and I, for one, would not be doing so) she would disappear back down the hole she was guarding. We all stared in awe of the furry monster for what seemed like a long long time and then finally moved on again to the more mundane business of grasshoppers and stick insects.

I slept incredibly well that night in the confidence that nothing would penetrate my very carefully tucked-in mosquito net. You see, to be quite truthful, despite having a Welsh surname, my love of animals has never quite stretched as far as physical contact, let alone climbing into bed with them. The nearest I've got has been allowing the occasional woman under the sheets and, between you and I, that too can sometimes be a pretty unsavoury experience.

When daylight came at 6am, it was time to get up. Not because the life of a junglee is so absolutely hectic, it's just that you've been asleep since 9pm and there's only so much sleeping one can do. Instinct took me back down to the river as soon as my T-shirt and shorts were pulled on and a little bench in a clearing high up above the water was a find beyond my wildest dreams. I really must buy myself a flat cap. Call me an old fart, but you've got to agree there really is something down-right bloody satisfying about watching a majestic river sweeping gently through the countryside. With this bird's-eye view I had two for the price of one, the spectacle of the gushing little river Gallocunca spilling out from between the trees into the very much larger and browner Tambopata. I sat there for a very long time enjoying the movement of the waters, the wonderful scenery in all directions and a delightful moment of solitude. Life was perfect; and in no small way because, yes, it was at that very moment I realised that Gordon was no longer with me. He had shrunk away in the hours of darkness and left me to face life all on my own. No hard feelings old mate, but it was great to be a perfectly balanced individual once again.

I sat there until it dawned on me I was becoming something of a couch, or rather bench, potato. It was time to get my act together, take the bull by the horns, and make the bold step of a solo exploration into the rainforest. There were plenty of paths and it was broad daylight and even a coward of my considerable standing should surely not find this prospect too daunting. So off I went in my sturdy boots, several litres of bottled water in my pack, camera and binoculars at the ready. These two most basic of traveller's gadgets were specially selected idiot-proof versions, but still no guarantee that in a moment of excitement I wouldn't confuse one with the other, hold them back to front or cut off my air supply by getting one or both of the straps tangled around my windpipe.

All was going swimmingly and with little activity to report for the best part of twenty minutes. It was hot, but quite comfortable, and life was just dandy. And then it happened, quite out of the blue … something unseen, but no doubt truly horrendous, appeared from nowhere and landed straight on to my naked arm. Now, it's at times like this that you can really test the speed of your reactions and it surprised me to find that I could actually move faster than the speed of lightning. Heart pounding to a deafening beat, I slapped violently with my free hand, swivelled 180 degrees and followed the action through with a kung-fu type motion that left both hands and one raised knee suspended in mid- air. What the HELL was that!? Get on your way you little bastard!

Had it gone? Did I kill it? Then I saw it, swinging gently from side to side. Long, narrow and a sort of dirty grey in colour. An embarrassing moment, but how was I to know the attacker was in fact the loose strap of my backpack?

Peru

OK, so I over reacted. But believe me there are lots of things out there in the jungle and they're nearly all hiding and watching your every move. Some of them are actually disguised as innocent every day objects, so you pick a beautiful leaf from a tree only to find that it suddenly changes colour, two slitty eyes are staring up at you and, before you know it, a nasty poisonous substance is swimming around in your bloodstream. Your breathing becomes difficult, vision starts to blur, you turn and head back for camp, but your legs turn to jelly and you collapse amongst more of the same deadly leaves. Unable to move or speak, your inert body finally expires and within seconds the circling vultures swoop down to remove the skin from your bones and strip away your last vestiges of dignity.

Perhaps I'd watched too many films. It was time to start behaving like a real man. So, after a deep breath, chin held high and chest puffed out I marched boldly on along the pathway. Things settled down, especially my heart rate. The birds tweeted and I relaxed enough to stoop down for several minutes to watch an army of leafcutter ants, a few hundred thousand of them transporting cargo to and from their nest. Incredible creatures, only found in the warmer regions of the Americas, they do, as Mr Ronseal would have said, exactly what it says on the tin. They cut up shiny green leaves and carry fragments so much larger than the size of their own bodies that it looks for all the world that the leaves are marching in an enormous line along the forest floor. A strange life being an ant, I decided.

A pleasing calm had come over me by this time, only to be shattered by another sudden heart-stopping sound. An urgent rustling in the undergrowth, a heavy weight crunching through the trees, moving at pace. I looked round quickly, expecting to see an animal at least the size of a small family car, but it turned out, in fact, to be nothing more than a lizard. And, though I hate to admit it, probably no more than ten inches long. I found myself wondering whether the young Tarzan had experienced this sort of beginner's panic or if he too had ever thought:

The Four-Letter Countries

"Stuff this jungle lark, I'm off to lie in my hammock and listen to Radio 5Live".

Unbeknown to me, and perhaps to you too, the BBC no longer transmits the World Service to South America. So bear in mind, next time you're a-hammock in an Amazonian rainforest, that your options are to try and pick up the football scores through the crackly Asian frequencies or pursue more intellectual stimulation: such as reading up on the local region.

Admittedly it was with a certain reluctance that I finally conceded, for an afternoon at least, that Henry Wickham should take precedence over Manchester City. Aha, so you don't know who Henry is then? Let me take you back to the rubber boom of the 1800s when the Amazon rainforest, of which 15% is in Peru, was the only place in the world that had the trees that yielded the magic latex. The Brazilians in particular were onto a good thing and not surprisingly decided that they should do everything in their power to hold on to this lucrative monopoly. Meanwhile, in faraway gloomy Glasgow, a Scotsman name of Charles Mackintosh had designed a raincoat and had joined forces with one Thomas Hancock, a man with some revolutionary ideas of his own. Thomas was quick to see that rubber was an essential ingredient if a Mack wasn't going to leak rain through the stitch holes so he went along to Kew Gardens to suggest they get to work growing some rubber trees. 'OK' they said, 'not a bad idea, Tom, but we'd need some seeds from the Amazon and the South Americans have declared it illegal to export them. We could always go and nick some I suppose…'

Henry Wickham was deemed to be the best man for the job. In 1876 he slipped over to Peru and somehow managed to slip out again with 70,000 seeds in his pockets, or wherever seed-thieves stashed their booty in those days. Within a very short time, rubber trees were sprouting up all over the British colony of Malaya, south-east Asia had become the most cost-effective rubber supplier in the world and Henry Wickham had received a knighthood for services rendered to the Crown. Well done Sir Henry.

Peru

Thanks to Henry the rubber market all but collapsed in Peru, but there was known to be gold in the region and still the outsiders came to the Madre de Dios to seek their fortune. They would almost certainly arrive by river because even today there is really only one road of note in the entire region, an area the size of Austria that is truly one of the Earth's last great wildernesses. It is home to maybe 100,000 people, amongst them some 10,000 Amazonian Indians, and almost all earn their living off the land: growing cotton, sugar, coffee and Brazil nuts or simply hunting and fishing as many have done for thousands of years. I felt very privileged to be there. Just think, where else in the world could one hope to see 152 different species of dragonfly? Not to mention 600 species of bird, 1,200 butterfly and an unthinkably deadly variety of spiders and snakes. It was time to get out amongst it again.

This time the jungle trek would not be a solo affair, but undertaken with people who knew what they were doing. A very much smarter approach, I figured, if you come from Manchester and even your neighbour's tortoise frightens you to death. So off we went, a small group of us, one guide at the front, one at the back. Just the way I liked it.

This time there were no dramas, just a few nice birds in the trees and a small but deserted clay-lick. Not a cliff, but a solidified mudpool, spotted by one of our guides, Juan Carlos (locally abbreviated to Juan Ca and pronounced Wanker, how we loved that), who explained that tapirs (sachavacas) also liked to lick the clay and had evidently been there a few hours earlier. Unfortunately this time we'd missed these odd-looking animals (they're like brown pigs with anteater's snouts), but perhaps we'd see some at the lake to which we were heading. It was, after all, called Lake Sachavacaya.

The lake appeared as if by a miracle, some time late in the afternoon. It was bigger and far more beautiful than I'd imagined, perhaps a kilometre across, and our camp for the night had already been set up almost at the water's edge. The huge wooden platform with a roof, like a house with no walls, was a permanent structure amongst the trees and, unbeknown to us, a support team had arrived earlier in the day to arrange rows of mattresses and mosquito nets along its length. They had also carried an impressive array of cooking equipment and were already preparing dinner as we got changed for an afternoon dip. This was definitely the smart way to do camping!

The light was fading, but local rules dictated that we must listen to a short presentation before swimming was allowed. You see, our busy team had also kindly prepared two small tents for our use, along a path from the camp and roughly thirty metres apart, and it was here that our toilet training briefing was to take place. And, because everybody understands that disposal of body waste is an important eco issue, we all tried extra hard to avoid grinning when it was explained that one toilet was dedicated to the depositing of liquids, the other for solids. These twin towers could most definitely not cope with any sort of excretory overlap. Oh, and there was a little bag of powder to sprinkle where appropriate. The system, as far as I could see, was designed to operate like a buffet in reverse, but was it etiquette to re-trouser between courses? The novelty seemed to grip the imagination of the male members of the audience, but was evidently of little concern to the ladies, who had already reached their unanimous but unspoken decision that death would be a more pleasing alternative than the indignity of a visit to the dumporium.

We paddled in a couple of dugout canoes to the centre of the lake and then spilled overboard, one at a time, into the delicious clear water. What a privilege to have all that nature almost to oneself, to lie back and see the colours of the sky and the sun through the trees and the small families of brightly coloured birds squawking overhead. It was far too good an experience to rush and everybody else was obviously of the same mind, only the impending darkness eventually coaxing us back into the boats. There we sat for some time, laughing, joking, getting dry as best we could. Then the sun finally slipped away and noticeably, almost as a mark of respect, so did all the chatter. It was time to let the birds and the animals take centre stage once again and this was all just too good to pollute with our own ugly sounds.

It was so spectacular on that lovely lake that we went out again a few hours later and then a third time shortly after 5am the following morning. We hunted for crocodiles by night and fished for piranhas at daybreak, yes, all this in our big lovely swimming pool. Probably sounds scary to you sitting in your armchair, dear reader, but when you're a fearless, rugged, outdoor type you don't blink at that sort of thing. To be absolutely fair, the crocs that we tracked down, lighting their eyes up by torchlight so we could take a photo were actually caymans and it has to be said little more than a metre in length. The piranhas I cannot comment on, because we didn't catch any.

The morning outing wasn't really a fishing trip anyway, the reason we'd got up so very early was to be back in our canoes for when the sun came up over the eastern end of the lake. We were, and it did, and wow, was it worth it. We watched in a collective trance as the pink sky away to our left slowly lit up the surface of the water, almost as though somebody with a dimmer switch between thumb and forefinger was in perfect control of all the arrangements. Then, suddenly, there came that now familiar shriek of the macaws and it was quite easy to pick out those distinctive bright red and green colours darting back and forth in the half light. We sat and glared into the stillness of the water, watched the snake birds – so named because their long black necks poke out menacingly above the surface like miniature Loch Ness monsters – and as the sun came up we stared down at the trees, all those individual shapes and colours, reflecting on the glassy lake, appearing in perfect duplicate. Yes, this really was some show.

* * * * *

Where do you go from there? Impossible really ... that whole experience was as good as it gets. It was the finale, la pièce de résistance and, for me, it was the end of that particular road. I was a long, long way from home and it was time to ponder the journey ahead. To get from somewhere in the centre of Lake Sachavacayal to somewhere inside the M25 was going to take a canoe, a long hike, a motorboat, a bus, three planes and a very serious amount of mental adjustment.

MALI

It took me a full ten minutes to convince Lyn at the club that this wasn't a wind-up. I really was going to Timbuktu.

She knew it to be somewhere mysterious and magical, but like most people she hadn't been too sure whether the place really existed. Wasn't it just a myth, something from a children's storybook? And if it was real, why was it so famous, and where was it?

Answering the last question first, I told her it was in Mali. Then I waited a few seconds, knowing exactly the conversation that was to follow. Dialogue is a very predictable business where Mali's concerned:

"Aaah, yes, my sister's son went to Bali last year, said it was a beautiful country."

"No ... er, actually ..."

"The pictures looked lovely."

"Sorry, but Bali isn't a country. It's an island in Indonesia."

A little bit of Basil Fawlty lives inside us all and I was fighting to keep him caged. The smile, the failed attempt at politeness and, ultimately, the grimace:

"She didn't mention Timbuktu though."

"That's because Timbuktu is in Mali."

"Mali? Is that the name of a country?"

"Yes madam. It's in Africa."

"Oh I remember. Didn't it used to be called Malawi?"

Funny thing, geography. Ask anybody in the world if they know where the UK, France or Germany is and most would have a pretty fair idea, even the Americans still reeling from the shock that Austria and

The Four-Letter Countries

Australia are not the same country after all. Then move your line of questioning on to the exact location of Mali. If you try it on a first date it could limit the likelihood of any physical intimacy, but it is a nailed-on guarantee to entertain your friends at a dinner party. When everybody has had their guess and the excitement has reached fever pitch you can hush the crowd, climb to your feet, and tell them this: "Mali is shaped like a big beautiful butterfly, sitting diagonally across the huge bulge that is northwest Africa. It is completely landlocked and shares borders with seven other countries. And, ladies and gentlemen, it is actually bigger in area than the UK and France and Germany combined."

By now you will have drawn gasps from your audience. Some may heckle or even contest your facts. Others will be shocked into silence, eyes and mouths wide open. But most will applaud loudly, so be ready with the encore. This is the point at which you can let them into the FLC world, give them something to remember you by, something they can carry forward into the rest of their lives. Simple, but ever so effective: "Togo is tiny. Mali is massive. Chad is colossal." And then you sit down.

* * * * *

The flight I took to Mali goes there every Thursday night from Ghana and stops on the way in Ouagadougou, which, as anybody with an anorak and a handy little hood will tell you, is the capital of Burkina Faso. What a fun profession it must be, a maker-up of city and country names. I know it seems a little childish, but the prospect of just landing at such an exotic-sounding place made me feel part of an adventure and I felt no resentment whatsoever towards the six passengers for whose benefit we had touched down. It was late at night, around midnight. No doubt most of the locals were already sound asleep. Would these be known as Burkina Fasoans? It was the first time in my life I had ever wondered that.

It was nearly two in the morning when we landed in Bamako. Not a time of day one would ever choose to arrive anywhere, but at least I'd pre-booked a place to stay, all I had to do was get there. The airport seemed so very tiny and had a feeling of closedness that most places do in the middle of the night, the only people around were there because of us. I felt almost obliged to apologise for keeping everybody up.

I grabbed my bag off the creaky conveyor and stepped through the exit door into a vast, dark, open space. It was eerily silent and there was nothing or nobody to be seen, save for one car on its own that looked like a small boat adrift in the ocean. The voice that came from behind me was the last thing I'd expected and the shock made my shoulders jerk into the air as though trying to lift my body away from the ground.

"Taxi?"

Despite the pitch darkness I could see that he was large. His skin was the same colour as the night sky and he wore a patterned skull-cap and dark glasses on his sizeable head which was cocked to one side as though too heavy for his neck. A chunky chain dangled loosely and the cigarette jammed between his gold teeth nicely rounded off the Rap gangster image. He pointed an invitation to the solitary vehicle.

"Are you an official taxi?" I heard myself ask in schoolboy French like a civil servant on his first trip abroad. Thank God nobody heard me ask such a dickhead question. Did I really think he would say no? Would a positive response somehow reduce the likelihood of my being axed up into small pieces?

I looked around to see that everybody else had gone home, just me and Al Capone left standing in the car park. Options were looking mighty thin on the ground and what seemed a hopeless situation was about to take a turn for the worse: somebody stepped out from the passenger side of the lone vehicle. My choice now was to climb into a motor in the dead of night with two dodgy-looking characters or to sit under the stars, miles from anywhere, outside a closed airport.

"Combien, monsieur?"

101

The Four-Letter Countries

The price he was asking wasn't unreasonable and his mate had already vacated the passenger seat by relocating to the back (to get his blade ready?). Like it or not, it had to be done.

The cosy threesome set off in what would have been complete silence had it not been for the deafening sound of my own heartbeat. Would they be able to hear it too? I didn't move a muscle except for a subconscious clenching of the fists and a slow, controlled bit of exhaling designed to prevent me from exploding. Should I get my phone out and fake a conversation or would the prize of a Nokia serve as a further incentive to take me out? I chose to just sit there, tried to look as hard as nails and watched for any movements through the corner of my eye.

We passed through places where a headless body would probably have gone unquestioned for months, but I felt slightly encouraged to see that we were at least heading in the direction of town. My logic was that if I was to be robbed and executed there would be no point in taking me for a drive first, thus the further we went, the better I viewed my chances of survival. Unless their torture chamber just happened to be a long way from the airport.

Twenty-five minutes later came the moment I'd prayed for. The driver pulled up outside the hotel, courteously carried my bag up to the entrance and, with the help of his friend, tried to attract the attention of whoever was within. They tapped on one of the tall gates, then tried a sharp whistle and, when that failed, gave a series of little shouts in a very foreign language. Nothing, not a murmur. I wasn't doing anything at all, didn't even care, was overwhelmed by the pleasure of still being alive though a little guilty at having classified these helpful young men as potential assassins. Then I decided to lend a helping hand which involved placing my hand on the gate and giving it a push. It was open, and had been all along. Everybody laughed, we all shook hands and I gave the boys the biggest tip they had ever seen.

Mali

* * * * *

The little family hotel was on the east side of Bamako in a suburb with the quaint name of Hippodrome. It was built around a lovely courtyard full of trees and had lots of books and magazines lying around and friendly staff who smiled and said hello a lot and had probably worked there all their lives. I instantly liked it and decided to spend a lot of my first day enjoying the home comforts. Who knew what might happen? I had never met anybody who had been to Mali or, for that matter, anybody who even knew anybody who had. So I was a tad curious to know what kind of people I might encounter.

I didn't have to wait long. The guests at breakfast on the first day were two Swiss guys who had just driven from Europe across the Western Sahara and an Austrian lady who had come by bus from Senegal. To talk to them about their adventures over baguettes and coffee brought home to me the real joy of travel: the characters that you meet, people who are determined to make life interesting, who don't calculate success by how much money they earn or whether the number plate of their twin-seater car sports their initials.

The following day was a chance to see Bamako, so, starting early in the morning to beat the sun, I walked the three miles from Hippodrome to the city centre. Let me try to set the scene.

There is no pavement, so we are walking along the edge of the dusty road, as close to the traffic as we think we can get away with, a line of emerald green buses hurtling past every few seconds. They billow filthy black pungent smoke, but even that is preferable to the stench of the waist-deep ditch that runs alongside. To describe exactly what it looks like in there or how badly it smells would be as much a test of my literary skills as it would be of your stomach. So I'll just ask that you close your eyes for a moment and picture how your garden might look if everybody in your town turned up one morning and emptied their dustbins over your wall. And then ... their bowels.

The Four-Letter Countries

Tramping through the dust and the debris with traffic fumes to the left, fetid ditch to the right and blazing sun overhead, it occurred to me that this was not everybody's idea of a holiday. But the roadside in Africa is where people live and work, eat and sleep, buy and sell. To find out what it looks like, how it works, and what makes it all tick, you have to be part of it for at least a little bit of the time. At least that was what I kept telling myself. I tried to keep up a sensible pace, but met competition for space on the roadside with others who were making the journey in the opposite direction. In fact at one point I had to step aside as about thirty of them bumbled along, sniffing at each others' arses as they wandered aimlessly into the morning traffic. These were not people, of course, they were goats.

A flock of animals taking a morning stroll through the capital city is pretty routine stuff in most of Africa. It certainly didn't faze or even interest the man at ditch-side who had claimed an area of dust as his own and was busy arranging his collection of brand new – still in the clear plastic wrapper – sofas and armchairs for sale. Next in line – they were like fishermen on a riverbank – a large lady sitting adjacent to an impressive pyramid of watermelons, twice the size of footballs and even larger than her sagging breasts. She kindly offered me a sample slice of the blood-red fruit, her huge smile of rotting teeth and the waft of raw sewage hitting me at just about the same time. As with the three piece divan, I politely declined. But I did need a battery for a borrowed camera, so my face must have been a picture of joy when, a little further towards town, an enormous Kodak sign loomed up away to the right. The adrenaline burst that ensued saw me leap the turd trench like a gazelle and scramble, somewhat breathlessly, across a pile of loose stones to a row of small, higgledy-piggledy shops. I peered inside, definitely more in hope and excitement than genuine expectation.

The camera store was a small windowless affair with benches around its inner walls reminiscent of a public park changing room for Sunday footballers. The only thing in its favour was the absence of that smell of muscle rub, beery farts and wet kit from the previous afternoon's match. Certainly there was no sign of any cameras or equipment. But there was a man inside and he was looking at me and I had to say something, if only to justify my presence in his ... er ... room. Questioning why I got myself into these wacky situations and mumbling incoherently in schoolboy French, I figured I might as well show him the camera.

He stared at it for quite a long time, then at me, and something in his manner told me we weren't going to be mates. When I asked him if he had a battery for that specific model he looked down at the ground, hesitated for about five seconds then jerked his head and said:

"Oui."

Sure Boris. So where is it? In fact where is ... anything? He made no attempt to get one from his stock because he didn't have any stock. In fact, he didn't have anything at all. OK then, let's see how he responds to this:

"How much is it then?"

"Five thousand CFA."

"That sounds too much."

"OK then, 4,000."

"I think they cost less than that."

"I could do it for ... er ... 3,000."

"So why did you quote me 5,000?"

"Are you arguing with me?"

"Yes, I suppose I am."

"Do you want one or not?"

"No, thank you. Au revoir"

Africans are naturally friendly people and any form of buying and selling always involves an element of playful banter. But this guy was not at all playful, he was cynical and aggressive, and I knew he was just trying to keep me in his hut while he could think up a ruse to try to extort some money. It was the first and only time I have ever haggled over the price of something that didn't even exist.

The Four-Letter Countries

By the middle of the morning I'd made it in to town. Not exactly an experience I'll savour until my dying day, but it had a pleasant Saturday morning bustle, some nice old buildings and there wasn't too much in the way of raw excrement. I wandered around until the heat made it hard work then took a cab north to the top of the mountain that overlooks the city, an area known as Point G.

Many cities look better from above than at ground level and Bamako is definitely one of them. I sat there for an hour or so in the relative silence, looking down from the coolness of the mountain, the same view that the President has from his palace. The absence of city heat and noise helped to put everything into perspective and here was my first real look at the River Niger, a broad band running right to left across the top of my picture, the distant southern boundary of the city.

And what a mighty river it is. It's an incredible 2,615 miles long, roughly the same distance as Timbuktu is from London. Think about that for just a few seconds, a river that would take more than five hours to fly along in a jumbo jet. Its journey from the uplands of Guinea across to Nigeria and out into the Atlantic passes through over a thousand miles of Mali, from the greener south-west of the country, where I sat now, right up to the edge of the Sahara. My plan was to more or less follow its north-easterly route for around 450 miles: the first two thirds by road and then, all being well, up to Timbuktu on the river itself. Sounded exciting, I couldn't wait to get on the move.

* * * * *

It took half a day in a minibus to get to Segou. The improbably straight line of tarred road had cut through miles and miles of unchanging landscape, a world of total flatness where blue sky and orange dusty earth met half way to form the horizon. But there was also plenty of green, hundreds and thousands of small trees and bushes dotted everywhere, usually standing alone or at most in small clusters. And as our driver had explained when he pulled on to the verge, there was a toilet behind every one (not really, just a joke).

The Hotel de l'Indépendance did not belong on the outskirts of a little town in one of the poorest countries in the world. It was modern, spotlessly clean and offered luxury en-suite rooms, a delightful restaurant on a shaded patio, waiters serving ice-cold beers and a well-maintained swimming pool set in lush gardens. This place and Segou itself, from what I could make out, seemed to be about a thousand years apart. I wasn't complaining.

The actual town held no surprises, though the wide roads that mimicked the boulevards of France's elegant cities gave it a certain added grandeur. But its most pleasing feature was the forest on the edge of town and the incredible mansions that sit so improbably at its centre. I walked along the paths between the trees, so pleasant and cool after the heat of the streets, and admired the stunning chateaux that were once the homes of the administrators sent out from France and still quite magnificent despite half a century of neglect. These incredible buildings would not have looked out of place on the banks of the Loire or the Seine; it was sad to see them largely abandoned and decaying in this way, such a pity that nobody will have the funds to restore the buildings to their former splendour. At least the local authorities allow them to be used as meeting rooms for the people of the town. A delightful little stopover was Segou.

Onwards in a northerly direction, traversing miles and miles and miles of more flat land and occasional small villages the same colour as the earth. There were very few vehicles indeed, the local people walked, usually barefoot, always using the tops of their heads to transport cargo however large or small. I even saw a man carrying a cup on his head, years of practice (or a very flat head) enabling him to move at a normal pace. The children yelled and waved as children always do: "Cadeau! Cadeau! Cadeau!" Not "hello" or "welcome", but the French word for 'gift' and usually spoken with an outstretched palm.

The Four-Letter Countries

So much space. Mali has a population of around ten million people in an area more than five times that of the UK and the sheer scale of this emptiness is like nothing I'd ever seen before. Thousands of square miles of nothingness, just occasional small, ramshackle villages, mostly just a series of mud brick walls, a row of rectangular shapes and some of those without even a roof. Were they houses too, the roofless ones? What was inside? I stood on tiptoes and peered over the top and the answer should not have surprised me. Absolutely nothing at all.

As in most of Africa, water would be collected from a central point by the womenfolk and carried back to the respective households where the children play and the men do very little. I noticed that in Mali people in the villages often walked around holding plastic kettles with distinctive red/green or blue/yellow stripes, but why would a kettle be made of plastic? After a few days, the penny finally dropped. The water in the container was not for making tea, it was to compensate for the fact that they have no flush toilets or little boxes of Wet Wipes.

Next stop was Djenné, a bustling market town and home to one of the world's most spectacular buildings. The Great Mosque at Djenné is reputed to be the largest mud-brick building in the world, a fact, I suspect, that few people are in a position to confirm or deny. It is impressive enough to be classed as a World Heritage site, it's Mali's Eiffel Tower, Big Ben, Empire State Building, Opera House, the one thing that people from all over the world would flock to see if flocking were ever to catch on in West Africa. It's an enormous creation with wooden struts sticking out of its sides, partly to hold it up, but also to serve as a ladder for the townsfolk who restore it every year when the rain starts to wash it away; rather like having a snowman as your main tourist attraction.

Fortunately for the mosque-repair team, rain does not happen often in Mali, it's usually bone dry for nine months of the year. When it does come, it falls from July to September and then, at the end of the year, the winds blow from the north-east and daytime temperatures can drop to as low as 30 degrees centigrade! Malians refer to this period as the cold season, which tells me it might be some time before they put in an appearance at the winter olympics.

Further north and finally to the port of Mopti, a chaotic, sprawling city of 100,000 people and the confluence of the rivers Niger and Bani. I'd made it to the middle of the big beautiful butterfly, just below the V between its wings and now more than half way to Timbuktu. I walked the hot streets and the endless market stalls where men of many different tribes came to trade clothes, jewellery, masks and even slabs of salt from the desert. The children followed me in small groups, each demanding a cadeau, preferably a pen: "Donnez-moi un Bic, donnez-moi un Bic". I didn't have any Bics handy and am not sure where I stand on the Bic front anyway. There's a body of people out there ready to tell you that these kids should not be encouraged and that the Bic-distributing travellers of yesteryear were a misguided bunch of hoodlums. Not drug pushers, but pen pushers, so-called do-gooders, they should have looked at the bigger picture, sense of values, the unhealthy and contagious precedent they were about to set for the rest of humanity. I think my own view is that the world has some bigger problems to sort out; people all over the planet are slaughtering each other every day of the week and, from what I can see, none of them seems to be leading the attack with a box of biros.

* * * * *

Travelling across Mali by minibus had to be done to get that sense of perspective. Yes it was a little monotonous, hours and hours of that unchanging landscape, but, like sailing across the ocean, the appeal lies in its extraordinary vastness and the sense of solitude that it creates. Here in Mopti at last it was time for a change, to leave road transport behind and transfer to a *pinnasse*, a lovely *Call My Bluff* kind of word that could be a shawl or a dance or a festival but turns out to be a motorised canoe. The vessel was about two metres wide and long enough to take fifteen passengers and a handful of crew. A small section towards its rear formed a simple galley and behind that a hole in the bottom of the boat served as a toilet, the users discretely out of sight of fellow passengers but in full view of everybody else on the river!

The other travellers on board had come from the UK and Brazil and USA and Canada for the River Niger experience. The usual mix of humans: some quiet, some who never stop talking, the funny ones, the nice but ever so serious, the fascinated and the unfascinatable. But most importantly they were all good fun.

We sat in pairs and watched the world go by from morning till night, the scenery of the semi-desert varying little, but with the sensations of the sun and the breeze this was an altogether different experience. The straw canopy above kept away the fiercest rays and also served as an upper deck for those of us (me, mostly) who wanted to sit on top and feel the warm air blasting our faces. I perched up there for as long as my body could take it, the 360 degree views and the absence of other people creating the weird illusion of being alone on the planet. It was good to be alive and what better way to celebrate those wonderful moments than by singing a little medley of Rod Stewart numbers, from the early ones like *Mandolin Wind* through to a corny, inevitable and embarrassing chorus of *I Am Sailing*.

We travelled up river for three days and it was fantastic. Every few hours our captain would cut the engine and nudge up to the riverbank, dispersing the ladies knee-deep in the river washing pots and pans or simply splashing water on their fully-clothed bodies. He would go into the villages in search of food, sometimes returning with bread or some fish or a chicken, but just as often coming back empty-handed. Meantime we amused the children, the hundreds of children that always mobbed us for cadeaux and yes, some of us even gave out a few pens.

The secret was to try to get to our campground by the late afternoon, when the sun was no longer so vicious, but there was still enough daylight to pitch the tents. The first camp was the one I remember best because it was the one for which I was least prepared, and more significantly, it was my first introduction to *cram-cram*. Nothing at all to do with that likeable Sunderland-supporting athlete who now graces our airwaves on behalf of the BBC, these are very sharp and prickly burrs that grow on the semi-desert grasses and attach themselves in large numbers to shoes, clothes, feet, anything at all.

It was late on that first afternoon, as soon as I jumped ashore, that they made for the velcro strap of my sandals, not one or two, but fifty or sixty of the little buggers. I hopped from foot to foot cursing, and pulled a few off, pricking my finger in the process, but there were too many for me to deal with there and then. Time was short, daylight was diminishing fast and tents had to be put up. The sand was far too hot to dispense with the sandals, so despite the pain and like a true man I stoically carried on and went about my erection. Best to get that one out of the way now.

Standing in a bed of razor sharp thorns is no laughing matter, nor particularly is putting up a tent while gallons of sweat pour down your face like ice cream melting on a cornet. So imagine my delight when several million mosquitoes suddenly appeared from nowhere and set about sucking all the blood from my ankles. The torture was complete. Cram-cram pricked, mozzies pricked AND buzzed, sweat flowed and so did expletives. I found myself asking whether life ever got any worse and whether it would help to let out a loud scream. Part of me even wondered whether I might actually be going slightly insane.

Now shaking, fumbling, writhing – a desperate man in an advanced stage of Parkinsons – I yelled all the rudest words I could think of. The mosquitoes were loving every minute, each taking turns to deliver that oh-so irritating and absolutely pointless high-pitched screech prior to diving in for another slurp. I screamed and I sweated, boy did I sweat, but somehow, against all the odds, I got the tent, the bastard tent, to stand up. I slumped unceremoniously inside, zipped it to the top, sprayed enough anti-mozzie poison to kill a rhino and lay there on the lumpy groundsheet, a sweat-soaked, cursing heap, staring up at the canvas and panting like a dog. It was completely airless and the heat was stifling and the venomous spray was stinging my eyes and throat, but I would gladly have stayed in there all night and risked suffocation ... had it not been for the sudden and terrible realisation that I was about to poo my pants.

The thought of going back out into that mosquito madness filled me with abject despair, but the sensation from below indicated that there was no compromise on offer. Oh no! Twice in only four countries, this time more extreme than the last, what punishment lay in store for my lower intestine in the many miles and months ahead? I dived out like a maniac into the night air only to find, to my joy and amazement, that the little horrors had all moved on. So, with torch in one hand, squashed loo roll in the other, and thorns like shards of glass in my feet, I shuffled to the nearest available bush.

To anybody not familiar with outdoor pooing strategies let me tell you the number one rule: upon reaching your chosen spot you must immediately and completely remove all clothing from the waist down-wards. Let me explain. Some movements, or lack of, demand the tight low squat to enhance performance whereas the looser bowel permits the luxury of a taller stance. Without the encumberment of garments you can enjoy the raw outdoor pleasure of emptying the Delhi Belly in a proud, upstanding, head forward and legs akimbo pose, not dissimilar to a giraffe munching on leaves, and also enjoy greater conversational options over the top of the bush (or at least a cheery 'Hello, I'm Doing A Poo' wave) as the action, and later the Andrex, unfolds. But more critical still is the need to change direction, or even location, at very short notice. I have yet to meet anybody who likes to share this moment of glory with flies, spiders, beetles, wild pigs, or heaven forbid, snakes and I can guarantee that you will not want knickers knotting your ankles when a python slides forward to check out your jobby. So get out there and enjoy one of life's greatest pleasures, take your undies in your left hand and stretch those legs whenever you can. Even take a little mid-session stroll to another bush, chances are you'll bump into somebody for a half-time chat. But please make sure you tread very carefully.

* * * * *

By dusk on the following night I was wearing long pants and lots of spray and walking very cautiously around cram-cram bushes. Experience is a wonderful ally and when tents were up and dinner eaten and hot red tea sipped by the campfire, I walked off alone along the sand to enjoy the beauty of the gently rippling water and the fantastic silhouettes of the sand-dunes illuminated by the full moon. Then I sat in the semi-darkness and stared at the stars and listened to the birds on the river and thought about the old saying that you only get out of life what you put into it. This moment was my reward.

Three days on the boat had given me plenty of opportunity to look at maps and do some homework on Timbuktu. Fascinating reading, and whether you like it or not, I have to tell you a little bit about this place. You see, Timbuktu, or Tombouctou as it is spelt locally, is in itself an incredible story. We start by taking eight of the largest countries on the planet and covering them, almost entirely, with sand. Three and a half million square miles of the stuff. This is the Sahara Desert and it goes from one side of Africa to the other, from the Atlantic Ocean to the Red Sea, an empty space that is just too big for the likes of you and I to really come to terms with.

The city of Timbuktu sits on the southern edge of this desert, exactly at the point where yellow gives way to white on the map. Fifteen hundred miles of sand to the north, another thousand to the west, more than double that to the east. You could walk the two and a half thousand miles to or from Cairo without passing another town. Or village. Or person. And you would be very thirsty.

The absurdity of its location was exactly the reason that Timbuktu prospered as a city. By the 14th century merchants were regularly crossing the desert to get to and from west and north Africa and it grew as a crossroads for people heading in all directions. It thrived as a trade centre for gold, slaves, salt, cloth and horses and went on to build a university that was to attract scholars from all over the muslim world. Word of this mysterious city travelled far, even to distant lands like Europe. For several hundred years it became the white man's obsession to get to Timbuktu as if it was some far off treasure, but until the 19th century all those that tried it had failed. They were overcome by disease or the tortuous heat or wiped out by the Tuaregs, a feisty bunch of nomads who did not take kindly to overseas visitors messing around in their desert.

In classic adventurist manner, the race was on to see which nationality could get there first and so keen were the Frogs that, in 1824, the French Geographical Society laid down a challenge – they would pay 2,000 Francs to the first European expedition to get to Timbuktu and back. In those days that would keep a Scotsman in whisky and fags for a good number of years and so it was one Alexander Gordon Laing who put himself in the frame.

Alex Laing had been on his way home from the alehouse in Greenock, twelve pints of strong ale and a fish supper sloshing around in his sizeable belly. The night was dark, cold and damp, for this was Scotland, and he was in a particularly bad mood. The supper hadn't cheered him any, just meant he hadn't been able to smoke for eight minutes. There was no-one around to pick a fight with, so he kicked out at an empty bottle lying on the pavement, missed it hopelessly and almost keeled over backwards off the edge of the kerb. It was the last straw. "Fuck ye, ye bastard, fuck the lot o' yers. I'm away t'ae Timbuk-fuckin-tu".

That was the story as I had imagined it anyway; just shows how wrong one can be. You see Gordon Laing (as he was actually known) was the son of a Classics teacher and at the age of 18 he went to Barbados and joined the York Light Infantry. Later promoted to the Royal

Mali

African Corps, in 1824 Captain Laing got his instructions: "to undertake a journey, via Tripoli and Timbuktu, to further elucidate the hydrography of the Niger basin." Quite a task I would have thought, particularly if you didn't know what elucidate or hydrography meant.

He left England in February 1825 and headed for Tripoli where he was received by the British Consul. And more interestingly, the British Consul's daughter. Her name was Emma and she must have been pretty tasty because Gordon decided to marry her there and then. History shows that they tied the knot on July 14th 1825 and on July 16th he set off to trek across the Sahara, leaving his bride behind. What they did on July 15th remains a mystery to this day.

Despite fever and attacks from the stroppy Tuaregs, Gordon Laing achieved his goal thirteen months later – it was August 18th 1826 to be precise when he became the first white man to make it to Timbuktu. He stayed on there for five weeks and wrote numerous letters expressing concern that the local chieftain was hostile and that the atmosphere was tense. In hindsight this proved to be something of an understatement. Laing was murdered two days after leaving town.

Only three other explorers had successfully reached Timbuktu by the middle of the 19th century. There was this Frenchman, a German, and an Austrian...

René Caillie was a little bit smarter than Laing and he went one better. He decided to disguise himself as a muslim and spent a year in Senegal learning to speak Arabic, arriving in the fabled city from the west in April 1828. The ploy worked. The Tuaregs welcomed him in as one of the lads and he became the first to live to tell the tale. He got confirmation of poor Mr Laing's demise a couple of years earlier, then went back via Morocco to Paris and a hero's welcome. And, presumably, 2,000 Francs.

Almost another thirty years went by before Heinrich Barth, a German explorer, arrived, supposedly doing his exploring on behalf of the British. Heinrich had taken the scenic route via Sudan, Chad and Nigeria and was so utterly knackered by the time he got to Timbuktu in 1853 he stayed for eight months.

And finally, in 1880, it was the turn of Austrian Oscar Lenz. He dropped in from Morocco and lived for a little while in town before going south to explore the Congo and Lake Tanganiyka. Incredible to think that these were the only four men who made their mark throughout a whole century of exploration.

* * * * *

Three days chugging up river had been exactly the right amount of time. It had been a fantastic experience to see Mali from the water, but more of the same would have been stretching a point, the landscape changed little and our routine not at all. It was time to hit Timbuktu, return to dry land, and find a shower.

The town is actually some 10km from the river, so a fleet of jeep taxis took us on a short but memorable journey to the checkpoint. All the passengers who sat adjacent to an open door or window ended up caked from head to toe in sand and my sunglasses alone collected a half-inch coating on each side. Better on the lens than in the eye I suppose. Next time I go to Timbuktu I'll keep myself well inside the jeep.

Half an hour later, a tired-looking sign welcomed us to Tombouctou and we crawled from the vehicle into the midday sun. We'd made it! The first move was to hand our passports over to the authorities to be stamped, a procedure that in most parts of the world is reserved for crossing international boundaries. Who cares, at least it was proof of membership of the very exclusive 'I've Been To Timbuktu Club' and a chance for the cash-strapped Malians to make some dollars. And so, here we were. This was it. Timbuk-fuckin-tu. We'd been warned not to expect too much.

"I found nothing but a mass of ill-looking houses, built of earth, situated in an immense plain of white sand". Not my words, but those of

Mali

the aforementioned René Caillie, who scribbled down these observations on his arrival in 1828. In the two centuries that have since elapsed, nothing very much seemed to have changed. The dusty streets were strewn with litter and broken, discarded items, even several old table football machines with the players hanging upside down on rusty rods.

There were some points of interest, however, and we were very grateful to be shown around the dusty alleyways by teenage students with an impressive command of English. They took us inside the mosques that were blissfully cool and showed us the plaques on the walls of the humble little houses that marked each of the sites where our four European explorers had stayed. Again it was a world of one colour, the sandy streets and the mud brick walls all blending into one to form a grey/orange mass on the edge of the desert. Or should I say "mess".

The clothes worn by most of the locals were generally unremarkable, though one little boy did stand out from the rest. He must have been about eight years old and my stomach churned to see that this lovely little Malian lad was wearing a Manchester United shirt, a sickening enough sight on a beer-bellied slob from Stretford or Bournemouth, but here we were in the desert in north-west Africa and this just wasn't right. OK, I know I'm a biased City fan and extremely sensitive to anything red, but surely he could have worn the colours of Timbuktu Tigers or Bamako Wanderers or Mopti Athletic or whatever teams they have in Mali? British football culture dictates that I should really have slammed my nut across the bridge of his nose, but as he only came up to my waist I decided to let him off with a scowl. Lucky for him he didn't push his luck and ask for a Bic, that's all I can say. Maybe next year he would be decked out in blue.

Or even blue robes. There were a few men in the streets of Timbuktu that really did stand out, dressed splendidly in bright blue robes and with veils covering most of their faces. Impressive and imposing, these were the Tuaregs, masters of the desert. So what were they doing in the city? Shouldn't they have been herding camels from one oasis to the next?

The Four-Letter Countries

I can answer that one. The Tuaregs have for thousands of years been a fiercely independent nomadic tribe, defending their territory resolutely and eradicating all those foolish enough to take them on. But now, in the 21st century, politics and nature are conspiring against them. The desert has become too dry to roam with herds of animals and international boundaries are starting to impose limits on wandering peoples. Their way of life has been eroded, as with many African tribes, and they now seek to earn a living as more traditional farmers or by selling their wares to dollar-rich tourists. And here they were in all their glory.

A couple of hours is as much as anybody would really want to spend trudging around a place so hot and ultimately dismal, so I found a hotel, negotiated the use of a shower, then went to an internet café to catch up on e-mail. "Sorry I haven't been in touch, you must think I've been to Timbuktu. Well ... actually."

By now it was well into Saturday afternoon, the sun was still beating down, and I knew exactly what had to be done next. You're going to hate this. I found a quiet little spot in the shade, plucked the short wave radio from my little bag and tuned in to the second half football commentary on Radio 5Live with Alan Green. Sad but true, Timbuktu or not, I wasn't about to change the habit of a lifetime.

Come 5.15, after bopping along to that fabulous theme tune to Sports Report, *Out Of The Blue*, and the classified results having been read impeccably by the inimitable James Alexander Gordon, it was time to move on. I was ready to head to another part of the country, to a place where some people had been in hiding for the last one thousand years.

* * * * *

This time we were in large, enclosed and very solid-looking vehicles that had apparently once been used for carrying water cannons for the German fire brigade. They needed to be sturdy now because there were no roads across to the Bandiagara Escarpment, just tracks at best through the miles of fields and sparse vegetation of eastern Mali. It took us a couple of days of bumping and bouncing with a camp stop en-route.

'This had better be worth it,' thought I.

It most definitely was. This remote region of Mali is not what one would call mountainous, but better described as flat with bits sticking up here and there. A peculiar landscape and quite interesting, but not in itself justification for what had literally been an overland journey. The reason we were there was the Dogons, a tribe of people who had fled the coast and gone into hiding some thousand years earlier to escape the wave of Islam sweeping north and west Africa. They had set up home in this region alongside several tribes of pygmies and eventually forced the little fellas to relocate into the jungles of the Congo further south.

So, decked out in thick socks and sturdy walking boots, a strange experience after weeks of sandals, we set off up 'the mountain' behind a local guide, heading for the Dogon villages. Some real exercise at last and, after a couple of hours of steady climbing, we reached one of the primitive settlements that was home to this ancient tribe. The houses were predictably simple, small rectangles of mud brick, but there were also smaller buildings scattered around shaped like our old public telephone boxes, but with little pointed thatched roofs. What were these peculiar little edifices – outside toilets maybe?

How many members of the Dogon tribe there are today depends very much on which report you read. The numbers seem to vary from 80,000 to three times that figure and that presumably just refers to the ones that are alive. Because as we were soon to see, the caves and crevices cutting into the rockfaces are the final resting places of several thousand years of Dogons deceased. This fiercely independent people worship their dead and are renowned for their ancient traditions and weird superstitions, ghoulish masks and unusual works of art. They live entirely off the land, descending to the fields by day and returning at night to their hilltop hideouts, an entirely separate entity from the rest of the country. Their wealth, or lack of it, is a direct result of their agricultural efforts. No surprise then that those strange little huts weren't outside khasis, but turned out in fact to be their personal granary stores.

It was a day to treasure. Never had I, or would I ever again, witness with my own eyes the existence of such a primitive, isolated community. But it wasn't just that. It was the geography, the experience of sitting in the sunshine on top of that peculiar escarpment and looking out at the vast, seemingly endless open spaces in all directions and this time from a completely different perspective. I stayed there for quite some time, reflecting on the things that I'd done and seen since arriving in Mali and decided that this really was a unique country. A voice broke the silence, that of one of my travel companions: "I think everybody in the world should spend at least one week of every year in Mali."

A sweeping comment, but I knew exactly where she was coming from. The different scale of time and space did something wonderful to the mind, provided a release of tension that you had never even realised was there in the first place. I knew I wouldn't go back every year, in fact more than likely I would never go back at all. No offence to you Mali, but an incredible journey like this just wouldn't be the same second time around.

Laos

Once upon a time, far far away in the mountains of South East Asia, lived a simple peasant tribe known as the Lao. They built ramshackle homes in the steep, lush valleys where they worked the land and pulled fish from the waters of the mighty Mekong River. Each small community had its own king and everybody prayed silently to Buddha for eternal peace and happiness. But alas, despite their devotion to this smiling, tubby little chap, all did not go well.

Over hundreds of years, with no provocation whatsoever, this hapless mountain folk were attacked by the Siamese, Burmese, Chinese, Japanese ... the very mention of any race ending in –ese would send them diving under their beds. At the end of the 19th century, it was the turn of the French, who seized power of the various Lao kingdoms and decided that henceforth these should collectively be known as the country of Laos (pronounced like house). Vietnam and Cambodia also fell ... and that was the start of sixty years of colonial rule in Indochina.

The French introduced their lovely language, created some elegant buildings and baked delicious bread, but despite all this the locals became seriously disenchanted with their lot. By the 1940s it was clear the European rulers were no longer welcome (were they ever, I wonder?) and in 1953 all ties with the colonial masters were cut. The Lao People's Democratic Republic (PDR) became a fully independent country for the very first time and to most of the world would be known, quite simply, as Laos.

The post-colonial honeymoon didn't last long. Across the northern border, the communist roadshow that was China and the Soviet Union was gathering pace. The hungry wolves were staring, drooling, and ready

121

to pounce – they had devoured the north of Vietnam in ousting the French and were heading in a southerly direction. Who could possibly prevent them from moving in for the kill?

Why, the American government, of course. What happened in the decade that followed is a gruesome and chilling story, but not for the telling here. Except to say this. That during the Vietnam War, Laos was supposed to be a neutral country, and incredible though it seems, wars have rules. Killing, maiming and torturing millions of people seems to fall within the accepted guidelines provided that the spectators at ringside don't get hurt. But those rules were broken, not once or twice, but more than half a million times.

From 1964-73 the Lao countryside was bombed by US planes at the rate of one every eight minutes, every day, for nine years. That comes to almost six hundred thousand bombs, more than they dropped in the whole of the Second World War. This was known as The Secret War and it gave Laos what will probably be its only ever world number one status. The most bombed country in the history of warfare.

How lucky I was to have the opportunity to visit Laos. In 1975 the communists had taken over after all and, as communists did in those days, they made sure the outside world couldn't see what they were up to. The borders had been closed and many of the Lao citizens that hadn't managed to escape (about 10% did get out) were sent away to newly-created 're-education' camps where they were locked up for the next fourteen years until the start of the 1990s, when the communist regimes around the world fell over like a pack of cards. From there, it all seemed to happen so quickly. The Berlin Wall was pulled down, Russia was no longer seen as the big enemy, South Africa made all the head-lines and Laos was opened to visitors…

I had done some background reading, but actual preparation and planning for my trip to Laos had taken less than three minutes. A glance at a map had told me the country was shaped like a falling tree and that the only two international airports were relatively close together in the bushy bit at the top. It made sense to book a flight into one city and out of the other. A visa could be obtained on arrival.

* * * * *

I flew in to Thailand from Australia then set off across the enormous terminal to catch the 10am Bangkok Airways flight to Luang Prabang, a city I'd never heard of on an airline I hadn't known existed. Such is the exciting, unpredictable life of the FLC traveller, I reflected with considerable satisfaction. Would I be the only westerner on the plane? The monster from another planet with non-black hair and huge round eyes? Here I was at last, gate 56, collecting a free fruit juice courtesy of the unknown airline, settling into my grey plastic seat. Questions would soon be answered and come to think of it, my jet-lagged eyes felt more black and baggy than huge and round.

The first passengers that caught my eye were certainly not Asian. These people were unwashed, scruffily dressed, grotesquely studded and had declined to use the seats in favour of slouching on the floor. Perhaps I wouldn't be the only Brit on board after all. I looked around at the hundred or so people waiting for the same flight and honed in on English, Irish, German and a large group of French tourists. I counted the number of Asian passengers. Zero.

The colourfully-painted aeroplane left bang(kok) on time and I got chatting in rusty French to a lady in the group from Paris (my French was rather rustier than hers, I noticed) about my trip and the flight over from Sydney. At that very moment her eyes widened and she let out a curious gasp and it crossed my mind for a split second that one of the springs in the seat might have somehow broken free and shot up into her anus. The fleeting image was shattered when she asked me to repeat where I had come from.

Sydney in Australia! It was too much for her to cope with. She immediately had to lean over and tell her mates across the aisle then swivel round and wake up the two couples behind with the breaking news. The impact could not have been greater had I arrived by parachute from Saturn. I couldn't bring myself to tell her that Sydney was in fact rather closer than Paris.

The two-hour flight north took us into lush undulating countryside and delivered an assortment of strangely-clad white people almost to the door of the modern airport building. More of an airstrip really, surrounded by mountains and palm trees, the deep green colours enhanced by the bright sunshine and a clear blue sky. It immediately felt like somewhere I was going to enjoy.

The arrivals hall reminded me of a neighbourhood supermarket, but here we were queuing for visas rather than paying for a trolley of groceries. I handed over my 30 US Dollars thanking my lucky stars that it wasn't a Sunday or a public holiday because, as the sign on the counter explained, an entry permit on those days costs 1 dollar more to cover the extra expense of staff overtime.

Visa obtained, quarantine form stamped, luggage collected, gaze from customs man averted, I was ready to head for the bank. I guess travelling just wouldn't be the same if it wasn't for the excitement and confusion that switching from one currency to another pretty much guarantees. I had done my best to prepare for it ... Thailand has Baht, Laos has Kip and Vietnam (my next destination) would be Dong. And like everywhere else in the world US Dollars would be king.

I stood in yet another queue at the small airport bank, but now with a very silly grin on my face. "I've been travelling all night and I just want to get some Kip!" There was nobody to share my little unspoken joke, but nonetheless it gave me immense pleasure. "Just wait till I get to Vietnam, I'll be getting my Dong out." Now I was really on a roll, so wrapped up in my world of stand-up comedy that I hadn't noticed it was my turn to step forward.

Five ten-dollar bills earned me 500,000 Kip, which I can assure you, is a very large bundle of notes when the largest is worth 5,000.

Laos

Thankful that I hadn't changed more, I emerged into the sunlight on to the front step of the airport where a crowd of some eight people had gathered. My mind flashed to Lagos in Nigeria where several thousand brightly dressed locals waving boards and pieces of paper arrive to receive every inbound flight and have to be held back by iron railings and squadrons of armed police. I was happy to be in Luang Prabang.

One of the eight sat perched on a wall and sold tickets for taxi transportation into town. He smiled and saw my confusion at being told the price was 50,000 Kip, invited me to pay US$ 5 or 200 Baht if that would be easier. This was going to be fun and games. I handed over part of my Kip bundle and he passed the ticket to one of the other seven men standing quietly behind him, all of whom turned out to be the taxi drivers. The nominated one smiled, lifted my bag into his white minibus parked right there and we gently pulled away.

We moved along very slowly towards the centre of town, but why were we going so slowly? There were no traffic jams, in fact no traffic at all. Just a few motor bikes, their riders steering with one hand and holding parasols in the other against the heat of the afternoon sun. They seemed to be going so slowly too. What was going on?

I watched my driver, who smiled back at me through his mirror as we dawdled along through the outskirts of the city. Then the thought came to me that we weren't necessarily going *that* slowly, it was just more slowly than I was used to, that's all. I had never been to Laos before. His general demeanour seemed friendly and trustworthy, but he couldn't speak any English at all. At least so I thought. In fact it turned out that he had mastered six words and after a sustained period of polite smiling he gushed forth with his first three: "You like waterfall?" An interesting opener indeed. He sensed my confusion and felt obliged to clarify, so much so that we had now pulled over and come to a complete stop. Had this been Colombia or Central Africa I would have been looking towards the bushes for masks and guns and insisting that we kept moving forward. But this man was no bandit, of that I was sure. He smiled again and shyly handed me some postcards of the local sights, postcards that I would be shown many times during my days in Laos. "I take you?"

I declined the waterfall offer and instead we made for the hotel Mouang Luang. The Mouang Luang at Luang Prabang, try saying that when you've had a few beers. Ten minutes later, a wave and another smile from the driver, and I was standing at the hotel's polished reception desk. It was impressive, and I don't just mean the desk. The place looked like a palace set in lush gardens: high ceilings, open archways, gently whirring fans, white walls and dark shiny wood. I was willing it not to be fully booked, and it wasn't. The price was US$45 per night, but would there be a discount if I stayed for a few nights? The proprietor smiled nervously, bowed his head and looked saddened and embarrassed in equal measure to have to deny me any form of a bulk deal. I couldn't quite put my finger on the reason, but I felt slightly shabby to have asked in the first place.

It was a lovely hotel and for most of my time there I had the place to myself. The French party from the plane stayed the first night, but as I looked towards their long table at breakfast I couldn't see my friend amongst the group. Instead I did notice a very attractive lady with short blond hair whose right nipple seemed to be fighting to get out of her white cotton shirt. I found myself wondering what had happened to the left one and why women's nipples often seemed to work independently. In the interest of broadening my general knowledge I decided one day I would try to find this out. Who might know? Who could I select from my Phone a Friend List in the event of a tit question separating me from a million quid? Then I realised I'd been staring at her chest for rather a long time and quickly started to fiddle with the seeds of my watermelon.

* * * * *

The main street of town was a ten-minute walk away and 25 degrees sunshine made for perfect strolling. I was relaxed, happy, it all seemed

126

so calm and peaceful and I was trying to figure out what made it different from other places. And then the penny dropped. Cars! There were almost no cars on the streets, no sound, just a few motor bikes and that great Asian invention the samlaw (or tuk-tuk), the motorised three wheeler that serves as a taxi. Everybody that walked by smiled and said 'Sabaii Dii' in such a cheerful sing-song way and I found 'Sabaii Dii-ing' back to them gave me an embarrassingly (for a grown man) enormous amount of pleasure. I figured it could only mean 'Hello' and once really into the swing I even mimicked the art of stretching the final bit so it came out as Sabaideeeeeeeeeeeeee, like a man falling down a well.

It was to be the only word of Lao with which I could claim any sort of fluency. Lao is a language very similar to Thai and which, when written, looks like a line of twisted paper clips. As though that isn't daunting enough there are six tones, so one word can have several completely different meanings depending on how you sing it. This must be a night-mare for any European mad enough to try to learn it. Wouldn't it be fairer to the tone deaf to just come up with some different words?

There were more westerners than I had expected and the town had clearly tooled itself up to cater for the backpacker's every need. Almost every commercial building was either a guesthouse, a restaurant, a laundry, a travel agency or an internet café, but it didn't do anything to detract from the immediate charm of the place. In fact I soon realised that in finding this town I had stumbled upon something a bit special.

I walked for a long time, got my bearings and watched the local people, many of whom were monks with shaven heads and dressed in very distinctive bright orange robes. They were mostly young lads, teenagers, and I found it all very intriguing. So much so that I decided to sit and have a beer, not surprisingly called Beerlao, and read a couple of paragraphs about monks and religion. (Two paragraphs, from experience, being my monks and religion threshold). Here it comes in a nutshell: In Laos all young men are expected to spend at least a short period of their lives as monks, during which time they live in one of the temples and are kept in food by way of donations from the local community. There are restrictions about when they can eat, they can't receive money, sleep on beds, consume alcohol or even think about sex. No surprise then that some of the lads prefer to do just a couple of weeks.

Buddhism is very much at the heart of Lao culture and the teachings of that religion are what has quite evidently shaped the personality of the people. The version practised in Laos is known as Theravada and it teaches that, above all else, the most important thing in life is to always keep one's calm and never outwardly show emotion. (I suspect very few car drivers in Rome are Therevada Buddhists). The other version of Buddhism, Mahayana, is followed in China and Vietnam and encourages a more assertive attitude, which explains a generally far more aggressive approach to life, particularly business, in those countries.

A spicy papaya salad went down well with the beer and the two paragraphs and now I was itching to get down to the banks of the River Mekong. I knew it was only a few hundred metres away, parallel to the main street where I was sitting.

Five minutes later and there I was, surrounded by mountains and staring in awe at yet another of the great rivers of the world. Suddenly my mind went back to Mali, sitting on the hillside above Bamako looking down on the Niger, and I realised that, at 2,500 miles, the Mekong is almost as long. I get misty-eyed looking at these vast waterways, always think about where they start out and all the different landscapes and communities they pass through. The point at which I was standing I guessed was probably very roughly half way along the river between its source in the mountains of south west China and the point in Vietnam at which it empties into the South China Sea. It was a fabulous sight, but the colour of it surprised and, though reluctant to admit it to myself, disappointed me. Not blue or black or even grey, but a strange sort of reddish brown.

The city actually sits in the angle of two rivers and so I walked along to the point where the other one, the Nam Khan, meets its big brother. An incredible contrast, this smaller river was almost bright green and it was fascinating to stand at the confluence and watch its clear water flow out into the huge expanse of the Mekong. It seemed so reluctant to mix with the sandy coloured water and the two colours co-existed side by side for quite some distance before it all finally blended into one.

* * * * *

Luang Prabang has mountains and rivers in abundance, but its main claim to fame is the city's incredible architecture. It boasts over 700 historic buildings, earning its official classification as a world heritage site and amongst these are some of the most spectacular temples found any-where in the world. You know it must be something very special if UNESCO has seven experts based there full-time to catalogue their findings.

I was utterly mesmerised by these beautiful, ornately decorated gold temples with their elegant pillars and layered concave roofs. To stand under the bright blue sky and experience such a wonderful sight was a truly humbling experience; at dusk, perhaps even more dramatic, like something out of a movie, a magical silhouette with the unmistake-able form of the palm trees completing the picture.

My favourite streetside café was right next to one such temple. A typical LP evening would see me sitting there under the stars with a plate of spicy noodles and a chilled bottle of Beerlao, no doubt tormenting the abstemious monks walking by. From time to time I would look over the road and watch the trees swaying in the breeze over the magnificent gold building and then I would turn my attention back to the live Premiership match on the TV in front of me. You just can't get away from it, can you?

It did strike me as somewhat bizarre to be sitting in a T-shirt in a beautiful warm mountain valley by the River Mekong watching the Birmingham derby live from Villa Park. A faraway world of darkness, wind and rain, spectators wrapped up in coats, scarves and gloves and still looking chilled to the bone. It also struck me that life couldn't get much better (mine, not the fans!). The food was delicious, as was the beer, and the cost of a heavy night was never more than £3. Or should I say 50,000 Kip.

The food in Laos deserves more than a mention in passing, it was fantastic. Whatever was on offer was always absolutely fresh and invariably introduced a tingling combination of lime juice, chilli, ginger, mint and coriander leaves. One of my favourites, known as laap, was all of the above mixed together and finely chopped with chicken or pork or beef. Great stuff this, mild and flavoursome until you hit a small piece of red chilli, then it became decidedly hot and flavoursome. Chillies so small, but enough to make you stop talking or even leap from your chair. Maybe that's where laap dancing originated?

Then there were the fresh spring rolls, quite a surprise first time round. The smiley lady popped them on the table next to my bottle of Beerlao, four of them lying parallel in the middle of the plate, each wrapped in a sort of clear plastic. "Are these spring rolls?" I asked in the manner of a man who knew a spring roll when he saw one. "Yes sir, fresh spring rolls".

The word 'fresh' was obviously emphasised for good reason and indeed this was what separated these little chaps from your standard deep-fried offering. I picked one up rather apprehensively as though it might go off in my hand. Was this some sort of practical joke? It wasn't just fresh, it was cold. This was the fun of being in a foreign country, I reminded myself. And so, ever so slowly, I started to unwrap the unusual little parcel, looking around to see if anybody was watching, or worse, sniggering.

There was. In fact the waitress was laughing loudly in a very un-Lao like show of emotion. "You think it's plastic don't you," she managed to get out between titters. She was loving every moment. At least I wasn't the first falang (foreigner) to make a dick of himself. The plastic was in fact a kind of rice paper and rolled inside it were prawns and fresh mint and all sorts of goodies that were to be dipped in a sweet chilli sauce. I soon got the hang of it and devoured them all in minutes, savouring every mouthful and knew that for the rest of my life a routine spring roll would never quite compare with a freshie.

Night-life in Laos, like in most of the developing world, for the most part involves going to bed. However the advent of TV has introduced a further form of evening entertainment and the later addition of the satellite dish, in the bars that can afford them, beams news and sport in from all corners of the planet. In a way it seems sad that a simple way of life has somehow been sullied, but then who are we to judge?

I was pathetic enough to sit and watch live English football in Laos, but not such a sad case that I didn't feel a little uneasy about it. The compromise was to get out of the bar as soon as the game ended, forgo the post-match analysis and instead of watching re-runs of dubious refereeing decisions I would take my evening stroll through the night market, one of the most impressive markets I have ever visited. Not particularly because of the merchandise on offer, but quite simply because of the sense of occasion that it created. Every evening as the sun goes down a section of the city is cordoned off and the local ladies bring goods in to town and set up their pitches in the middle of the main road. No stalls or structures, they all just sit patiently on their carpets several metres apart, each pitch lit by an electric bulb suspended from a metre-high "gallows". It is a spectacular sight, such a homely feeling with several hundred small lights like candles illuminating the street in the darkness of the warm evening.

The ladies who work the market will most certainly be poor but their appearance did little to give that impression. These quiet, gentle folk always looked clean, manicured, well-dressed and ready with a generous smile. What a pleasure it was to be amongst these people, to exchange a little banter and have a quick peek into their mysterious lives. I had no wish to buy anything, but I never missed my evening walk through the market.

The Four-Letter Countries

* * * * *

I knew that at some point the waterfall had to be done. My legs weren't exactly trembling with excitement at the prospect, so I consulted one of the many travel agencies on ways to spice up the outing. Exercise was also on my agenda so the best suggestion was to take a guide and go there by bike and boat, returning by bike and elephant. Yes, elephant. It already started to sound more fun and I booked to go at 8.30 the next morning.

Lair was my guide, a man in his late twenties who looked ten years younger and spoke remarkably good English. We cycled along the dirt tracks and climbed up out of the town through the trees, the low cloud that always hung in the early morning providing welcome protection from the sun that would soon burn through. We stopped to chat, and in my case sweat, and drink water from our transparent plastic bottles. He talked about his life, his time in the monastery, the contrast of working with falang as opposed to his own people. His work took him on three-day treks with foreigners and he recounted how only the week before two ladies from Belgium had suggested that he and his friend kept them warm for the night! He had been shocked, amused, flattered and very tempted, but decided that his job would be on the line. It could get back to the company and was simply too much to risk. He didn't know their official policy, but suspected that bonking Belgian clients would be a dismissable offence. Oh, and he had a wife and baby at home.

The scenery was magnificent and our journey through the trees reminded me of the landscape where I'd gone in search of the famous Togolese butterflies. By mid-morning the cloud had given way to the sun as it always did and, as I huffed and puffed up the hills, the shirt was getting wetter and the face and neck were starting to glow.

Some three hours later we dropped down a track into the forest and parked our bikes at a half-built guest lodge overlooking the Nam Khan river (the one that runs into the Mekong in Luang Prabang). The building was being financed by Lair's boss, the German owner of the tour company, and Markus himself was there to monitor the progress. He talked excitedly about this little paradise by the river and how the project would contribute to developing the country's fledgling tourist industry. I wondered whether he had ever thought, as a little boy growing up in Frankfurt, that one day he would own a guest-house in a jungle on the other side of the world. Incredible how life pans out, isn't it?

A small motorised boat took Lair and me to one of the most unusual waterfalls I have ever seen. The crystal clear water ran over several tiers of improbably white boulders, each of which appeared to have been positioned in a wide arc for maximum effect. Cascading down through an opening in the trees it all seemed too perfect to be true – surely this was a giant water feature from a nearby garden centre? Like the other dozen or so tourists, I paddled and gawped for a couple of hours and enjoyed some spicy fried rice that appeared from a small hut half hidden in the trees. It never failed to astonish me how the Asian ladies could always produce such tasty food with the most basic of facilities at their disposal. I sat there thinking how the motorway service stations in the UK, which have all the resources known to man and a constant flow of customers, are unable to progress beyond greasy, tasteless, overpriced stodge. What a thing to think about in one of the most beautiful places in the world! Get a life.

It was agreed that I would return to the lodge by elephant, not because it was any easier or quicker, but because I was a tourist and should experience a ride aboard the greatest mammal on earth. The elephant is a key symbol of the country since Laos has a population of around 1,150 of them and yet only 4.5 million people, the highest elephant/human ratio in Asia at 3,913. As Eric Morecambe used to say, "not a lot of people know that".

Once on board it was quite comfortable, though I must admit I'd never given any thought to how one goes about mounting an elephant. Would you have expected him to kneel down obligingly so you could use his folded leg as a step? They are certainly not the speediest form of transport, in fact they actually walk more slowly than you or I. And that's not including branch-munching breaks and several phenomenal poo-stops (elephants don't seem to be able to poo and walk at the same time, but neither I suppose would you if you were depositing a jobby on that scale). Sitting up there a few metres above the ground, rocking from side to side often through dense undergrowth, was really fantastic and offered a vantage point that would never be possible any other way. I'm so glad I did it.

My legs were a bit stiff the following day and this seemed an ideal time and place for the long-awaited massage. I had passed quite a few little houses during the week with makeshift cardboard signs outside written in English and so, a little apprehensively, I tapped on the door of one of them. "Massage?"

The delicate-looking teenager ushered me into the family living room, memorable for its vast collection of assorted chairs, a lady having her breast sucked, and a man on a stepladder surrounded by tools. Her parents and baby brother I assumed. Thankfully there was also an adjoining room, completely empty except for a mattress on the floor, and it was into here that I was duly ushered. Not knowing what else to do I took off my T-shirt, lay there in my shorts, and wondered what might happen next.

A few seconds was enough to convince me that this young lady knew exactly what she was doing and that in this business size was to count for nothing. Working her way very slowly and purposefully around my body she used her palms, feet, arms and elbows to lift, stretch and twist me in ways I could never have imagined possible. At times she lay her entire weight onto me and, like you, I was more than a bit curious to know how far she was prepared to take this.

As though reading my impure mind she pressed her thumbs into the back of my calf muscles, a move the Nazis would have been proud of. My head jerked upwards from the mattress like a condemned man in the electric chair and at that very same moment the baby next door let out a blood-curdling scream. The drill then screeched from the top of the stepladder and in that split second the world had been transformed from a model of tranquility into a place of total madness. Then all went absolutely silent and once again perfect order was restored.

The whole body took a full hour and a half, excluding the shorts which she'd indicated in an embarrassed sort of way must definitely not be removed. She smiled a lot, but spoke not at all, except at the end, in confused English, to ask my age. I told her how old I was, then returned the same question to her. The answer, after a lengthy pause, was somewhat different from what I had expected. "Seventy two thousand," she said with a nervous smile.

I handed over the three dollars, smiled as appreciatively as possible to the whole family (their respective duties now apparently completed), and returned to the brightness of the sun-baked street. A glance at the watch, wow! Almost two hours had gone out of my morning. I now had to catch up on e-mail, pick up my laundry (washed and ironed for 50c a kilo), have a swim AND watch Liverpool v Man U live from Anfield. This was turning out to be one hell of a busy schedule. I decided to get a taxi.

LP was becoming too comfortable and it would have been very easy not to leave, so to focus the mind I booked on a flight to depart two days hence. I would go east to Phonsavan, forty dollars worth of plane ride on Lao Aviation.

Now I had to get my act together and, like it or not, the trip to the famous Pak Ou caves had to be done. The plus side to this was that even if it was a tourist flytrap it involved a boat ride along the Mekong – the river breeze in the face and sun on the back would be worth the tedium of trawling round with the clicking cameras.

It took an hour each way and I had a great fish lunch on the opposite side of the river whilst chatting to a lady from Denmark. The caves were a bonus, a gaping hole in the limestone cliffs where thousands of statues of Buddha in all shapes and sizes had been taken many years earlier to create a riverside shrine.

It was a good day out and perhaps the most memorable part was the outward journey. I had missed the early-departing tourist boats, so for the princely sum of ten dollars chartered my own skippered craft for the day. As the solo passenger on a boat built for more than twenty people I felt excruciatingly pompous cruising by the other tourists – did they think I was too stuck up to ride along with the hoi-polloi? I was soon to make their acquaintance.

Shouts from one of the boats drew our attention to the fact that it was in mid-river and going nowhere fast, so we chugged over to investigate. Its poor little skipper was struggling with his engine while a dozen or so tourists of mixed nationalities sat there grinning and joking, but seemingly enjoying the unusual experience of drifting silently along the mighty Mekong river. All except the American lady. She was red in the face and leaning forward and screeching in one of those CNN newsreader kind of voices that would normally send you diving for the MUTE button. She told whoever was prepared to listen that the situation was intolerable, that she was no longer willing to put her life at risk and that she demanded an immediate transfer to a safe and reliable vessel.

The main danger to her life as I could see it would come from the fellow passengers who seemed ready to dump her overboard and take it in turns to hold her ugly fat head under the water. Or was she concerned at the threat of starvation, the opportunity to have gorged six pizzas having been lost while trapped on board? She carried on ranting. We were told that a spark had emerged from the defunct motor, a fire on board was thus a distinct possibility, and that she was not prepared to be burned alive far away from her loved ones back in the little old US of A. And so, despite the pleading of their captain for a few moments patience, she masterminded a mutiny. I was no longer travelling alone.

Laos

As it turned out the stricken boat kicked into life shortly after and when we stopped for a break at a riverside village my tenants, including The Voice of America, returned to the floating fireball.

The little communities we visited were fascinating, they survived by weaving fabric on ancient wooden looms and distilling strange alcoholic potions in enormous tin drums. Another little sideline was renting the use of their toilets to passing tourists. They were spotless to the point of being shiny, a measure of the pride and cleanliness of even the poorest of people.

* * * * *

The last day in Luang Prabang was spent doing what, logically, I should have done as soon as I got there. The town sits at the foot of a small mountain and a walk up to its peak offers spectacular 360 degree views. Most people do this at the end of the afternoon to watch the sun set, but I decided to go on my final morning. And I'm so glad that I did. To stand up there next to the Phu Si shrine and look down on the two great rivers and the temples and the mountains and the little airstrip was a memory I will always cherish. I stayed up there for a couple of hours to soak it all in: it was too good to simply turn up, take a picture and head off back to town. I didn't know when I would be back in this gorgeous place, just hoped that one day it would definitely happen.

Back at the hotel the reception informed me that a visitor had called in my absence, asking for me by name, and that he would be back. Spooky indeed. Who in the whole country knew me or where I was staying? It had to be a mistake. Didn't it? A few minutes later I was summoned back to the lobby where a smartly dressed local gentleman was waiting to see me. He was from the office of Lao Aviation and had come to return the Visa card that I had (unknowingly) left behind the day before. How's that for service?

The Four-Letter Countries

The last night in LP was a few Beerlao and England v Wales at rugby. A lively crowd had gathered in the bar, but it wasn't a great performance by England, or in the eyes of many, the referee. One of the revellers, a public school chappie from London, had obviously been quenching his thirst all day and spent the entire evening standing on his chair directing abuse very loudly towards the screen. I found myself wanting to disappear under the table and wondered whether the local people tiptoeing by had ever, in their well-ordered lives, witnessed aggressive human behaviour of any sort, let alone a man screaming obscenities at a television set.

Richard had sobered up by the next morning and was very much quieter sitting next to me on the little plane to Phonsavan with the ten other passengers (again no locals). He confided that he'd had a few tipples in a bar the night before and I told him my story of the almost-lost credit card rather than mention that I had also been watching the match (and him). We agreed it could have been a bad day all round but England had won in the end and we'd both averted disaster.

Whether the good run would now continue was not something we could take for granted. *Lonely Planet* had gone to great lengths to warn against flying with Lao Aviation, dodgy planes and poorly-equipped airports seemingly not to their liking. But as we boarded the plane at 9am on another beautiful sunny Monday morning in paradise, I could only feel a great sense of privilege. I thought of people in the cold and dark UK, grey faces waiting for delayed trains, motionless cars in miles of traffic on overcrowded motorways. What a lucky boy I was.

The short flight east was spectacular, over tiny and presumably very remote villages, perched on pale lime green mountains with clusters of dark trees that looked like broccoli from the air. Half an hour later we were in Phonsovan, the capital of Xieng Khuang province. This region had been made famous for two entirely different reasons and the best person to tell me all about it, I had been assured by a fellow traveller, was the owner of the Maly Hotel. He always meets the flights at the airport.

Laos

Except, it turned out, on Monday mornings. Richard also had his heart set on the same hotel and, as there were no cabs, we found a minibus owner prepared to take us there provided we agreed to view and consider his own guest house first. And anyway "the Maly has a large group in and is full today." We viewed, considered, and rejected his dismal premises and our hitherto smiley driver sulked all the way to the door of the Maly. Inside the hallway we found the famous Mr Sousath standing behind his grand reception desk and quickly checked on availability. "Group? What group?"

He turned out to be quite a character did Mr Sousath, but then any person who had experienced what he had could hardly be anything else. The newspaper article on the wall was written by the *Bangkok Post* and it told his story roughly like this:

When he was a small boy in the 1960s Laos was caught up in the terrible war between the Communists from North Vietnam and their powerful enemy from the USA. The people of the country had to choose to join one side or the other, or simply run for dear life. Sousath's father had feared for the safety of his son and in desperation packed him onto a bus with a crowd of others fleeing to China. The terrified boy was 10 years old. He hated China and eventually managed to escape back across the border to his home country, taking refuge in a cave with a group of adults who were too frightened to go anywhere else. And there he lived for five years until the end of the war, by then a teenage boy. They were eventually to hear that the fighting had stopped when a helicopter of the Lao army swept the skies of the north of the country to spread the happy news. The aircraft actually landed close to the cave that had been Sousath's makeshift home and when the pilot jumped out of the cockpit it turned out to be none other than his own brother.

If this happened in a movie you would dismiss it as being too far-fetched but this is in fact a true story. The part of Laos where I now found myself was the most seriously affected by the Vietnam war, in fact the most bombed region in the most bombed country in the history of warfare. And remember that Laos was supposed to be a neutral country. So why did it happen? I will try to explain.

Imagine the north of England is at war with the south. The gruff Yorkshiremen, Scousers, and Geordies in black and white striped shirts are on the rampage and heading for London. The respectable folk of the Home Counties are terrified, beside themselves with fear that their flower beds will be trampled on by vulgar, urinating people wearing cloth caps and so they erect barriers from Hilton Park Services on the M6 right across the Midlands (something most of them felt should have been done anyway many years earlier). So how do the marauding north-erners respond? It's obvious. They head west into north Wales and defi-antly march through the mountains of Snowdonia. Now the Southern Softies really start to panic, they are determined to resist this invasion at all cost. They turn for help to their rich allies with airbases in Ireland who are only too keen to get in on the action. Within days, the Welsh mountainside is being bombed to pieces and, just to make sure, the bombing campaign is kept up night and day for the whole of the next decade.

The joke is there to explain the geography and roughly how it happened, not in any way to diminish the seriousness of a brutal and pointless war. The North Vietnamese were marching through Laos, the Americans were determined to stop them and it was from their air bases in Thailand that they flew in to drop more than half a million bombs on the country throughout nine years of insanity. The Secret War was no big secret, but neither side was allowed to acknowledge their presence in a neutral country.

* * * * *

By now you've probably forgotten I said that this part of Laos has two great claims to fame. The other is not related to the war in any way, but in fact goes back hundreds, even thousands of years before then. The

Laos

region is known as the Plain of Jars and we were soon to find out from Mr Sousath Junior what it was all about. Richard and I dumped our bags upstairs and a few minutes later we were in the back of the Land Rover and ready for a half-day guided tour.

To set the scene we are driving through lush, gently undulating countryside, but in the distance on all sides we are looking at a landscape of delightful rolling mountains. After half an hour or so, surrounded by fields, we stop and get out. The sky is deep blue, the sun searing hot, we stand by the vehicle and look out to the fields beyond. What we see is really very unusual. Around 250 stone creations, several metres apart, but in no discernible pattern. They differ in heights from that of a small infant to a tall man and some look like mushrooms with chunky stems and large overhanging tops. But the majority of them do not have lids, or rather they are lying on the ground close by. We are invited to sit under the shade of a tree to have our first lesson of the day.

Young Sousath had inherited the enthusiasm and determination of his father, of that there was no doubt. Together they had studied the three main sites of the jars, researched everything there was to know and led their own searches for more or similar. These expeditions had taken them all around the country and were scheduled to extend into other parts of Asia, the Sousath boys were the true experts when it comes to the Plain of Jars. Whether true or not, his presentation was polished and extremely convincing:

There are three main sites and several smaller ones in the country-side around Phonsavan and the first Westerner ever to see the jars was a French lady in the 1930s ('around the time my parents were born,' was my first thought). We are at the biggest, known as Site 1, other sites have somewhere between maybe 50 and 150 jars. But what are they, who built them, when, and why? I'll give you the short answer and put you out of your misery. Nobody really knows.

There are many theories, though, and the Sousaths are convinced that theirs is correct. More than 2,000 years ago a nomadic tribe swept in a south easterly direction and trekked right across Asia as far as Indonesia (similar sites in other countries support this view). Their religion/superstition dictated that at the end of their lives they donate all their wealth to the gods and so, when the time came, they built hollow jars of granite and sandstone and encased their treasure within. But it wasn't the gods who raided them, it was those nasty Chinese who came over the border to rape and pillage some years later.

Nobody has ever found anything inside the jars, nor have any been located with their lids still secure. Some historians have suggested that they may have been used as tombs, but then surely there would have been human remains to support that theory? The mystery will be solved once and for all if an untouched site can be found, but searching for new ones is a very dangerous business. The terrain of eastern Laos looks very beautiful, but is littered with unexploded ordnance, one foot in the wrong place and your leg, or your life, is no more. And, as though that isn't bad enough, there are still American-trained 'soldiers' of the Hmong tribe living out in the mountains who are not convinced the war is over and are liable to take a pot-shot at any passing archaeologist!

The Sousath boys have, they claim, discovered an unmolested site and it will answer the unanswered when the tops are finally prised off those virgin jars. All they need is a sponsor to render the site safe and to bring machinery and experts and cameras to the Plain. Until that support is guaranteed, together with the publicity and lots of money they feel they deserve, the whereabouts of the lost site will remain a secret behind the doors of the Maly Hotel.

Richard and I sat and listened, mesmerised like two small children, not sure what to make of it all. Were we privy to something that would change the history of our civilisation? Or just a couple of gullible tourists being fed a pile of horseshit?! Maybe one day we will know the answer to that one.

We walked around the site and took endless photos, commenting that they would all look exactly the same but snapping away at more nonetheless. We posed for pictures standing inside the jars and studied damage caused in recent years by bombs and bullets. Then we got back in the jeep and drove to the other fields where we did pretty much the same thing all over again.

The scenery was awesome and the location of the sites would be a dream for any serious photographer. At the final stop, having driven past a capsized Russian tank, we caught sight of some other people for the first time that day, a local man and a couple of westerners. Our guide shouted out a greeting and exchanged a few words and it was only as the small group grew closer that I realised the person he was talking to was the Plain of Jars' other specialist, his own father.

The Maly Hotel was much more war than jars. It was like a museum, wrecked bits of aircraft all over the place, guns, grenades, bullets hanging from the dining room wall, even the cutlery was made from crashed American aeroplanes. It was a walk through time, a history lesson without the boredom, and the food and beer was pretty good too.

I had planned to stay more than just one day but Sousath Senior was honest enough to admit that there was really little more on offer to stay for. He chuckled at the fact that he was doing himself out of business and then called Lao Aviation to book me on the next flight to Vientiane. Richard opted for a nine-hour bus ride to Vang Vieng and, as travellers do, we shook hands and went our separate ways. It had been twenty four hours we wouldn't forget in a hurry.

* * * * *

Laos isn't a big country, in fact it is very close in size to the UK (for stats bores like me, UK is the 77th and Laos is the 81st largest country in the world. It stands at number 7 amongst the FLCs.) However that is where the similarity ends. The population is only about 8% of the UK's and Laos's infrastructure is almost non-existent. There are only around 5,000 kms of tarred roads in the whole country and, until the 1990s, the only way to get to the south from the north was by river. Things are changing, but ever so slowly; distances that could be covered in a few hours in Europe would take days if not weeks in Laos. For that reason I decided to concentrate the trip on the north of the country and leave the south for another day.

Phonsovan airport was really nothing more than the equivalent of a small house next to a landing strip. So when the plane to take us to Vientiane failed to appear the tourists simply went outside, lay in the garden and soaked up the sunshine until the buzz of the aircraft came within earshot. A very civilised and stress-free way to travel don't you think? As is often the case the wait was far longer than the flight itself, but I was safely in the capital later that day.

The taxi ride into Vientiane was a culture shock. Traffic, noise, scruffy buildings, more traffic, oh dear, oh no, what have I come to? Please take me back to lovely, calm, peaceful Luang Prabang, I don't want to be part of big city life. Jenks, Jenks, Jenks, pull yourself together. This is absurd. You're in a little city in South East Asia and behaving like a small child denied more sweeties. Get a grip!

Well I did, sort of. It took me five attempts to find a hotel that wasn't full but I got a room in a travellers guest house for US$15. This, I was assured, entitled me to an en-suite room with air conditioning and satellite TV and, of course, breakfast. Wow, how life had changed for the backpacker since I was a lad. Satellite TV! En-suite bathroom! In my day son it was shared cold water – if you were lucky – and, at best, a crackly bit of news on the short-wave radio. And I vowed that I would never sound like my Dad.

On closer inspection the en-suite bathroom was actually a shower cubicle with a toilet in it. I am never sure how these things are quite supposed to work, but can only assume that there is somebody out there who knows how to take a shower without reducing the toilet roll to the consistency of mushy peas. In my humble view, what this arrangement needs is an external dispenser whereby dry sheets can be drawn through a slat in the cubicle wall. Maybe I should patent that? Or perhaps be the first to create waterproof toilet paper? It could even be used in swimming pools.

I lay on the bed for a few minutes then drew back the curtains to have a look through the window. But there was no window, just bricks where a window used to be. So my room was actually a sealed box at the end of a corridor at the back of an old building on the sixth floor. In case of fire it was clear there would be only one course of action: telephone next of kin, say goodbye and hope to die as quickly as possible from smoke inhalation. I decided it was time to go out again.

The streets of Vientiane offered all the usual things that one would expect to see in an Asian city plus a few more sophisticated touches left behind by the French. There was nothing to love or hate about it, but certainly no oozing of charm, and the concept of cars on the roads was something I was still not reacclimatised to. Did I really want to be in a city anyway?

* * * * *

I woke up next morning feeling more positive, spurred on by the fact that I hadn't been charred to death, and decided to ponder my next move over the pineapple pancake breakfast. As ponders go, this was a good one. It was our old friend *Lonely Planet* that told me of a place called Lao Pako, an 'ecological resort' some 55kms to the north-east. I wasn't sure. The word 'resort' sounded a bit Butlins, but then it was intriguingly fused with the always-a-winner 'ecological'. The fact that I couldn't decide what an ecological resort was helped to make the final decision and the taxi driver couldn't believe his luck.

The road takes you as far as Somnamai ... and then you hope to find a motorised canoe to complete the journey. Anywhere else on the globe that would perhaps seem a chancy arrangement, but not in Asia. I have been travelling long enough to know that if a service is required in this part of the world then somebody will be ready and willing to earn themselves some money. (In Africa it's OK to just ask for money, in South America they find it more convenient to nick it). Sure enough a boatlady was there and I was guided along the quiet river, just a man and his bag, like a character in a 1950s movie.

I am still not much clearer what an ecological resort is, but was delighted with my thatched cottage high up on the bank, looking down at the river snaking through the trees. Eight or ten fellow ecologists had made it to this clearing in the jungle from various parts of the world and we all swapped stories at the evening sessions in the sauna. Yes, that's right, sauna.

Perhaps not so different from what the Finns originally created, this looked like a garden shed set in the undergrowth. The sauna master, as I shall call him, was responsible for gathering and burning foliage a few yards away and the vapours it gave off passed through a pipe leading into the floor of the little wooden hut. A crude arrangement maybe, but it sure sounded a great idea. Everybody went for the sauna, partly because it was a novelty and I suspect partly because there was bugger all else to do.

The truth of the matter is that once inside the shed, which could seat six at a pinch, it was just a fug of dense woodsmoke that made it impossible to even see if another person was in there. You simply opened the door, muttered an expletive as you stumbled in, and then rather tamely asked if anybody was home. The length of time spent within was established by your tolerance for burning eyes and the extent of your determination to have some fun. Thankfully there was a small natural pool outside and it didn't go unnoticed that people spent rather longer in that than they did sitting on top of the bonfire.

There was actually one other ecological pastime and that was known as tubing. Not the most scientific of sports, one sits on the inner tube of a tyre on the river and enjoys the thrill of being swept along by the current. The town of Vang Vieng is famous for this, but as I wouldn't be going there on this trip here was my big chance to sample the experience. So off I went to reception, collected my tyre and was told where to enter the river and where to get out several hundred metres further along. This was going to be fun.

Once on the river the first move was to position myself atop my new ring, so to speak. Calculating that my pert buttocks would fit neatly through the hole I hauled myself up and out of the water only to find that each time I did so my body weight would force the hitherto horizontal tyre into a vertical botty-rejecting position. No matter. If at first you don't succeed try, try again ... keep on trying until you have plummeted head first into the murky water so many times you are screaming out loud and can feel the first symptoms of cholera taking hold. And then give up.

Thankfully the splashing and the histrionics had not attracted any onlookers and it was time for an executive decision – I would try again once more, but this time just holding onto the side of the tyre. And so, finally, facing downriver, elbows in the air, legs outstretched, head tilted backwards, I was ready for the off.

And I might indeed have set off, except for the fact that the water was more or less stagnant. This brought back memories of the fresh spring roll, is there a guffawing ecologist behind every tree waiting to see what I do next? I jerked my head shorewards but saw only jungle. Wait a minute – I am ... am I? ... Yes, I'm moving, I'm moving, here we go.

I think I span round three times and then, ever so slowly, I moved ... backwards. Surely not. "Please let it be true that rivers can't – on a whim – just start flowing in the opposite direction," thought a now slightly panicky man clinging desperately on to a ring of inflated rubber. "Who knows where I might end up?" That was enough to get me swimming, or at least splashing, such that now I was right in the middle of the river.

The current did pick up, there was finally some movement in the right direction and, still waiting for the exhilaration to kick in, I drifted very slowly downstream. Some minutes later I drew level with the path where I'd been instructed to rejoin land and, relieved that the whole ludicrous episode was drawing to an end, I made a dash for the bank as soon as the water looked shallow enough. What happened next was an odd and grizzly sensation. My feet sank into the soft mud, first to my ankles, then up to the shins, and by the time I'd scampered to the river bank the lower halves of my legs were completely grey and crusted. All I now had to do was walk barefoot through stones, broken glass and prickly plants back to the resort, shivering and still carrying a fucking tyre. I haven't been tubing since.

The experience ensured that my final day was restricted to the hammock and the sauna and to having a beer with two great ladies from Hertfordshire. They had left their boring husbands at home mowing the lawns and decided to go off with backpacks to follow in the footsteps of their own daughters. They laughed a lot, and on the morning I was leaving, their howling could be heard from the river, across which they had decided to paddle in a small canoe. Unfortunately for them they had just gone round in circles, a familiar story, and they were forced to return to camp to plan an alternative way to get to the other side. Their luck was in as I was about to get a motorised boat back upriver and they were still laughing and waving as my boatman dropped them off on the far bank. They were great fun and I was still smiling as I chugged along the river to my waiting taxi. But there was one thing that suddenly troubled me. How the hell were they going to get back?

The taxi driver from earlier in the week hadn't been able to make it, so he had kindly sent one of his mates instead. It didn't take long to get back to Vientiane and since this was my last day in Laos we went straight to the Wattay International Airport, a sparkling glass-fronted building that any country would be proud of and no doubt looking forward to a time when it handles more than 47 flights a week. It was clean, tidy, almost empty and a very pleasant place to be. Come to think of it, there couldn't be a better way to sum up this delightful little gem of a country.

CHAD

The challenge of exploring the Four-Letter Countries was always going to take me to some of planet Earth's most unlikely places. I suppose that was the appeal. From that fateful moment, squinting at the list of country names in the middle of the night, almost all of them had become an object of fascination within my susceptible mind. The fabled city of Timbuktu, the lost civilisation of Machu Picchu, the islands of Fiji, the ancient kingdoms of Persia. It all seemed so ... well, exciting, and the ones I hadn't yet made it to seemed to be getting more and more enticing with time. But then, lost entirely in all this eager anticipation, there was Chad.

I tried my best to conjure up an image of this little-known country, but nothing very much seemed to happen. So I gave it another go, a teeny bit harder this time, like sitting round a ouija board waiting for something to start moving. But it was no good, nothing was out there. My mind was Chadless in the extreme.

It was time to start turning those big wide pages of the atlas. Always an impartial friend is Mr Collins, he pulls no punches, lays out the bare facts, tells it as it is. And this is what he told me, in no uncertain terms: Chad is right slap bang in the middle of nowhere. Or to be more precise, right in the middle of north Africa, so very in the middle that it has immediate neighbours that reach to the seas on three sides of the continent. It is the third largest landlocked country in the world and one where very few people live, and no doubt even fewer choose to visit. It is entirely surrounded by other countries jostling for position in the premiership league of Places You Wouldn't Go To If You Lived To Be A Million

149

The Four-Letter Countries

Years Old: Niger, Libya, Nigeria, Congo, Central African Republic, Cameroon and Sudan.

You might have seen a similar map on the UK evening news. Ever since the Sudanese government launched a brutal campaign to eradicate its country's darker-skinned tribes, arming gangs of Arabs to the teeth and despatching them to the west of the country, the poor desert folk of Darfur have been fleeing across the border to the relative safety of eastern Chad. Yet another African tragedy and more haunting images of wretched, starving people, too weak to even brush the flies from their gaunt and frightened faces.

No laughing matter, certainly, but this only served to confirm my growing feeling that this is the decade of the Four-Letter Countries after all. Conflict in Africa, the war in Iraq, nuclear weapons in Iran, Cuba on the brink of change, political instability in Fiji ... Would the BBC finally recognize the need for a dedicated FLC newsdesk?

* * * * *

We travellers are a pampered bunch these days. Thanks to backpackers and suitcase-wheelers past and present there is a veritable library of guidebooks to tell us the best and worst places to eat and sleep pretty much anywhere in the world, what to do when we get there, what to say and who to say it to. They even have a section detailing the kind of toilets to expect so you can get in some practice before leaving home.

Lonely Planet, the king of guides, started out with a yellow book helping us across the vastness of South-East Asia and now, a generation later, produces a dedicated manual to almost every village on the globe. Or so I thought. In fact, as my increasingly desperate, frantic and ultimately fruitless attempts to find a guidebook on the shelves of the UK's finest shops and in the warehouses of its online retailers proved, Chad, the twentieth largest country in the world, more than five times the size of the United Kingdom of Great Britain and Northern Ireland, has been boycotted by the entire publishing industry. Could there be a reason for this, I suddenly started to wonder?

So how to get there, what to expect, who to turn to for help and advice? I was bereft of ideas. Then it came to me, a brainwave, I remembered the name of the man who knows the Sahara inside out. A desert nut who spends his life in sand or writing about it. He's called Chris Scott and he's crossed the Sahara numerous times in every way you could possibly imagine. To him, a trip to Chad would be like a housewife popping along to Sainsbury's. I couldn't get to the internet quickly enough and soon found a website describing the adventures of the great man.

The euphoria didn't last long. In fact didn't even get beyond the opening sentence: "Since 1982 Chris has undertaken twenty expeditions through the Sahara visiting every country except Chad". Except Chad! Chris Scott, Sahara Man Extraordinaire, has done Libya, Egypt, Niger, Sudan, etc. but for some reason has decided that Chad is not for him. Is he some sort of five-letter country weirdo? Frustration was creeping in.

The prospect of travelling into the complete unknown suddenly seemed a trifle daunting, but I still had one last throw of the dice, the British Embassy in Chad. My chance to cash in on the years of paying all that tax to Her Majesty's government? Who knows, they might prove to be a source of inspiration and guidance. Back on to the internet forthwith, my boy.

And so I did, but only to suffer another demoralising blow. Well, a blowette really. I suppose I should have seen this one coming. *Lonely Planet* don't go there, the intrepid desert adventurer doesn't go there, so why should the British Embassy see a need to set up camp in the desert? (One vowel, three consonants, that's why). Instead of a Chad embassy or consulate, they settle for the comfort of the Cameroon and dish out instructions via the web to any of their subjects potty enough to contemplate striking for Africa's dusty interior.

The Four-Letter Countries

This was the first time I'd ever logged on to the Foreign and Commonwealth Office Travel Advice page, a memorable experience in itself. If you've got the stomach to read it, this was the advice for anybody foolish enough to be thinking of travelling to Chad:

"The political situation in Chad is unstable and security uncertain. Armed clashes have recently flared up in N'Djamena, the capital. There is rebel activity in the east of the country. Extremist groups are active and dangerous in the north. Roadblocks and kidnappings are becoming frequent in the south. There has been fighting in the Lake Chad area to the west. There is a general risk of indiscriminate terrorist attacks. Travel at night is unsafe due to highway banditry. Travel by road is subject to delay and harassment by police and military. Local air travel is unsafe, unreliable and not recommended."

(Further advice for those still alive). "There has been a fatal outbreak of measles. There has been a fatal outbreak of cholera. There has been a fatal outbreak of Hepatitis E. Meningitis outbreaks are common. AIDS and malaria are prevalent at all times. Medical facilities are very poor. Hospitals have been affected by strikes and are even less responsive than usual."

The concluding advice, though I really can't imagine why, was that British citizens should not travel to Chad except for "all but essential" reasons. How exactly did one define 'essential'? I felt decidedly gloomy, but something instantly brought a smile back to my face. I read the next paragraph entitled "Local Laws and Customs" in which it explained with a curious choice of words that in Chadian society "some sexual acts between members of the same sex are illegal". Fascinating stuff. So which particular acts would they be? Does the Department of Sexual Mores produce booklets with notes and diagrams to provide a sort of highway code for the gay community? And how is it monitored? A local inspector who creeps around at night caning the buttocks of over-zealous homosexuals? (If so, wouldn't that just be playing into their hands?) What a funny place.

Chad

Bollocks to it. Hanging on until Chad was deemed a safe place to visit would be like waiting for Manchester City to be crowned European champions. I couldn't risk going through life with that double disappointment. I would go, see what it was all about, and if it really was that scary, I would run home to my Mum and have a nice cup of tea and a ham sandwich (with the crusts cut off and a scraping of mustard pickle).

It was fast becoming obvious that few tourists venture into Chad. The people who do visit go because they have to, music to the ears of the accountants at Air France and Ethiopian Airlines, the only services available from West London to Central Sahara. Each airline has one hand loosely caressing your scrotum and you, the passenger, get to choose which one of them does the squeezing. For the price of a flight to Chad you could go to visit the pyramids or the Great Barrier Reef or Disneyland or probably take a whistle-stop tour to include the seven wonders of the world. Surely the least that God could have done was to arrange cheap tickets to visit the hellholes of the planet that he so lovingly created?

There were three good reasons to go via Ethiopia rather than Paris:-

1. I had never been there.
2. I wouldn't give an obscene amount of money to the Frogs.
3. I could get my Chad visa in Addis Ababa.

Point three was actually a major decider. For those of you not familiar with the lunacy of the visa system it goes something like this: the more desperate a country is for hard currency, the more obstacles it places in the way of the would-be tourist to pay a visit and inject a fistful of dollars. This visa is simply a stamp or sticker in your passport issued in exchange for some completed forms, a couple of photos and, of course, whatever fee is deemed appropriate. When they are issued on the spot at airports – a service offered by customer-friendly countries – the whole process takes about five minutes in total. But to those nations hell-bent on inflating egos and wasting as much of everybody's time as possible, five minutes is quite simply an unacceptably short process. So you telephone their embassy or consulate to establish the procedure.

This is the first of many challenges that they set you. You ring, full of optimism, first thing in the morning, but there's no answer. You try again a little later, five or six times, but still it just rings on. You're just on the point of checking the number with a lady in Mumbai when this time the line is busy. Your hopes are raised. It stays engaged for five hours, then it goes back to ringing without an answer. The same happens the next day and the day after. After five days of this, as you are just about to hang up for the 127th time, somebody answers the phone. Certainly not a greeting, or a "Hello, this is the Embassy of The Republic of Turdova, how can I help you sir?" It's actually more of a grunt, as though you have disturbed somebody in a hotel room in the middle of the night. You check you have the right number.

"Turdova?"

"Yes" the voice snarls in an accent you don't recognise.

So surprised are you to be talking to somebody, you can't actually construct a whole sentence. But it doesn't matter, their dialogue is never tailored to the caller's questions anyway:

"Bring two passport photos, it takes two days."

You gain your composure and formulate a question, but after the third word you realise nobody is there. You're talking to a dialling tone.

Two days is the norm for the ambassadorial arm to be raised and the rubber stamp hammered on to a page somewhere in the middle of your passport. So you give up half your working week and head off into London to the embassy of the impoverished Republic of Turdova, a small marble palace in Kensington or Mayfair. The visa section opens for a twenty-minute window each morning and afternoon, not at all on their public holidays. These occur approximately five times a month – the dates vary from year to year according to the moon. Always best to call in advance to check they're open.

Chad

Having played this visa game for so many years I really thought I'd seen and done it all. But the Chadians, bless them, had one extra card up their sleeves. A three-day excursion into London wasn't going to be enough time-wasting to satisfy their needs, so to really test you they have cunningly located their nearest consulates in Paris and Brussels: anybody thinking of taking a hol in Chad first needs to build a Eurostar Citybreak into the equation. Either that or, so the grumpy bloke in Brussels told me, have their passport sent back and forth by DHL. If ever you needed proof that the world has gone completely fucking barmy …

* * * * *

I like the name Addis Ababa – even though I don't always get it right – and was quietly amused at the prospect of a few days there. What hadn't occurred to me was that I wouldn't be the only one to succumb to the allure of this unusual name. To my astonishment almost every hotel in town was full and it took several hours of driving around in one of the bashed-up Lada taxis before finding a room, ironically almost back at the airport. No matter, I was in the city on visa business and as it turned out the Chad embassy was somewhere just around the corner.

They don't really do addresses in Ethiopia – 'behind the Palestinian Embassy on Bole Road,' was the best anyone could come up with – but I arrived at the converted house at the same time as the lady who worked there. I got the feeling that not many tourists passed that way, but she treated me politely and indicated that they would issue my visa there and then if my paperwork was in order. Did I have the letter of invitation?

I explained that I was a tourist and that tourists generally do not work on an invitation basis. OK, did I have any sort of a letter? Thankfully I could produce a typed piece of paper to say who I was and where I worked, an entirely worthless document, but one that seemed to satisfy their requirements. All I had to do now was confirm that I would be staying in a hotel. (The Chadians must have fallen foul in the past of hordes of British travellers trying to claim housing benefit and they were taking no chances on me). I gave them the full name and address of Le Meridien, thankful of the internet and my own preparations for this big interview. The dollars were handed over, I sat patiently for an hour admiring a photo of the President above a huge vase of plastic flowers, and the job was done. I really was going to Chad.

The rest of my time in Addis was spent wandering the markets and dodging beggars, some of whom proved to be quite a challenge. It had been many years since I'd had to deal with severely crippled people lunging into my path and on several occasions I had to feign passing them on one side, drop my shoulder and then sidestep quickly the other way. Though I say it myself, my nimble footwork completely out-manoeuvred them and they simply couldn't cope with my turn of speed and lightning change of direction. Of course I had extra limbs and didn't depend on a makeshift crutch for support, but it was satisfying to know that I could still cut it at inside-centre if the house rugby team ever invited me back.

I was ready for Chad and didn't want to spend any more time in that weary little hotel room. It was Valentine's Day, never a high point on the traveller's calendar, so to cheer myself up I invented a little song, based on the old Smokey number:

Now I've got my visa
I really wanna go
What I'm gonna do there
I don't exactly know
I've spent 24 hours just livin' next door to Addis
(ADDIS, ADDIS – GET ME OUT OF ADDIS!)

24 hours,
on my way to Chad
the biggest shithole in the world

Chad

I must be fuckin' mad
I've spent 24 hours just livin' next door to Addis
(ADDIS, ADDIS – GET ME OUT OF ADDIS!)

I set the alarm on my mobile and went to sleep early, but it wasn't the alarm that woke me. It was the phone in the room, the one I didn't even know was there. Why? Who? It was midnight.

"Is that Mr David Jenkins?"

Heart beats faster. "Who is this?"

"Chapan Airlines, sorry to bother you?"

"Japan Airlines????"

"No, Chopean Airlines."

The penny then dropped. It was Ethiopian Airlines, but because she was Ethiopian she didn't know how to say 'Ethiopian' properly. That's just typical of foreigners isn't it?

The lady was calling to say that I needed to be at the airport in five hours' time because the flight to Chad had been brought forward. It sounded like a great wind-up and one to bear in mind for the future, but this had to be genuine. Nobody else knew I was there.

Five hours later, still dark, I checked in. It transpired that there weren't enough passengers to justify the scheduled flight over to the Ivory Coast (via Chad) and another one to Ghana, so just one plane would go round and drop people off. Those of us lucky enough to be bound for N'Djamena would be the first out, three and a half hours after take-off.

The thrill of sitting by the window was somewhat diminished by the fact that there was no perceptible change to the landscape for one second of the journey; just sand and scrub with occasional trees and the reflection of the odd wispy cloud on the scorched surface below. No roads. No lakes. No rivers. No cars. No people. No buildings. At least none that I could see, although I must admit to spending more time watching the Chopian Airlines stewardesses and wishing they were my very close friends.

The Four-Letter Countries

The plane had almost landed before I saw a building of any sort, though the river Chari did come into view just as we dropped into N'Djamena. It was just after ten in the morning.

A little tentative and deeply contemplating my foreignness, I started down the steps of the aircraft. Whooom! Within a nanosecond I was struck in the side of the face by a jet of white hot air, the force of a baseball bat driven into the solar-plexus. My instinct was to look towards the engine of the plane to see if it had caught fire, but the heat wasn't coming from there and in fact it wasn't just hitting my head. It was all around, it was stifling, overpowering and, of course, it was coming from the sun. Welcome to Chad.

Ours was the only plane and we parked more or less in front of the terminal building. Immigration was fairly routine, though my writing the word 'tourist' on the arrival card seemed to confuse the officer in charge. This was an entirely new concept to him and I could see from his patting of pockets it gave him the urge to write something down on the form. He had no pen, but like a true teacher's pet I was more than happy to lend him mine.

Baggage collection was less routine. The passengers, mostly berobed and bearded, a few wearing suits and carrying laptops, gathered hopefully alongside the single conveyor belt. When fifteen minutes passed without any bags nobody seemed too concerned, most people just responded African-style by sitting patiently or lying down on the non-conveying conveyor. The heat was increasing with every passing second and although there was an air-con unit, the system was, naturally, broken. Half an hour, no bags, still general apathy, but one passenger was getting sticky and irritable and that, you may have guessed, was me. What was going on? I needed some answers.

And thus it was explained to me by a friendly banker on a business trip from the Comoros Islands: "Today the President will travel and the law dictates that when he flies out of the airport nobody is allowed to move until his plane has taken off. Once His Excellency is safely in the air and

158

the red carpet is returned to the cupboard the conveyor will again be allowed to roll."

In this case, the conveyor was allowed to roll 1 hour 55 minutes after our plane had landed. It had long since become clearer to me why some passengers had struggled into the cabin with all their luggage and I mentally apologised for having cursed their stupidity. It was me who was the plonker after all.

I was surprised to find the main street of town was just a few hundred metres from the airport and the pleasant Hotel Sahel somewhere between the two. Not cheap, for what it was, at US$100 per night, but half the price of the two international hotels and almost certainly a greater sense of character. The owner was a smart chap from Mauritius who had obviously been so sick to the back teeth of beautiful women, turquoise sea and golden beaches that he'd decided Chad was the place to head for. "There 's plenty to do," he assured me. "Life is pretty good here." To prove his point he recommended a restaurant, a bar and a travel agent and I resolved to check them all out within the next 24 hours.

To avoid the danger of the dark streets at night, the Hotel Sahel provides a driver to take you where you want to go (and bring you back) for US$1. I wanted to go to the Taj Mahal, recommended as the best of the restaurants, and it turned out to be a former residential house in what was clearly an affluent part of town. Behind the large gate and the high wall the tables had been arranged on the driveway, along the terrace and around the swimming pool, one end of which had been boarded over to form a stage for the evening cabaret. All very civilised, a curry house under the stars. One of those magic travel moments, I sat there wrapped in the warmth of the evening, staring up at the twinkly sky with an ice cold Gala beer in hand and a big grin on my face. Perhaps Chad wasn't going to be so bad after all.

It was interesting to see that almost all the customers were 'blancs' as the local refer to us white-skinned folk. Same again in the bar that came recommended, a large outdoor place with live music and a line of prostitutes (all from neighbouring Cameroon I was told) yawning and filing their nails in the way that ladies of the night do the world over. The temperature was perfect for sitting and sipping a cold beer though probably still too hot for sleeping without a fan, or air-con, or both. What on earth would it be like during the day? Thank goodness I had chosen to visit in the winter.

The only way to get anything done in that sort of climate is to get up very early, so by 7am I was ready to hit the streets. There was already plenty of bustle, hundreds of people on motorbikes and others crammed into pick-ups to get them to their places of work. Somewhere below my feet was a layer of tarmac, but all the roads and pavements were covered in sand, ideal for the orange-bellied lizards that darted around all over the place, often in groups of ten and sometimes as many as fifteen. Elegant trees lined the streets, but sadly, as is always the case in Africa, garbage was piled everywhere and open troughs/gutters at the side of the pavements collected even more. Memories of A Saturday Morning in Bamako (a great title for a song?).

I can cope with most of the negatives in Africa, but the unnecessary filth always gets to me more than anything else. It seems that the locals are completely oblivious to it, treat it as a way of life, ever willing to create more rubbish and live their lives alongside it. I suppose there's no reason they should think any differently, but it never fails to amaze me in such places that disease doesn't completely take over. Isn't it incredible that the human body can develop resistance to all this?

The Avenue Charles de Gaulle runs right across the city of N'Djamena and this, the western end, was by all accounts the posh bit. Everything is relative and if you were lowered in by helicopter from St Moritz then posh wouldn't be your immediate choice of word. This was more the wild west, though the attractive bakeries and cake shops were living proof that the French had left behind a few refined touches after their forty seven years in charge. They went home in 1960 and as with most African countries post-colonisation, this marked the start of a long period of unrest. More of that later.

Toumai Air Tchad was not an airline I'd ever heard of and I could only assume this was the dodgy outfit our Foreign Office had made reference to. No matter, their uniformed staff in the smart, cool office welcomed me in off the already hot and dusty street and proudly handed over their timetable for my perusal. A single sheet of A4, it listed the days of the week and the destinations their plane (singular) serviced on each of those days. Three times a week to neighbouring countries, a trip to and from eastern Chad Mondays and Fridays and two days off. (Maintenance and repairs? Keep dreaming lad. Not enough fuel, more likely).

The city in eastern Chad was Abéché and if I wanted to fly somewhere this was where I would be going. Chad is a big country, as I mention at every given opportunity, but will try not to harp on about too much more. If you imagine it as a rectangle it measures about 1,500kms from north to south and 1,000kms from east to west. N'Djamena is in the far west, close to the Cameroonian border, and about two thirds of the way down, so it would take an hour by plane back across the empty landscape to get over to Abéché. Could I resist the temptation? Cautiously I made a provisional booking, but didn't hand over my precious Central African Francs.

Do you remember the currency story from my other African jaunts? The CFA, as it is known, used to be pegged to the French Franc at 100 to the Franc, but now is tied in to the Euro. When I worked it out the exchange rate hadn't actually changed that much because I was getting 655 to the Euro, around 950 to sterling. So it was a fairly easy one to work with, thinking in terms of 1,000 to a pound. Just had to make sure I didn't get the zeros mixed up.

Which I nearly did on my visit to Tchad Evasion, the ever popular tour operator. I introduced myself to the large sweating man as a tourist interested in any sort of adventure he might be able to offer. Surely a dream start to his day? Well, not exactly. His response was to stare at the floor for a long time and then gradually puff out his cheeks and blow air slowly downwards. From my limited experience of life this wasn't usually a promising sign. "Difficile" was the first and only word he uttered after this period of intense reflection.

He asked me what I had in mind and I told him quite truthfully that I was open to suggestions. Still he looked a very troubled man, his large head now moving from side to side to indicate that my requirements were way beyond anything he could deliver. Very reluctantly he then mumbled the option of a trip to Lake Chad. A day out in a private vehicle that would cost around CFA 250,000. Minimum.

See what I mean, the big numbers do throw you. If a thousand is just over a quid, then 250 of them is just over £250. More or less two hundred and sixty notes. To go and have a butcher's at a lake. He read my face: "Oui – c'est cher."

"Tres cher," I confirmed. Would that include food or accommodation?

"No, day trip, you sort your own food. But if there's more people you could perhaps split the cost. Anyway, have you registered with the police?"

In response to my confused look he brandished a form and explained that as I was a foreign visitor this would need to be completed and taken along to the local police together with a passport photo. To my astonishment he then took my passport, completed the form on my behalf and drew a map to direct me to the right building. He then smiled for the first time and reminded me that the Lake Chad trip would work out cheaper if we were a group. A nice man, he obviously just wasn't a morning person.

* * * * *

Where would I find more people? Everybody here was with a company or a charity organisation. I was probably the only person ever to have set

Chad

foot in this strange country with the intention of having a good time. Now I was puffing cheeks and looking a little bit miserable.

I thought about £260. For that money back home I could take a cab to the airport, a flight to Verona and back, hire a car to drive around Lake Garda, enjoy a delicious meal overlooking the Alps and wash it down with a fine bottle of Chianti from the cellar. And still have change for a beer on the way home.

Lake Chad was fast losing its appeal. And by all accounts it was fast losing its water too. In fact this is some story. It is reckoned that a few thousand years ago Lake Chad was a huge body of water measuring 400,000 sq kms, that's a square with all sides over 600kms. When it was measured in the 1960s the lake was only six percent of that size and today it is a further twenty times smaller. If the world needs a reminder about global warming here it is before our very eyes. Or could be. Was I going to fork out £260 to see a big puddle?

Wondering what I was going to do next, I headed back into the fierce mid-morning sun and bumped into the German solar engineer I'd met at breakfast.

"Fancy a trip out to Lake Chad, Reinhard"?

The most probable answer I figured was that he would require a detailed itinerary supported by a cost breakdown from which he could create a spreadsheet on his laptop and thus assess the impact of any decision on his current cashflow status. In fact he just said 'yes', but would have to speak to his colleagues.

In the meantime I started asking people about Abéché, what it was like, were there any hotels there. The answers were much the same from everybody. Dunno, never been there. Hotels? Oogh, I doubt it.

Reinhard came through with the news that he couldn't get the time for adventure and the opinion/wild guess that Abéché would have accommodation to cater for the aid workers over on the Sudanese border. It seemed a fair shout, but still the prospect of being dumped in the desert until the solitary plane came back to pick me up brought out the true wuss in me. Something a little more concrete was needed to cheer me up, to convince me that if this zany expedition east were to be undertaken I wouldn't be left to shiver in the sand and forced to live off a diet of goats' milk and camel droppings.

I walked a lot around the sandy streets of N'Djamena, got into air conditioning wherever possible, returned for cold showers in my room at every opportunity and drank a litre of bottled water almost every hour. Thankfully most parts of the body regenerated quickly, but my feet weren't used to the round-the-clock life of sand and sandals. They were sore, hard, cracked and despite my best efforts always looked and felt as though they belonged to a tramp. I decided not to look at them too often.

It was interesting and quite unusual for Africa that most of the local people paid very little attention to me as a foreigner, I wasn't hassled by anybody, but nor was I greeted with any particular warmth or affection. No reason why I should be, just that in so many countries the westerner gets used to being the centre of attention. Certainly there was no feeling of danger or intimidation, at least not until I decided to take a photo.

Let me tell you what happened. I was heading off to the police station for another dose of bureaucracy when I saw what to me was a comical sight. Two bicycles had been stored in the deep trough at the roadside which was otherwise filled with litter and I thought it would make rather a good picture. I took the camera from my small bag, but just as I was about to shoot an elderly gentleman came over and politely explained that photography was not advisable. The building behind me was apparently a military establishment and ... He hadn't even finished his sentence when a uniformed officer with a maroon beret appeared in front of my face.

"Vous avez filmé. Pourquoi?"

"Non monsieur, je n'ai pas filmé."

"Vous avez filmé."

He didn't raise his voice, but stared at me with pure hatred in his eyes, the look of a man whose mother had been violated. This looked nasty, very nasty and I was relieved that the elderly chap came to my defence to explain that I hadn't taken the picture. They then started arguing amongst themselves for quite some time and since they were paying no further attention to me I decided to quietly move away.

Remember the scene from *Colditz* when the escaping British POW dresses as a German officer then walks calmly out through the gates, teeth and sphincter tightly clenched, just waiting for the dogs and sirens and gunfire from behind? That was me, mincing along the streets of N'Djamena, wishing I could blend into the crowd but knowing there was nowhere to hide.

About ten minutes had passed and my heartbeat was starting to level out when the voice came from behind.

"Vous avez filmé."

He was back, now on a motor bike, and he had come to nail the foreign fugitive. My heart and my bowels went into overdrive, I was in very serious trouble.

"Non, je n'ai pas filmé."

"Vous avez filmé."

"Non, monsieur."

"Vous avez filmé."

"Non, non, non."

"Etes vous sur?"

"Oui. Absolument sur."

Then silence. More staring. What was he thinking?

I know what I was thinking. I was thinking that I was in very deep shit and might be getting marched off to prison for spying. Left to rot in a stinking cell in Chad. Who would know I was there? Not even a British Consulate to beg for my mercy. I so did not want to be arrested.

The staring was too scary, so I decided to break the silence. Not really sure what to say, but to show what an honest and decent chap I am, I decided to tell him I was on my way to the police to get registered. More staring. Had I dug my own grave, would he come with me and report me for my subversive activities? You jerk Jenkins, why didn't you just keep your mouth shut? His response was to tell me that the police station was in the opposite direction. Then more staring.

"Oh silly me I am just a stupid tourist and I don't speak very good French and I am so so very sorry for the fact that I speak your beautiful language very badly as I would love to communicate better with you beautiful Chadian people and explore your lovely country and please if you just raise your arse ever so slightly from the seat of your motorbike it will be the greatest honour for me to get down there and shower it with kisses ..."

It was probably even worse than that and delivered with a huge sickly smile and an outrageously enthusiastic handshake. I'm not proud, it worked. He decided to let me off this time without so much as a mention of a bribe. He even offered to give me a lift to the police station, an offer for which I thanked him profusely before explaining that I needed a good long walk. The transformation on his face from anger to confusion was quite spectacular. What sort of person would want to have a good long walk when it's 42 degrees centigrade in the shade?

* * * * *

The Chadian Ministry of Job Creation and Time Wasting has dedicated a section of a building within the huge police compound for the registration of foreigners. Therein sits a bank of warped, rusted filing cabinets and three officers whose job it is to load said cabinets with utterly useless data. Each person sits there in the semi-darkness and the stifling heat behind a rickety desk: one transfers the information from your form into a ledger, one stamps your passport and another hands your passport back. It keeps them off the streets, and if I played my cards right, would hopefully keep me out of jail.

Chad

Looking around at the military people all over the city it was obvious that there was something of a security paranoia about Chad. Tourists, or should I say tourist, were treated more with suspicion than curiosity, there was the fiasco with the bags at the airport and then the hullabaloo about my camera. Why was this? Who were they scared of? Was it always like this? I read a little about the history of the country.

The French had left in 1960 and for the first fifteen years of independence a Monsieur Tombalbaye was the head of state. He was a man from the Christian south of the country who ruled with an iron fist and upset the Muslims in the north. In 1975 he was assassinated (US$1 million cash was found in his house) and replaced by another southerner, General Malloum, who formed an alliance with a commander of the northern rebels. But it all quickly fell apart and by 1979 there was a north v south battle with the capital city stuck in the middle and suffering thousands of civilian casualties. It was to get worse when Libyan forces joined the north and actually occupied N'Djamena until the French joined in and forced them back. What had started as a civil war was now effectively Libya v France. The retreating Libyans tried to occupy northern Chad, but the northerners didn't want them there and managed to push them back over the border.

In 1990 another warlord from the north, Idriss Deby, returned from exile and with the strength of his own private army took over power. He is still there, and like every other African leader he makes sure he always wins elections, his photograph adorns the walls of every building and the airport downs tools whenever he's around. Peace is at best fragile, democracy is questioned, northerners still feel hard done by, Libyans feel the urge to invade periodically, Nigerians lay claim to land around Lake Chad and Sudanese bandits come raiding from the east. Perhaps it's not surprising that security is so visible after all.

One morning I got up very early and took a taxi to the centre of the city. The Marché Central is really the hub of N'Djamena and the early part of the day, I figured, the best time to see markets. We headed east along Charles de Gaulle and surroundings became noticeably shabbier, streets full of rubble as well as the usual piles of garbage. The market hadn't really got going and what activity I could see was scarcely engaging. In short, I was standing amongst a scruffy, ramshackle collection of market stalls and wishing I was somewhere else. Down by the river perhaps?

I started to drift away from the market and decided that a photo of its entrance, a little unusual in that it was built like a fort, could not cause any offence. To avoid attention, I stepped back quietly away from any crowd and slipped my camera out when nobody was around. It wasn't a very smart move. Why hadn't I learnt from my previous scrape? No sooner had I taken it from my bag there was a man in a track suit screaming and shouting and waving his arms with a level of ferocity that in itself was truly frightening. My heart missed a beat, in fact may have stopped altogether. Déjà vu. Oh no, the military people would be over any second now. They'd given me a second chance and I'd blown it. This was it. The End.

He was incensed, truly incensed. Why had I been taking pictures, I had no right, I should be arrested, vous avez filmé, vous avez filmé, vous avez filmé! ... He was yelling at the top of his voice, hysterical stuff. Under normal, non-Chadian circumstances only drugs or insanity could provoke an outburst on this scale. Everybody in the market must have heard the commotion. I was a dead man. Louder and louder he screamed and yelled and I realised, perhaps too late, there was no point in my standing there any longer. The lunatic then took a few steps towards me, arms raised, teeth bared, as though prepared to kill for his cause: "Fuck Off and Don't Ever Come Back" (or words to that effect) he yelled in nutter's French.

Disturbed minds think alike. I turned and ran very, very fast down an alleyway, clambered over rubble, into a side street and ran and ran and ran and ran as though my life depended on it. Or should I say, because my life depended on it.

Chad

Sweat poured out of every part of my body and I kept running until my lungs just couldn't take any more. I stopped and almost keeled over, stared at the ground with hands on knees and then, still panting like a rabid dog, desperately tried to engineer a smile for the bemused local people standing in front of their shacks. A sitting duck, I had to get away. The motor bike, the maroon beret, they would be coming around the corner at any moment. Capture, torture, imprisonment. Death of The Camera Man.

More running, a busy road ahead, a taxi. It was probably the road out of the market where I'd started and where the motor bikes would be looking for me. But I had to chance it and by waving my arms from a concealed position in the side street I managed to get the taxi to stop. The US Embassy please!

I don't know what made me choose there, but then raw fear is a very funny thing. There was nothing for me at the embassy and once we'd pulled up outside its huge walls and I'd started breathing again I changed my mind and asked to go to Le Meridien. The hotel would be safe, I could blend, sit in the garden, take coffee, look out over the river and thank my lucky stars.

* * * * *

I had the address of the Ministry of Tourism and it turned out to be a kind of military barracks close to my hotel. Everybody I had asked about Abéché had shrugged their shoulders and said they'd never been there so this had to be my best, in fact probably only, chance.

The man looked somewhat surprised to see me, possibly - I mused - because he had never seen a tourist before. When told of my proposed visit to Abéché and asked of the hotel options there he answered with a phrase that I was quickly getting used to. It translates as: "Dunno mate, never been there." Then he added, rather more surprisingly.

"Try the Ministry of Hotel Development in the next block."

169

The Four-Letter Countries

In for a penny, in for a pound. I found the tiny, dark room with three empty desks and a very bored person sitting behind each one. Their faces lit up on seeing a visitor, a white one who spoke garbled French. This was something that didn't happen often in the world of Chadian hotel development. I asked the usual question and got the now familiar answer, this time in triplicate. Nobody had ever been out east, but they would find out by calling the Ministry of Hotel Development in Abéché.

The man at the other end of their mobile was, I was told, Monsieur Waza and he was very much looking forward to meeting me. The friendly trio then questioned me about my reasons for visiting Chad (tourist? You are a tourist?!), life in England, our cold weather and, of course, most important of all, David Beckham. Handshakes and smiles were offered all round and I was sent on my way with Waza's phone number in one hand and a large brown envelope in the other, the latest hotel plans that they'd been working on!

I was off to Abéché whether I liked it or not. Toumai handed over my ticket and in response to my call Waza assured me that he would be waiting to receive me later that day. How did I get myself into these strange situations? This was going to be a week-end with a difference.

However much one enjoys the thrill of Africa, there is always a tangible feeling of relief to return to a 'normal' environment, one that doesn't include overpowering heat or dust or filth or noise or some form of chaos. That is exactly what was going through my mind as I sat on the cool leather seats of the spotless aircraft, waiting to take off for eastern Chad. I was smiling, relaxing even, the screaming and shouting and all the mindless jostling at the check-in now a fading memory. The bizarre security check at the wooden table placed in the sunshine on the edge of the runway (45 degrees Celsius) had finally been completed. At least I would have one hour of sanity.

It turned out we were waiting for two more passengers, both of whom eventually boarded the plane in some style. The first was an ema- ciated man with an uncontrollably shaking body and very stary eyes. He had to be carried up the aisle by the stewards, one holdings his arms and the other his legs so that he drooped in the middle like a hammock. They plonked him on the seat diagonally behind me for what could well have been his last ever journey and I couldn't help looking across towards the pathetic trembling figure. His mad wide-open eyes stared straight at me and with true Christian compassion I prayed that whatever was wrong with him was not highly contagious.

Last, and definitely, not least was a younger man dressed in a Barcelona FC track suit, training shoes and a blue and burgundy striped Barcelona shirt. He could have stepped straight out of the Nou Camp except for the fact that he appeared to be clinically insane. He was screaming and bawling like a man who'd seen a camera, though thankfully this time I was not the source of the problem. It seemed he was pointing at one of the stewards and was so incensed that once the plane started to taxi he unbuckled his belt, jumped up from his seat and started to remonstrate in the aisle.

The arguing continued, take-off was aborted and the pilot drove us back to the terminal building where we parked up once again. The door opened, some more people got on, then everybody stood up (except the ladies breast-feeding their children) and started shouting at the same time. Never in my life had I seen anything like this on an aeroplane. The captain, absolutely furious, came out of the cockpit and forced his way to the back of the plane. He gave it to Barcelona in no uncertain terms like a schoolteacher dealing with a naughty infant: the plane would not be taking off unless all passengers stayed in their seats.

I sat there watching this bizarre scene unfold, but couldn't figure out what it was all about. The only other non-African on the plane was a Japanese aid worker from Yokohama and he had managed to keep up with the drama: Barcelona was convinced the steward had stolen his wallet and insisted that the police be called to investigate. The reason he had suddenly stopped ranting and was now staring silently out of his window was not so much down to the bollocking from the pilot but because he'd just found his wallet in his sock. So much for an hour of normality.

* * * * *

The plane seemed to fly very close to the ground and an hour later we touched down in Abéché. It felt like the remotest place on earth. The desert landscape was altogether predictable, but I did notice an odd little range of mountains that created interesting shapes in the distance away to the north, a strangely comforting phenomenon in a world of almost total emptiness.

One side of the runway was packed with people – or should I say men – waiting for the plane or its passengers, all identically dressed in white with perhaps just a little variation on the headwear. The scene that followed was more like a party than the mere arrival of an aircraft, a simple event turned into a celebration with lots of big toothy smiles and laughter and slapping of backs that Africans do so well. Everybody seemed to be getting at least one hug and several handshakes and even The English Tourist with his little blue bag was about to join in the fun. A tall and very handsome man stepped forward with his hand outstretched and I was given the official welcome:

"Monsieur David. Bienvenue a Abéché" said Waza.

He took me over to his friend the policeman who greeted me warmly and stamped my passport (yet again) and off we went on the back of Waza's motorbike. As we weaved along the sandy streets of Abéché I pinched myself ever so quickly just to check that this really was happening.

I finally had the answer to my question, there are no hotels in Abéché. The envelope I'd handed over from M. Donon in N'Djamena was a plan for one that may be built in the future, a dream that would only be realised in the highly unlikely event that some money was made available to pay for it. Still, the Ministry of Hotel Development was alive and kicking and who was I to complain?!

Chad

The place to which I was taken by the friendly Waza looked more like a small school, but was in fact an 'auberge', a kind of hostel for aid workers. The room wasn't cheery, definitely more prison than hotel, but it was clean and offered everything the humble traveller could possibly have wished for, even a fan and air conditioning. All told a very satisfactory result, particularly if the electricity were to come back on. Waza had done me proud.

I put my bag down, looked around at the stone walls of my cell, and wondered what to do next. In fact what to do at all. From what I'd seen of Abéché, and I suspected I'd already seen most of it when crossing the town, it wasn't exactly Las Vegas. Crumbling houses, sand, camels, mosques and motorbikes just about summed it up. It reminded me of Timbuktu, perhaps the most backward place I'd ever been (until now), but even that dismal desert outpost had a few hotels and restaurants. Daylight was now fading and the power still off, so I decided to sit and eat the bread and drink the water I'd carried from the plane. Live it up; after all, it was Friday night.

Fully satiated, a walk under the stars in the hot night air won out over my other two options, which were sitting on my chair or sitting on my bed. The sandy street was pitch dark, but people wandered along in small groups and I could hear their chatter long before their silhouettes became visible. I had headed left from the auberge, the town now behind me, but after just a couple of minutes there was somebody racing up alongside, a young guy and obviously out of breath. He seemed friendly, at first I didn't know what he was saying to me, then I recognised a key word and it all fell into place. "Dangereux". He was our security man – the one who had opened the gate to let me out – and he had come to tell me that night strolling was definitely not a safe thing to do.

His name was Mohammed Sharif, he was 18 years old and as we headed back (no, I didn't put up a fight) to the auberge he told me stories of bandits that come out to rob at night. Men from The East, even as far away as Sudan. Daylight hours though were completely safe and tomorrow, to prove his point, he would be my guide.

A few thousand francs got me the use of a motor bike and for the next two mornings my new-found friend and I toured the sights of Abéché. It was even more basic than I'd expected, motor bikes and mobile phones seemingly the only advancement in the last two thousand years. The streets were almost entirely of sand and, of course, garbage. A few wide ones formed the main routes in and out, but mostly the town was a maze of alleyways, market stalls, crumbling walls, wandering animals and dead carcasses. It was in truth pretty depressing stuff and the heat from mid morning onwards was utterly stifling.

It was 45 degrees Celsius once again and this was the cool season, in a few months it would be five or ten degrees hotter still. Then it would rain for several weeks, turn everything to mud and bring a plague of malaria carrying mosquitoes. How did people live in a place like this? I watched a disabled man struggling to get his wheelchair through the sand and found myself wondering if he really believed in God. Surely very few people on the planet could have drawn such a short straw in life as that poor bloke.

The blazing heat meant that our hours of exploration ran from 7am until it was just too hot to move, which was about three hours later. I had pretty soon worked out that in Abéché it's too hot to do anything in the daytime and too dangerous to venture out at night, something you might want to take on board if you're planning a holiday in Chad this year.

Our plan on the first day, once the city tour was complete, had been to head out into the 'countryside', but a puncture quickly put paid to that. I spent half that morning sitting under a canopy at the roadside repair shop, watching herds of camels and packs of donkeys being driven across the desert by nomadic herders. What a bizarre existence, walking miles and miles every day through the sand with every inch of your face and body wrapped in fabric to protect against the swirling wind and ferocious heat. This had to be even worse than working at Tesco.

Chad

I did try an evening walk that day and even briefly entertained the idea of eating in a restaurant. It would entail returning in the darkness, but that would only take minutes provided I memorised the way back and, for that, the fly-covered carcass of a freshly killed dog turned out to be a useful landmark. But in hindsight it wasn't the smartest plan. The trudging through sand and garbage was not particularly enlightening and at one point led me into a square where several hundred men were getting pumped up by a man on a stage bawling into a microphone. It sounded aggressive and the whole scene reminded me of passing through Taleban areas of Pakistan a few years earlier just ahead of the New York attacks. What was he saying? I hoped he wasn't telling them to go and scalp the first westerner they could lay their hands on! My delicate mind flooded with visions of the assembled mob turning 180 degrees as one and charging towards me with arms raised, possibly making noises like Indians do on cowboy films.

I moved very quickly around the corner and into the calm of the only restaurant around, L'Etoile d'Afrique. The Star of Africa, a romantic name for a courtyard of battered tables with a grubby cordoned off area on the far side that was obviously the kitchen. I use the word obviously because there was nowhere else the kitchen could be, not because it looked remotely like a place for preparing food. To my amazement I sat down at one of the tables and listened to a verbal rendition of the menu before finding myself staring speechlessly at the filthy waiter:

"Qu'est-ce que vous désirez?" he enquired, with all the charm of a serial killer.

There could only be one serious answer. To get the hell out of there and never, ever return. I stood up, said: "Merci, Bon Soir," and headed as quickly as I could back towards the dead dog.

* * * * *

The Four-Letter Countries

Mohammed Sharif and I did make it out into the countryside the following morning and the feeling of immense space instantly eradicated the hopelessness and misery of life in the town. This was Africa, the harsh, rolling landscape, a vastness that is hard to explain or imagine, a sense of timelessness that serves as a reminder that the planet is so much more powerful than we humans will ever be. To be precise this was The Sahel, the area between the green south of the country and the barren north, rather than The Desert.

We scrambled up to the top of a hill and sat together on a pile of huge boulders, ate our picnic breakfast of baguettes and La Vache Qui Rit (Laughing Cow) and admired the fantastic views. As we looked away down the valley – yes CHAD VALLEY – across the miles of sand and stone, small trees and bushes, and the odd shaped miniature mountains, I asked Mohammed Sharif how one would know where The Sahel finishes and The Desert starts. He thought about this for quite a few minutes, worked it out in his mind and then gave me his very considered answer: "In the desert there is a lot of sand".

* * * * *

I really enjoyed the motor bike adventures and it was a pity that the sun forced us – well, me – back indoors so early. By 11am I was showered and ready to focus on the other two challenges of the day:

1) resume worrying that the flight back to N'Djamena would be cancelled
2) the purchasing and consuming of lunch and dinner

Shopping was made convenient by the fact that a purveyor of groceries operated from a little hut opposite the auberge. Fresh baguettes were regularly delivered there from an unseen bakery and his bottled water was sometimes chilled, depending on the power situation

Chad

at the time. The electricity was generally on for some hours of darkness and occasionally during the morning so thrice a day I would stock up on bread and water and supplement the diet with the ever-dependable La Vache Qui Rit cheese triangles. 'Was there anything else to buy?' I hear you asking? Funny you should mention that ...

In my early reckless days of Abéché life I spotted a tin of sardines upon the dusty shelf of the grocer's hut and decided to give them a go. To be frank it was a purchase I was unsure about from the start and my first tentative nibble, together with the inhalation of those fishy fumes, convinced me to abandon the project in favour of something more tried and tested (La Vache Qui Rit). The smelly little can went in the bin down the hallway and I noticed later that day the resident cat had enjoyed the feast.

One of the great things about food shopping in Abéché, and to be honest there aren't that many, is that opening hours are from 6am until 10pm. So to add a sense of structure to the holiday I designated 6.30am as the time for the breakfast shopping spree, 1pm for lunch and somewhere around 6pm for dinner. It was after one such evening visit that I stepped back into the cool hallway of the auberge to find a large pool of brown liquid outside the door of my room, a consistency and odour that wasn't immediately familiar. Then I heard the sound of the cat, realised what the mess was and congratulated myself on not having eaten the sardines. Thankfully the manager arrived as I was surveying the scene, but how would I best explain that le chat had shat all over his nice clean floor?

A life of bread and water, no booze and very little to do other than twenty hours a day of reading and sleeping should have made me thoroughly miserable. But it didn't. Even when nursing the daily rations in my prison cell on a Saturday lunchtime, reflecting that the boys at the golf club would be polishing off their lunches and tucking into their second pints, even that brought a smile to my face. Three days of battery charging and abstinence from excess eating and drinking was no bad thing (reminded me of early days in Oman) and in fact I felt mentally and physically much the better for it. But I still worried like hell that the plane wouldn't come back for me, that it might suffer a technical problem or be grounded by a strike in Nigeria. Did I have the stomach for a 23 hour bus journey back to N'Djamena if one of the wings had fallen off?

The plane did come back and I made a point of being the first person at the airport to check in for it. Unlike the day I'd landed there were a few other aircraft around – small planes carrying UN people with laptops and a helicopter full of African Union (AU) military personnel, all of whom were trying to do their bit to stop the carnage a hundred miles away on the Sudanese border. A few weeks earlier this to me had been a news story on the TV, somewhere remote and very far away. Now it seemed so strange to be on the edge of it, to sit alongside people from all parts of Africa and the rest of the world who were on their way back to the teeth of the conflict. Part of me wished I was going too, to do something to help make a difference, but the other part of me wished I was heading back to N'Djamena for another curry at the Taj Mahal.

Landing in N'Djamena this time round felt so much different from my debut visit which – incredibly – had only been the week before. Compared to Abéché this was Manhattan and a place I felt that I knew. There was unfinished business to attend to, a few sights to see, a few meals to eat and definitely a few bottles of beer to be drunk. It was great to be back!

First port of call was the American Language Center where I'd been made so welcome the previous week. In response to my offer to give a few English classes (in proper English) they had invited me to a pre-term open day and I owed them an apology for having run away to Abéché. Then next door to the patisserie, one of several of N'Djamena's surprisingly pristine eateries and a place that had occupied my thoughts during the moments I'd felt over-Vached. A friendly group of Americans invited me to join them and it was good to hear their tales from spending three weeks in the bush delivering medicines to remote areas: "So who are you here with?" I asked the table in general, perhaps not choosing my words carefully enough. It left the door wide open and the chattiest of the group was not slow to seize the opportunity: "Well you see, Jesus asked us to come …"

A little bit of a soliloquy followed, the gist being that they as Christians give medication to needy Muslims and who knows … one day the worshippers of Allah might come out and bat for the other side.

Still excited to be back in the big city I charged around in the choking heat, forgetting the basics of survival in the tropics. Feeling dehydrated and a little nauseous I was heading back to the room for some shade when I passed a man on the street trying to blow his nose using just his thumb and forefinger for control. I have read somewhere that women can pee standing up by using a similar system, correct placement of the fingers and the build up of adequate force being paramount in ensuring a clean and effective delivery. I tried to look away from my fellow pedestrian, but wasn't fast enough to avoid the sickening spectacle of several very long strands of snot ejecting from his nose and stretching like chewing gum all over his hands, chin and shirt, to name but three. Let this be a warning to you ladies – make sure you practice your technique in the shower before taking to the streets.

The more time I spent in N'Djamena the more I came to appreciate that parts of the city were actually quite pleasant. Sadly there wouldn't be time to sample the new restaurants I'd stumbled across, but there was The Tourist Attraction; I was determined not to miss out on that experience.

The National Museum of Chad, it has to be said, is a dismal little place. Twice I went there to find it locked up and could easily have been convinced that it had closed down years earlier had I not been assured otherwise. Indeed there is somebody in attendance in the mornings, a pleasant young man who will take you into each of the five rooms and talk you through the various artefacts. I could only follow so much in French, but the short tour did give some insight into Chad's troubled past and the many years of tribal warfare. Throughout the history of the country its small population, only 9 million even now, has battled amongst itself for supremacy and it was easy to see why even modern day N'Djamena would need to be prepared at all times for attack.

There had indeed been much talk of a coup in Chad and a possible attempt to oust, or kill, the President. It was yet another reason why the Foreign Office advised that only essential visits be made and now I realised the extent of my good fortune that all had remained calm throughout my short stay. Apart from the photo incidents which had left me with no photos of N'Djamena, it had all gone very well and in a way I was sorry not to have been able to spend a bit more time in this most peculiar of countries.

* * * * *

The airport was probably only 1,200 meters from the hotel, but with a bag, in the sand, under the midday sun, you take a cab. I had carefully saved my last few CFAs to pay for the journey and as we approached the airport building I pulled the crumpled bundle of notes from my pocket. Time for a little smug reflection: I had done it, nothing spectacular, nothing to be particularly proud of, but at least I'd made it around the country without any mishaps.

And then, as though reading my mind, the engine cut out and the car became absolutely silent – 100 metres from the departure terminal and we had run out of petrol! The driver cursed and slammed his hand on the steering wheel as we freewheeled very slowly along the flat airport road and I must confess that it took a big effort on my part to keep a straight face as we came to a natural stop directly in front of the airport door.

The guy who sat next to me on the plane was a Chadian who had emigrated to Canada and had been back to Abéché for a family visit. It was fascinating – and sad – to hear of his frustrations with his native country, particularly his conviction that Chad's oil was being sold at artificially low prices to line the pockets of its corrupt officials. There was no future in Africa, he reflected mournfully, so he'd had to go and live somewhere else, somewhere the outside temperature was 26 degrees below zero!

His lament finally came to an end when the gorgeous stewardess drew up alongside with a meal trolley. After a few weeks in Africa I was more than ready for something hot and tasty, and she was indeed … I ripped off the aluminium lid with great excitement and peered down into the carton placed upon the tray. Unfortunately readers I don't recall the detail of the starter or the main course because my attention was immediately drawn to the far left hand corner, wedged in just behind the plastic carton of water. It was a small triangle lodged on top of a cream cracker and of course I recognised him at once. He seemed to be smiling up at me and in a funny sort of way I was quite pleased to see him. My trusty old friend, La Vache Qui Rit.

The Four-Letter Countries

CUBA

As centuries go, surely the twentieth must rank as the most significant so far. Two world wars were viciously fought, science and technology changed lives beyond anybody's wildest dreams, we even watched live pictures of fellow humans being deposited onto another planet. Out of all this glory and pain the names of many individuals will long be remembered, though perhaps history will record that the lives of two remarkable men, from very different parts of the world, will stand out above all others. When the new millennium dawned Nelson Mandela was 82 years old, Fidel Castro just eight years younger.

I had been privileged to visit South Africa many times and eventually see the changes we all feared would never come. And of course a lot has since been written about Nelson Mandela, his struggle, his years of isolation. But what of Fidel Castro? This was a story that had largely passed me by even though it had been running for the whole of my life. Sure, I'd heard of the bearded man and Cuba and communism and bits and pieces of stories, but what was it really all about? Well, thank goodness it's a Four-Letter Country or I may well have never found out.

Let me give you 450 years in three sentences. The Spanish claimed the island in 1492, killed off most of the locals and then realised that to cut down all that sugar cane they actually needed some dark-skinned chaps after all (I know a-nothing, I come from Barcelona). In came thousands of slaves from Africa and for the next four centuries things ticked along OK, unless of course you happened to be a slave. At the end of the 19th century the Americans declared war on, and defeated, the Spanish, but were kind enough to offer Cuba their independence on condition that they, the Yanks, could lay their hands on a major Cuban seaport or two. Hence the now famous Guantanamo Bay.

By 1950 Cuba was a mess. More than half the island was owned by foreign companies, mainly American, and a military dictator name of Batista was running the country in a way that made him very rich and almost everybody else very poor. Castro, who had trained as a lawyer, didn't like it one bit, so he cobbled together a small army and tried to overturn the regime. It didn't work, most of his mates got killed and he was sentenced to fifteen years in prison, though he ended up serving only two. Batista had him released early in an effort to win public support, a move that he would soon live to regret.

Fidel sloped off to Mexico, grew a beard and teamed up with an Argentinian doctor turned freedom fighter called Ernesto Guevara, soon to be nicknamed Che (you couldn't be taken seriously as a freedom fighter with a name like Ernesto). Together these two young men plot the revolution, sail back into Cuba aboard a boat known quaintly as *Granma*, and with their small army and a growing band of disenchanted students on the island, they take on Batista's troops. After two years of bloody encounters the War of the People was finally won, Fidel Castro became the national hero and the new Prime Minister (and later, President) of Cuba. Long live the Revolution!

That was back in 1959. Who would have believed that 48 years later Fidel would still be ruling the roost? This was definitely the time to visit Cuba, the leader was frail and on his last legs (he would eventually resign in February 2008) and leaning ever more on his younger brother Raúl for support. I couldn't wait to get there.

* * * * *

I closed my eyes and for the next few minutes just listened to the incredible high-pitched sound that filled the air. A lake in East Africa, thousands and thousands of pink and white birds shrieking that identical shriek, that single sound, the only sensation for miles around other than the dust between your toes and the heat of the sun overhead.

It was a lovely daydream; opening my eyes actually revealed the sunlight-free blandness of an airport arrivals hall. The screeching was in fact that of the aching baggage carousels at the José Marti International airport, Havana, upon which no baggage at all had been sighted during my first fifteen minutes in Cuba. Rather than stare at the empty belt any longer I went to the bank at the back of the hall and swapped some Euros for Cuban Convertible Pesos, conveniently almost a one for one trade.

Back at the carousel I inspected the bundle of notes, oblivious to the surge of excitement that was about to course through my veins. Because never before, not ever, amongst all the shabby and torn and tatty and so often utterly pointless banknotes that have been stuffed into my wallet, could I recall being handed a note to the value of THREE. A 3 Peso note! They say that small things amuse small minds and whoever 'they' are they are probably right. But I just could not conceal my pleasure at this break from the dull convention of operating in multiples of five. Why indeed shouldn't we have a three-er? In fact why not have one that is worth 9 or 27.4? Nice one Cuba, I was happy, very happy ... and I hadn't even collected my bag.

Not at all sure what to expect, I stepped out into the afternoon sun, slid into the back of an ageing taxi and headed into Havana. My driver spoke excellent English and he was really quite charming, more than could be said of the decaying buildings that appeared in clusters on either side of the road. They looked grey, abandoned, something from a bygone era, only the laundry hanging from grimy windows to suggest there was human life within. I had pre-booked a room at the Hotel Plaza and was starting to wonder what the place might look like or whether indeed it would still be standing.

My fears were totally unfounded. I was soon to discover that a small percentage of Havana's colonial buildings have been preserved and, in some cases, beautifully restored and as I stepped into the huge lobby it was clear that this was most definitely one of them. Wide cloisters, shiny floors, tropical plants and a wonderful feeling of light and space. The height of my room was probably greater than its length or width with little to complicate it other than long thin shutters and a grumbling a/c unit, but it felt simple and homely and I liked the whole place very much.

Minutes later and I was out, exploring. Wide squares, narrow streets, crumbling buildings and everywhere, seemingly every single bar and restaurant, five or six musicians knocking out a cheerful tune. The place immediately felt happy, so full of life. Nobody had prepared me for the fact that Havana is in fact just one big party (I might have got more dressed up if I'd known) and there seemed to be so much going on to compensate for the fact that the city is largely a collection of sad forgotten buildings. A warmth and vibrancy not easy to find in an unfamiliar place and amidst all these ruins it was evident that pots of money had been invested in some improbably luxurious hotels. Mr Castro had finally realised that tourism was his last throw of the dice.

I found a table in a restaurant that seemed very popular though the menu, when it finally arrived, was rather less than inspiring. Chicken or pork or fish, rice and beans or potatoes.

"Chicken with rice and beans please."

"Sorry, no chicken."

"Fish then please."

"No rice and beans, just rice."

"OK. Fish and rice without beans then please."

The place was fun. Like everybody else I drank mojitos, a delightful mix of rum with ice, sugar and mint leaves, and watched all sorts of people wander by along the narrow street. The band played and the ambience was such that the hour-long wait for a piece of grilled fish mattered little. But the fact that when it did arrive the rice was entirely burnt could – on a worse day – have provoked a less polite request of the waiter:

"Any chance of some potatoes instead of the burnt rice?"

Cuba

"Sorry sir, potatoes finished. You can have a free mojito."

Given that the mojitos were excellent and the food decidedly below average I took him up on his offer, stayed and listened to the band and read a bit more about this weird and wonderful country.

What Castro did when he took over had been as spectacular as his rise to power. He asked the people of Cuba if they would like to have free education and a free health service. They roared in approval. OK then responded The Mighty One, so what we need is socialism.

The story of Cuba's economy, or rather, lack of one, goes back to the start of the Revolution (not referred to as a past event in Cuba but rather an ongoing situation). Fidel announced in 1961 that the state was assuming control of all the island's land and property, starting with that of his own father, and told the Americans in no uncertain terms that they could effectively write off all their assets in the country. The US was not at all happy to learn this and by way of response decreed that all business with Cuba should cease forthwith and that its citizens would be forbidden from travelling to the island.

Things were to get worse for the US when Fidel decided to look to support from Mr Kruschev and the boys at the Kremlin. The Russians were only too delighted to have a commie enclave just 80 miles off the coast of Florida so they poured money, technical manpower and all sorts of nasty weapons into the island. And that's what happened for three decades. The good citizens of Cuba got free health and education instead of a proper salary and for as long as the subsidies rolled in Castro could pretend that his system was a great success.

Then, if you'll excuse the expression, the shit hit the fan in a rather big way. The Soviet Union went bust, the men in fur hats flew back home and Fidel, like a teenager who had always lived with his parents, was left to ponder who would be paying the bills. Oh shit and double shit. What now? Mmm ... better give a few more speeches and tell people how lucky they are to be Cuban, to be part of a Socialist paradise. That'll do the trick.

The Four-Letter Countries

It didn't work and people started to get hungry. I was told that some were so desperate that they kept live chickens or even pigs in their bathrooms as an insurance policy against starvation. Castro knew that Cuba needed foreign money and, without any rich friends to call on, this had to come by way of tourism. Hotels and restaurants were needed, even a little bit of – dare I say it – enterprise?

* * * * *

It's only a four hour time shift from UK to Cuba, but to a pansy like me that would be a guarantee of four days jet lag. The question was: where should I go to do my lagging? There was a very slight temptation to head a couple of hours east along the north coast to the white beaches and turquoise waters of Varadero, the package capital where most Brits go for their all-inclusive 14 day feast of sunshine and Cuba Libre (the cocktail of rum and coke "invented" to celebrate independence).The pride of Europe would be there now, by the pool, having breakfast: Bacon, Beer, Bacardi and no doubt a packet of Bensons. How very appealing. Surely I wasn't becoming a snob?

I answered my own question by hopping on a local bus outside the train station and heading off towards another section of the coast, not far from Havana, but a very long way from Varadero.

There are several large ugly buildings along the beaches to the east of Havana and sadly for me they turned out to be the hotels from which I had to choose. The enormous pale blue monster I had taken for a disused hospital was, it turned out, a Soviet version of a holiday resort, but I couldn't bring myself even to get close up to that one. Instead I opted for somewhere smaller, less ugly and only mildly depressing. My home for two nights was an all-inclusive deal with as much food and drink as I could consume. Gulag-By-The-Sea.

The food at Gulag was, I suppose, pretty much what I had been told to expect in Cuba and a measure of things to come. Like most greedy folk, gastronomy is a subject very dear to my heart and, regrettably, an extremely serious rant will at some point have to come your way. If it's OK with you, we might as well do this now, all in one hit, get it over and done with. Then we can move on, as they say. So here goes ...

Eating in a hotel or restaurant in Cuba is a more bland, boring, unimaginative, dismal experience than my literary powers could ever possibly convey. It doesn't change, the food always looks the same, it is only ever lukewarm and it is utterly sodding pointless. It won't actually harm you, but there is a danger that your taste buds will simply become so redundant they will shrivel up and die. It's fish or pork or chicken. No seasoning, sauce, herbs, spices, garnish ... NADA. The regular alternative is congealed pasta, never hot, in fact usually stone cold, with a tomato sauce if you can manage a few lumps of that.

Ever heard of the expression more-ish? Now think less-ish. Yes, that just about sums it up. But why? Does communism eradicate self-expression to the point of creating a culinary vacuum? Is there a secret department that forbids flavour and has people flogged and tortured for meddling with ingredients? In a land that could grow almost anything at all, with neighbouring countries all around serving up the most flavoursome of dishes, how can it be that every single chef in the whole of Cuba wheels out the same tasteless crap morning, noon and night. (The rant is nearly over). The country is fantastic, I implore you to go there, but forget packing clothes or toiletries or hair dryers or whatever normally finds a place in your bag. Be smart: take black pepper, chilli sauce, basil, rosemary, lemon grass, HP, Lea and Perrins, anything, anything at all you can carry with you. This is my only piece of advice, it marks the end of my rant and I promise not to raise the subject ever again.

The beach was long and lovely and I took care not to step on the many small, blue jellyfish washed ashore. A storm had passed through and left a murky sky, but it was as good a place as any to unwind and re-set the body clock. What would I do when I woke at 4am next morning I pondered? Write to Richard Branson perhaps and ask what one needs to do to knock down all ten skittles when playing in-flight Virtual Bowling? I'd played it all the way on the flight over and I swear it's programmed to deny everybody that final pin. Maybe I would even challenge him to a match ...

The flight into Havana had been my first Virgin Atlantic experience. The fact that Branson's train service had so spectacularly failed to grapple with the paltry 184 miles between London and Manchester had always raised doubts in my mind about entrusting his empire to the challenge of crossing time zones. Wouldn't I be risking a three hour unscheduled stop in the Azores or being diverted to Uruguay where a bus would be waiting to complete our journey? As it turned out the flight had passed extremely smoothly, bowling aside. Thanks Sir Richard. PS. Sorry about your Cola.

Two days in the Gulag served its purpose and I returned to Havana feeling refreshed. The sky brightened and it was fun to spend some time taking pictures of the incredible buildings – an engaging mix of splendour and squalor – and the huge old American cars built half a century earlier. So brightly coloured they wouldn't have looked out of place in a circus, these were the only cars anybody could afford, or were permitted to own, unless the government decreed vehicle ownership necessary to one's profession.

In the world of communism you don't really own very much more than the clothes that you stand in, nor are you allowed to earn any money except the pittance that the government pays you. Nor are you allowed to travel overseas or own a passport unless the government wants you to. Nor are you allowed beyond the lobby of a hotel even if somebody was prepared to pay for you to stay there. This is communism. You can have dreams, hopes, ideas and opinions so long as you keep them very much to yourself.

I stood in Revolution Square where Castro had been so rapturously received by his adoring followers all those years ago. A large rectangle of some considerable size, but impressive it most definitely wasn't. In fact a complete non-entity, an expanse of concrete and weeds that looked like a disused car park, a huge waste of space surrounded on all four sides by ugly government buildings. In a city that boasts so much grandeur it struck me as odd that it's most historical site didn't even run to a fountain, a tree or even a bunch of flowers.

It is said that everybody knows that Castro ran the country from an office just off the square, but strangely nobody has any idea where he lives. Did nobody ever think to follow him home from work during his forty odd years in power? The reason for all the secrecy is that the CIA spent the best part of half a century trying to bump him off, in fact, if the figure is to be believed, there have been over 600 documented attempts on his life. If at first you don't succeed...

If Revolution Square was depressing then the smaller one in front of the cathedral was positively a joy to behold. A great atmosphere, I sat there in the sunshine with a glass of Bucanero, the tastier of the local beers, listened to the bands playing and watched a parade of men on stilts that appeared from around the corner. These two famous Havana landmarks really did show both sides of the Cuban coin.

A couple of blocks further along, the city's sea front was something of a disappointment. The weather-beaten buildings that look out across the Straits of Florida are lashed by hurricanes for four months of every year and it was no surprise to learn that every week in Havana several of them simply collapse. In truth most of the place seemed to be falling apart, so to find a suburb of tree-lined streets and extravagant-looking residences not far from the city centre was the last thing I expected. Who could possibly own such places?

Well, domestic servants, actually. Apparently these houses were owned by the rich Cubans that fled to the USA when Castro came to power and they left their maids in charge while they waited in Florida for the fuss to die down. Suffice to say they are now either dead or seriously fed up of waiting, meanwhile the servants continue to live in mansions on the leafy streets.

The Four-Letter Countries

About 12% of Cubans live in the States and more are trying to get there. The story goes that when the US actively encouraged people to emigrate from Cuba, Castro backed the policy all the way and opened the gates of his prisons. As thieves and rapists dived into the sea and started swimming, the US quickly changed the law: anybody that makes it there is still entitled to stay and become a citizen, but those caught drifting amongst the sharks now immediately get turned back.

I could have stayed longer mooching around Havana. Such a colourful city, with the buzz that downtown New Orleans used to have before it was tragically flooded, yet in many ways so sad. Cut off from the real world yet still full of little surprises. Who would have expected to find a bronze statue of John Lennon sitting on a park bench next to a children's playgound?

* * * * *

It seems odd to me that Cuba is a Caribbean island because in my book Caribbean islands have to have a cricket team. (Come to think of it, this is my book.) It is, in fact, bigger than all those other famous islands added together and what's even more fascinating, an oft-quoted gem, is that it boasts the same overall area as Bulgaria. To which I can only say this: who the hell has the slightest idea how big Bulgaria is?

The main island is long and thin, around 1,250km from west to east, too big to cover the whole lot in one visit. Because of this wealth of riches, I had planned to do a lot in a short space of time and had resolved to explore the western half by bus and bicycle. So I joined a small guided group that was headed that way from Havana.

The countryside was lush, the sky a deep blue and the roads just perfect for cycling. The wide open fields offered graceful palm trees, banana and coffee plantations, bright colourful flowers and smiley, waving people who were genuinely pleased you had passed by and been a part of their day. Tiny schools appeared improbably on the roadside, most no bigger than your front room with maybe eight children playing ring-a-ring-a-roses in the defined little garden that was their playground. Cars were very few indeed, the people of the country more often passed by on a pony and trap or the occasional motorbike with sidecar (remember those from old war movies?). It felt as though I'd been transported in a time capsule to a bygone era, to a happier world, a place unpolluted by the miseries of modern life. Then along came a truck billowing thick black smoke from its rear, perhaps not so unpolluted after all.

It was hillier than I'd expected, a test of the lungs and a constant battle against the rivers of sweat running into the eyes. Regular stops were absolutely essential and a welcome opportunity to savour those wonderful views, assess the wetness of my clothes and briefly contemplate the miseries of incontinence. Our guide, by contrast, was totally in control and he grinned a lot, clearly amused at the sight of these breathless, capitalist punters roasting in their own juices. His command of English was pretty impressive too:

"Jeezus, Dave. You're sweating like a cornered virgin."

Would my Spanish ever reach a level of fluency that I could make jokes about cornered virgins, I wondered? And this from a man who had never set foot outside his own country.

The further west we went the more spectacular the countryside became. The cycling was challenging, but the scenery of the Vinales valley was more than just reward for aching limbs and a soggy shirt. Where else in the world could you find scenery like this with no traffic or tourists? This really was a valley in the true sense of the word, a wide fertile corridor with huge oddly-shaped limestone hills in the distance both left and right. Karst, I believe is the geological term, a landscape more commonly associated with that of southern China.

The end of each afternoon was marked with a cold Bucanero and a swim in the hotel pool. The latter a luxury I hadn't expected, but there was a surprising number of rural hotels with good, if slightly run-down facilities. From a distance these small chalets set in deliciously lush gardens could earn 5 star ratings anywhere in the world, but sadly the flaky paintwork, bashed up furniture and dangling wires were a reminder that this was Cuba, the communist state, after all.

One of the most interesting stops was in the village of San Diego de los Banos. It was my second night into the countryside, having cycled from the forested hillsides of Soroa, and the splendid looking hotel offered spa baths and massage services as its speciality. 'Oh yes please,' thought I.

All seemed perfectly normal as I was lead away from the smart hotel reception area until I saw the building that had been rather fancifully designated as the leisure annexe. It could at one time have been a hospital, more likely a lunatic asylum, possibly even a secret centre for human cloning, indoctrination or just straightforward torture. It was an enormous, eerie, and almost derelict building and as I was ushered through the long, silent unlit corridors I couldn't help wonder what had happened over the years behind all those metal doors.

A glass panel in the wall served as a small counter behind which a few bored-looking ladies carried out their administrative duties. It was a relief just to see that normal human beings actually existed within this scary edifice and the urge to turn and run became slightly less pronounced. Did I want a sulphur bath? If 'yes' I would have to be prepared to throw away any garments worn therein as the chemicals would destroy them beyond repair. The choice was mine.

Had I packed a disposable wardrobe for the purpose of spa bathing? Hardly. Is this what other people do? Could it explain why some tourists lug around suitcases the size of a small house? From now on I would always look upon those enormous grey cases and their lopsided owners in a very different light, for they clearly had it all worked out. I pictured the two distinct compartments within the Delsey luggage: clothes to return home with on one side, lunatic asylum bathing gear on the other.

Cuba

The other choice was a massage, 10 pesos for half an hour or 25 for an hour. Nobody could explain the logic of such a wacky calculation, in fact it seemed I had been the only person awkward enough to question the rationale behind their pricing formula. We agreed on 45 minutes and the ladies set about completing the necessary documentation. Now I have never been to the NASA space station, but I would guess the amount of paperwork involved in despatching a rocket into orbit consumes pretty much the same amount of time as it did to get me onto a massage bed. Thankfully I was in no big hurry.

The rooms behind the steel doors were no less austere and certainly no more welcoming, strangely empty except for a few flat beds divided by makeshift curtains. Then my lady appeared, a fresh-faced young thing who barely looked old enough to have left school – as with policemen, a sign of ageing is that masseuse just look younger all the time.

She indicated for me to undress and lie on my front, but er ... just how much undressing was one supposed to do? I didn't want to appear either a prude or a pervert so decided to leave my swimming trunks in place and looked up inquisitively to gauge her response. I thought back to my massage in Laos and that young lady's reaction to my proposed nakedness. (Had she sweated like a cornered virgin?). This one shrugged, appeared to deliberate and then nodded to indicate that kit fully off would really be better. I must admit, if I was forced in to giving a lady a massage, I would probably have reached the same conclusion.

For the first twenty minutes I lay there, face down, elbows out, All Back and Buttocks. (Whatever did happen to Derek Nimmo?). The absence of my shorts was not an issue at this stage, but I (we?) knew that the moment of truth was looming. 'Was this a regular situation?' I wondered, or was I actually the first client to give her the full monty? In fact had she ever even seen a naked man before? What would happen at the moment when she asked me to spin over? A gasp perhaps? A nervous giggle? I really didn't know what the reaction would be – from any of the three of us – but I was soon to find out.

For twenty two and a half minutes I lay flat on my back as naked as the day I was born. Not once in that whole time did she bat an eyelid, raise a smile or even start panting uncontrollably. She simply rubbed the fragrant oil into each of my muscle groups and then, job completed, she walked silently from the room.

* * * * *

Back at the pool the world seemed so strikingly normal and a lively crowd were obviously having fun at the bar. I hurled myself into the sparkly water and then went over to join the party..

The fun, it turned out, was really a very loud and rather inebriated one-man show, the local schoolteacher demonstrating his vast wealth of knowledge of all things British to anybody interested or polite enough to listen. He had just been paid (about £10 for the month) and was in celebratory mood:

"Hello my friend, where are you from?"

He was looking straight at me.

"England." (Just the answer he was hoping for)

"Aaaagh. England. I know England. I love England. Ask me anything you want about England. English history. English geography. English literature. Anything, anything at all and I will tell you … I know Surrey, I know Hampshire, I know Yorkshire, I know Somerset..."

"A drink, maybe?" I interjected.

"Yes please. Another glass of rum please … And history. Ask me about William the Conqueror. Queen Victoria. Edward the Confessor … who lived from 1004–1066, King of England from 1042, or ask me about Ethelred the Unready and, of course, Godwin, Earl of Wessex..."

A nice guy, his knowledge and enthusiasm uncontestable, but, like Ethelred, I was decidedly unready for an afternoon of this. A return visit to the pool would be my way out and I looked longingly towards the beautiful glistening water, only to see that it was almost entirely covered in a film of what looked like oil. In fact it was oil, massage oil. Oh dear, how very embarrassing.

* * * * *

Cycling in the west of Cuba had been nothing short of fantastic, a place I wanted to go back to before I'd even left. I'd never associated Cuba with such spectacular scenery and the decision to see it from the saddle had most definitely been one of my smarter ones. Now it was time for what I hoped would be an equally sensible move, to head towards the centre of the island and to visit a few of Cuba's more famous towns and cities. But first to a bay on the south coast that just had to be seen.

The Bay of Pigs was, in fact, nothing short of pig ugly. A dreary hotel and a sad little museum is really all that marks the coastline where the famous US-sponsored invasion took place in 1961. The Americans had trained 1,400 ex-Cubans to attack their former homeland in ships and planes repainted under the Cuban flag and, as the world has now come to expect from the US military machine, it was the usual cocktail of tragedy and farce. Within three days 200 of them had been killed and the other 1,200 captured and the US had to spend $53 million of taxpayers' money in ransom aid to get them back. (Sergeant Bilko and his boys then headed off to work their magic in South East Asia. Remember Laos?)

From there, on to Cienfuegos, the kind of place I like. It has no particular tourist attractions and there is nothing you feel you are supposed to be looking at or taking pictures of. Just a straightforward pleasant place, a typical regular working city, and what better way to spend a Monday morning than to watch people working.

Like all towns and cities in Latin America it has a square with lots of trees and a bandstand and an impressive array of statues and busts

The Four-Letter Countries

of important people you and I have never heard of. I sat in the coolness of one of the colonnades and sipped a coffee, very contented, admiring the pastel buildings of blue and green and pink that formed the rectangle, each with enormous doors and slatted windows that must have been twice my own height. I watched beautiful women, of which there were many, so elegant with white shirts and jet-black hair, short skirts and long brown legs. Smiling teenagers, most carrying small rucksacks, walked by in groups chatting and giggling. And as always, by total contrast, there was the Weird-White-Legged-Tourist with the silly hat and the red face smeared with sun cream, a monster from another planet with various pieces of equipment dangling round his neck.

There was nothing at all typical about the next town I visited. Trinidad is a world heritage site on the Southern coast of the island, a series of narrow cobbled streets and traditional old buildings and the place that all the tour buses will flock to once Cuba is really on the map. Small shops and market stalls complete the picture – and what a picture this place is. A gathering point for artists, musicians, poets, people with lots of beads, women with frilly skirts … getting the idea?

I stayed a little way out of town in the hotel on top of the hill, looking down over the rooftops and the Caribbean Sea beyond. At 6.30 every evening this was definitely the place to be, Mojito or Bucanero in hand, gazing out at the horizon and watching the sun like a huge ball of fire slide gracefully into the water. The sunset in Trinidad is one of those experiences that will stay with me for the rest of my life.

There are also a lot of other things I will remember about Trinidad and one of them is definitely Andrew; a wonderful and very amusing man from Maidenhead who decided to 'come out' one evening as we were slurping mojitos and enjoying the sunset. Andrew wasn't declaring himself to be gay, it wasn't that sort of coming out, but he had chosen that moment to tell me of his very special achievement, which was this. He had, throughout the previous twenty years of his life, set himself and achieved the target of watching every professional English and Scottish

Cuba

football club play a match on their home ground. Just think about that for a moment.

I can't tell you how good this conversation made me feel. Here was a man who had come home from work in Berkshire on a cold Friday night in winter, gone to bed and set the alarm for 3am Saturday morning in preparation for the nine-hour jaunt up to Elgin. Once there, along with 400 or so locals, he bought a pie and a programme (he always bought a pie and a programme), watched what he described as the worst game of football he had ever seen, then drove non-stop all the way back home to Maidenhead, arriving around 3am Sunday morning.

There have been times, many times indeed, when the whole FLC project has struck me as nothing more than an infantile waste of time and money. Then, when you least expect it, fascinating people like this come along and suddenly things don't seem so silly after all. I had no hesitation in telling Andrew about the journey to Chad, I knew he was one of a handful of people in the world that would completely understand. So, wherever you are mate, here's to you!

The hotel there was great, the pool was delightful ... well, apart from the dead cockroaches, and the chambermaids created beautiful animal shapes from the fresh towels they left on the beds every after-noon. A nice little Cuban touch this, and probably so much more fun than cleaning the rooms. What was not great, of course, is the you-know-what, the stuff we have agreed not to speak about. If you can picture a very downmarket version of Watford Gap Services then you'll understand why two of us decided to forego the buffet dinner one evening and see if there was anything better on offer in town.

A bit of bad luck really that just as were dropping down towards the maze of narrow streets all the power in the town went off, a not uncommon occurrence in Cuba. It was eerily dark and silent on the cobblestones, a scene from a Sherlock Holmes film, but it didn't stop the locals approaching us by torchlight to invite us to take dinner in their homes. This was a commercial deal, not an act of pure kindness, an alternative to an official restaurant and an imprisonable offence for the owner should he/she be rumbled. We had no idea which would be the best option or where exactly we would be taken. It was a blind decision in every sense.

Our host checked that nobody was looking, then we slipped through a doorway into an anonymous courtyard where a glowing candle was the only discernible feature. We sat down at a plastic table and studied our surroundings: high walls on all sides, house behind, darkness, absolute silence, no sign of other people. Just a slight breeze and a few million stars overhead, I stared up at all those twinkling dots, tried to work out the constellations that other people seem to identify so easily, failed as usual, resolved one day to be able to understand it if only just a little bit. Then I realised I was getting a stiff neck, so tilted back down to rejoin the absurdity of the occasion.

This was to be a dinner with a difference, particularly if our throats were cut from behind and we were left slumped over the table until all the blood had oozed from our bodies. Anywhere else on the planet I would have felt horribly vulnerable but – strangely – my only worry here was what would appear from the kitchen, if they even had a kitchen. The menu came verbally from a dark man whose features I could barely make out: chicken or fish? (Mmm, now there's a surprise). We opted for the latter then just sat there silently in the darkness sipping the beer that had appeared from somewhere. Talking would have seemed too normal an activity under the circumstances, so we just focused our attention on a huge spider crawling in the candlelight across the wobbly table.

What exactly was happening behind the door to my right was something I would have preferred not to dwell on, but the need to release a few Bucaneros forced me to go over and give it a couple of taps (the door, that is). One of the smiling hosts invited me in and pointed to the comfort station, thankfully the first door and close to where I was standing. The absence of proper light spared me the detail of the kitchen, though I couldn't avert my eyes from the Dickensian conditions and a couple of guys stooped over the gas flame frying up our dinner.

Issued with my own torch, I surveyed the smallest room. If you have ever been to a house that is in the process of being built you will be familiar with walls of plaster and loose items of sanitary ware waiting to be plumbed in. In this case the said item was a toilet bowl, not new, but not plumbed in either. Not surprising then that the only liquid within had arrived directly from the human body, an unnerving panful of very watery diarrhoea to be precise. I found myself wondering whether this had been deposited by one of the chefs or perhaps even a previous diner, as though the origin of the smelly faeces was somehow important to the enjoyment of the evening. Perhaps Watford Gap services wasn't so bad after all.

The food was less memorable than the event itself and we left with thanks, smiles, handshakes and no doubt several million bacteria. It had been no better or worse than the usual fare, but this was not one of the country's best 'paladares', as these home restaurants are known. I did visit a few more during my time on the island, sitting in people's gardens and front rooms and car ports, and some in fact were very good. Particularly surprising was that lobster became a feature of the private menus and extremely tasty it was too.

These meals with rum and beer cost on average US$15 per person, equivalent to a monthly salary in Cuba, so no surprise that many are prepared to run the risk of a government official lurking in the bushes. But how can people be expected to live on the equivalent of 30p a day? The money situation needs a little explaining. The regular local currency is the Peso and this is used exclusively by Cubans. From 1993 to 2004 foreigners were expected to use US Dollars, but the government decided to introduce their own second currency to replace that, hence the Cuban Convertible Peso. So we have two types of Peso and effectively two monetary systems – a pound would buy you 1.5 convertible Pesos, but 36 local Pesos, if you could do anything with them.

The Four-Letter Countries

Local Pesos are used by Cuban nationals to buy basic commodities and each citizen is entitled to a monthly ration of these items at a heavily subsidised price. Special shops dish out eggs and rice etc and individual purchases are recorded in their ration books. This ensures basic survival, but anything beyond must be purchased in Convertible Pesos at real market prices. Small wonder then that everybody wants to sell you some cigars or take you back to their place for a nice home-cooked dinner.

I loved Trinidad. The electricity eventually returned and stayed on for most of my time there and I slotted into a nightly routine of a few leisurely sundowners on top of the hill followed by a walk down into town to see the show. Every evening at 9pm the music gets under way just up the steps off the central square and anybody is welcome to go along, join in the dancing or just sit and watch. This is, I can assure you, entertainment of the very highest order.

Dancers, in my opinion, fall into one of three categories. There are those who feel less than compelled to join in and who, if the truth be known, would rather just stay at the bar. If they do get dragged onto the dance floor their heads and arms and legs jerk about self-consciously in all directions as though afflicted by a disease of the nervous system. They are rhythmically spastic, an unpleasant sight to behold and their gyrations serve no purpose other than to produce a large and seemingly uncontrollable amount of perspiration. I am not particularly proud of it, but at least smart enough to recognise that this category is very much where I belong. Promotion to a higher division has never been remotely on the cards, not even an outside chance of the play-offs.

The next group is made up of people who can move around a dance floor and actually look as though they are enjoying it. Not especially talented nor in any way extrovert, but able to glide around harmlessly in time with the music. Sane, balanced individuals.

Then there is category three. You don't see many of these, particularly when you grow up in England. True performers, people born to move to the sound of music, a chosen few from another world whose hips and legs move so effortlessly yet with a sense of purpose and in perfect time to the music and the steps of their partners. Poetry in motion, so utterly mesmerising; a gift bestowed upon the people of the Caribbean by their ancestors from the African continent.

Every night, as soon as the band got into their stride, these remarkable, graceful athletes would take to the floor. They would dance the Salsa into the early hours of the morning and for me it was something very special indeed to just sit there beside the swaying palm trees, watch the show unfold and sip on a mojito or two (ok … neck mojitos as though there was no tomorrow).

* * * * *

Early one morning I saw Andrew at breakfast and there was something in his demeanour that hinted all was not well. Had it suddenly dawned on him that he'd never in fact made it to Stenhousemuir or that he'd forgotten to record pie quality at Hamilton Academical? He was staring at his omelette, or rather the half-sprout served as garnish on the edge of the plate, and was eager to recount his experience of earlier that morning.

A scorpion! He'd been bitten by a scorpion as he was putting his shorts on. Not surprisingly it had caused him a lot of pain and even more panic, but the pool attendant, no doubt highly trained in all matters of tropical medicine, had assured him that if he didn't become feverish there was nothing to worry about. Andrew wasn't entirely convinced, but he did, I noticed, manage to polish off his omelette and sprout and I could sense he was already drooling at the prospect of The Scorpion in the Shorts story over half-time Bovril at Maidenhead United.

That day I took a ride on a steam train into the lush countryside, through the beautiful rolling hills of the sugar fields (long, thin leaves) and

The Four-Letter Countries

the banana plantations (short, fat leaves). This had been a very important region in the sugar-producing heyday, hence the existence of this old train line that now carried tourists instead. We stopped for coffee in one of the fabulous old colonial houses where the masters had resided, alongside tall watchtowers that had served to keep an eye on the slaves in the fields. What a beautiful place this was, as long as you weren't working 15 hours a day in the plantations.

It was soon time to leave Trinidad, maybe too soon really, so I treated myself to one last wander along the cobbles, a few more waves to people sitting on their doorsteps (Cubans do a lot of doorstep sitting), and a quick visit to the eggs and rice shop. This was a dark little store with a wizened old lady behind the counter, eggs stacked up against one wall and bags of rice against the other, in fact pretty much everything you would expect an eggs and rice shop to be. You would go a long way to find anything so deathly uninteresting and on that basis alone I asked the lady for permission to photograph her wares. She was absolutely delighted just to have an overseas visitor in her shop, though I suspect somewhat bewildered that a grown man would want to include sacks of rice amongst his holiday snaps.

* * * * *

My last stop of any note was the town of Santa Clara, the scene of a bloody battle where Che Guevara and his men had fought Batista's troops and forced the dictator into exile. When Che's remains were returned to Cuba in 1997, some thirty years after his death, it was here that they chose to lay him to rest. The enormous memorial to Che and his comrades who fell in battle is extremely dignified, certainly the most impressive of its type that I have seen anywhere in the world. Visitors are permitted to walk inside the mausoleum, read the inscriptions and see the carved faces of the men who perished. A fresh flower is attached to each one of the memorial stones and an eternal flame burns in the corner, which of course was lit by Fidel Castro himself. I found it very moving, so tastefully done, a great tribute to those that were lost and a credit to the country.

Although Che's name and face appear on every street corner wherever you turn in Cuba (and humdrum exhibits ranging from his handkerchiefs to his socks are proudly displayed in each town's 'Museum of the Revolution'), it was only here that I could really appreciate the impact that this man had had on the world. The museum next to the mausoleum covered every aspect of his life, from boyhood and medical school in Argentina to his part in the struggles and wars of Latin America and Central Africa. Incredible to think that he accomplished so much and yet was only 39 years old when the CIA caught up with him in Bolivia and ordered him to be shot.

I had learnt a lot that morning, in fact the trip to Cuba had taught me more history than I'd ever absorbed before. But it didn't seem like history in the true sense of the word, it was recent, happening in my lifetime, Che Guevara had been alive when England won the World Cup in 1966!

It was a fitting way to finish the trip, reflecting on how Cuba had got to where it was. But how long could it all last? What would happen next? Would the changes, when they did eventually come, make the country a better place or would they destroy its unique charm? The truth is that nobody knows the answer to that one. What I do know is that it's a really beautiful island of charming friendly people and a place that I'd felt very privileged to visit.

It was time to go back to Havana and I made a point of having one last mojito in the Bodeguita del Medio – the little bar next to the cathedral made famous by Ernest Hemingway. The Nobel and Pulitzer prize-winning American novelist had loved the country, made it his home for twenty years and won so many friends there until he returned to the USA in 1960. Sadly he took his own life a year later, maybe he should have stayed in Cuba after all? So this was it ... a toast in earnest to Ernest and

The Four-Letter Countries

Ernesto – Hemingway and Guevara, one who came from North America and one from the South, yet strangely, who will always be remembered as two of Cuba's greatest heroes.

FIJI

"Hello Mr Prime Minister, this is Frank. And to be perfectly frank, we think your government is corrupt, ineffective and failing miserably to take this country forward. So we'd like you and the cabinet to leave please, or we'll come over next Tuesday and throw you out anyway. Enjoy the long weekend, Mr Qarase."

It sounds like something from a James Bond film doesn't it? But Frank Bainimarama was, and still is at the time of going to press, the head of the Fijian army and true to his word, on Tuesday 5th December 2006, he led his squadron round to the government offices and announced that with immediate effect he and his men would be running the show. It made world headlines for a couple of days, but sadly for the media there was nothing of excitement to report. The government slunk off with barely a whimper and, with the exception of a few road blocks and soldiers in the streets, nothing very much happened at all. The country carried on with business as usual, while the journalists and cameramen sat around waiting for the blood to start flowing. But nothing, not so much as a handbag raised in anger. So what would happen next?

I don't want you to get the wrong idea, think I'm a hard nut or anything, but I decided to go and find out. My flight to Fiji had been provisionally booked anyway and what better preparation for dropping in on the present and future war-zones of Iraq and Iran than a fresh, hot-from-the-barracks, military coup. It would be my first ever and a nice, sedate, bloodless little number to ease me in gently.

Once again I found myself flying from Sydney, which as all those humble Aussies will tell you, is The Griydis Ciddi In The Entoyah Fakken

The Four-Letter Countries

World, mate. A week there had dealt with the worst of the jet lag (do other people do jet lag for an entire week?) and as the Air Pacific flight made its descent into Nadi that buzz of expectation, and just a hint of a silly grin, started to kick in. Whatever little I had achieved in my life, however stupid and futile and utterly ridiculous this Four Letter Adventure was deemed to be, at least I could say with a smidgen of pride that I'd made it all the way to the opposite side of the globe. Pathetic I know – and how much more of an achievement it would have seemed had I done it on a home-made raft or a pogo stick – but at least I was here, FLC number 8, and a glorious 12 hour time shift from the UK.

It was dark as we descended and as the plane got lower I could make out the glow of a mass of water below. Not surprising you might think, given that Fiji's territory is almost entirely made up of water, but alas this was not the Pacific Ocean. And just to prove it … THUD, we had landed.

The rain was pouring down in diagonal lines under the airport lights, stretching the already huge puddles right across the runway. The surrounding fields were obviously under water and as I peered out into the wild tropical night, my first thought was for those poor girls in their short grass skirts. Would they get soggy and start to disintegrate? (The skirts, silly). And something I'd never thought of before: 'do they wear grass knickers too?'

Nadi, which funnily enough and quite inexplicably rhymes with randy, was well and truly flooded. The pounding of the rain was further exaggerated by the tin roof of the airport terminal, a scenario which might well have dampened the spirits had it been a December arrival into Luton. But how can you feel gloomy when a group of men with flowery shirts and big smiles are bashing out a cheery tune on guitar and ukulele to welcome you to their country? This just never seems to happen in Bedfordshire.

I talked floods with the taxi driver and learned that, on the back of a long drought, it had been raining heavily for a week. Looking ahead through the headlights, it didn't seem to be letting up one iota. He dropped me at the Nadi Bay Resort, a curious name for a backpackers' lodge cum budget hotel, but an instantly likeable place it was. The bar was buzzing, more flowery-shirted men were playing more guitars and ukuleles, and the food delivered from the kitchen looked exquisite. Wow, what a life, I think I might become a backpacker again one day.

I sipped my first cold Fiji Bitter and contemplated a map of this very unusual country. Four hours by plane east of Queensland and three hours north of New Zealand, Fiji is far and away the most remote of all the FLCs and certainly the smallest. Picture this in your mind, if you will: I'd like you to draw a square in the South Pacific, all sides 1,000kms. In the centre put two tiny islands diagonally adjacent and scatter seven or eight groups of even smaller ones all around. You now have as many as three hundred islands in total, but only 2% of the square is land, the rest pure blue ocean. If the picture isn't clear or you drew it wrong the first time round then please go back and do it again.

Nadi is on the west of the larger of the two main islands. This one is known as Viti Levu (Great Fiji) and with 70% of Fiji's population (total 850,000) it's very much considered the main hub of the country. Compared to the other specks in the ocean it looked enormous on the map, but I calculated the coast road all the way round would be no more than 500kms. There seemed to be a few other roads too, cutting into the mountainous interior, another dangled carrot as I contemplated the over-all game plan. The more I read about Fiji the more I realised how much there was to explore. Rain or not, I had better get a move on.

Less than twelve hours after landing in the country I went back to the airport, booked a 4WD for later in the week, then checked in for the flight to Vanua Levu, big island number 2. The town on its south east corner bears the irresistible name of Savusavu and it was a very large man from Air Fiji who explained during bag weighing that we would more than likely be calling in at another island along the way. And then a polite and rather unusual request:

The Four-Letter Countries

"Could you just pop yourself on to the scales please sir."

Another big smile and a nod to confirm this was a genuine requirement. (They probably don't have Candid Camera in Fiji anyway). I stepped on.

"Oogh sorry to tell you this sir, but we can't take fat bastards like you to Savusavu". No he didn't really say that, he just gave me another reassuring smile, made a note of my weight and handed over the boarding pass for seat 1A .

The flight was to be an unforgettable experience. The plane was tiny, only six of us, and I sat just behind the two pilots who didn't even close the cockpit door. It was a perfect hijacking opportunity, but looking out of the window on that clear, beautiful morning, it was a safe enough bet that nobody would ever demand to be taken anywhere else. The sight below was something quite extraordinary, a feast of colour to prove that neither man nor machine will ever be able to create beauty to rival the magic of nature.

The sea was a patchwork quilt of deep inky blue and the palest of green, as though somebody lying on the ocean floor was creating the effect with a series of powerful lights. I spotted hundreds of tiny islands poking out above the surface of the transparent water, each one surrounded by pale yellow sand and a ring of toothpaste-white surf, a sharp contrast to the lush forested silhouette of Vanua Levu hovering in the distance. I tried to take it all in and begged time to stand still. There are so many beautiful things that I'd been privileged to see in my short lifetime, but this, no, I couldn't recall anything in the world that could quite compare to this.

Our brief stop was in Taveuni, known as the Garden Island for very obvious reasons. Even more bewildering greenness, gorgeous trees and flowers, even posh houses with manicured lawns at the water's edge. Foreigners Live Here, and who could blame them?

There is something else to say about Taveuni, something of real geographical significance. For it is here that the 180 degree meridian passes through, the oft-talked-about-but-never-seen International Date Line. This is officially The Opposite Side of the World. In theory once you cross this line time moves back to the day before, so keep moving east and you get the same day twice (ideal for a long weekend). Of course it would all be very confusing if the residents of this little island lived on different days of the week, so the date line obliging swerves to the right and the whole of Fiji stays on the eastern half of the globe.

We were a little behind schedule into Savusavu (only myself and the pilots were still on board), but the owner of the guest house I'd e-mailed was waiting there as promised when we taxied in. Identification was a uncomplicated process: a small shelter just large enough to swing a cat (and it would be a very nervous cat) and one man sitting alone inside it. His name was Beat, which he pronounced Bayat, not because he was from Fiji but, to my surprise, from … Switzerland. Initially a slight disappointment that, I'd expected a man in traditional costume with a neck like an elephant's thigh, but Beat turned out to be a very likeable bloke.

He'd built his own house on the side of the mountain and within fifteen minutes I was sitting under my mosquito net on a four poster bed with a view of Savusavu's gorgeous harbour filling the room. It was quite a spot, a pity that the clouds were starting to roll in once again and the sweat, as ever, began trickling down my face. This was the damp, humid season and the weather was doing exactly what it said on the tin.

* * * * *

It was late afternoon when I scuttled down Beat's steep driveway and along the coast road into town. No real distance involved, but the humidity was oppressive and thankfully there wasn't much to do there other than check e-mail and have a beer on the terrace of the sailing club. Savusavu the town was uninspiring: a line of outdated, slightly tatty shops and a taxi rank full of bored, under-worked men trying to scratch a living; my first reminder that this tropical paradise and mooring point for millionaire yachties was also a third world country struggling to make ends meet.

I sat and admired the lovely views, sipped a Fiji Bitter and watched the yachts in the harbour, all of which made up for the soulless street and the feeding frenzy of the mosquitoes on my already lumpy and now bleeding ankles. With dusk it was at least getting a little cooler, my shirt was finally drying out and life was starting to seem rather pleasant. Then Beat dropped in for a beer, we chatted about his past life as a dive instructor in Grenada and then joined an English couple, who, after a few minutes of small talk, told us a very gruesome story.

Jim and Sue had been living in Spain for fifteen years and thinking of moving house when they saw an ad in the local English-language paper. A house in the country was on offer at a bargain price so Jim called, met the owner at an agreed place and followed him by car on a 90-minute journey to view the property. Another man was waiting when they finally got there, but Jim, deciding there and then it wasn't for him, declined to go in and view. The matter was forgotten until several weeks later when a retired couple from North Wales went missing and the evening news showed a picture of the house they had been to see. It was that same country property and the poor souls had been robbed, murdered and buried in the house while their families paid ransoms in the hope of securing their release. The 'owners', it turned out, were two Venezuelan guys who had just been renting the property and once Jim had given his evidence to help get them convicted he and Sue decided it was time to leave Spain and travel the world. He wasn't actually called Jim, but to throw the Venezuelan mafia off the scent I thought it would be a sporting gesture to change his name.

The conversation moved on to Fiji, the recent coup and the previous, nastier ones of 1987 and 2000. This little island nation had certainly seen more than its fair share of political strife, particularly since independence in 1970, but what was it all about? I'll keep it as brief as I can:

Fiji

Go back a couple of hundred years to the 19th century and Fiji was, to use modern Britspeak, well dodgy. All sorts of people were trying to stake a claim on the land, so the local folk responded by killing and eating anybody that could be chopped up and added to the pot. A gory custom and a very ungodly way to behave, so missionaries from England were despatched to the south Pacific armed with bibles and, more than likely, lots of tempting new recipes. Slowly but surely the cannibals converted to Christianity, though it came too late for the poor Reverend Thomas Baker who was invited over for dinner one night...!

The self-appointed King Cakobou eventually decided that there was too much squabbling over land so in 1874 he invited the British to take over the running of the country. They immediately introduced a law whereby native Fijians should own the land, but the hard work in the fields would be done by somebody else. And as there was lots of hard work to be done – cotton was booming and the Civil War had depleted the output from America – the Brits turned to a colony with a plentiful supply of labour. Over the next forty years 60,000 Indians would be shipped in as 'indentured labourers', a polite term that sounds so much more PC than slavery and it can't have been that bad because most of the labourers chose to stay beyond their three year 'contracts'. The Indian community grew and grew, but integration with the locals was actively discouraged by the Brits, a situation that largely remains to this day. By 1970 they represented half of the population and ran most of the country's businesses, but tensions were rising: the Fijians owned the land whilst the Indians, who in their own eyes had no voice and little power, were doing all the work. What better time then, after 96 years at the helm, for Britain to grant Fiji independence!

The coups that followed were predictably along ethnic lines: the Fijians eager to protect their culture and the Indo-Fijians to establish their rights. But this latest, 2006 coup was different and seemed to have the support of both sides of the commnuity against their erstwhile leaders. This was about cleaning the country up, stamping out corruption and

213

putting an end to organised crime, from which the Indo-Fijian community suffered the most. But would it work and how long would Frank's "interim" government need to be in power? These were the questions everybody was asking, but it seemed that nobody had any idea of the answers.

* * * * *

At 10.30 every morning a rickety old bus leaves Savusavu on a journey that travels eastwards along the length of the Tunuloa Peninsula and after two and a half hours it arrives at Buca Bay, just across from the island of Kioa. I knew this because I'd read it in my guidebook and checked it out with one of the bored taxi drivers the night before. I'd also read a fascinating story about Kioa, how the people who lived there weren't originally from Fiji or even Melanesia (as this part of the Pacific is known), but in fact they were Polynesians. They actually came from the Ellice Islands – very much further north – where the Americans had set up base during the Second World war and given them the chance to earn some money. But what would they do with the dosh? Their whole country, a few specks in the ocean and now known as Tuvalu (its greatest claim to fame the much-coveted www extension .tv), was only 10 square miles in total, so they decided to invest in a fertile island with a bit more space down in good ole' Fiji. It was in 1947, despite the scary stories of the cannibals, that they made the big move south.

I left my main belongings locked up at Beat's place, told him I might not be back for a day or so and set off in search of Koia with just a day-pack. It was too hot for clothes, so I figured a pair of swimming trunks, money, documents and a camera should just about do the trick. All I needed to do before boarding the bus was stock up on bread, water, bananas and, of course, sevusevu.

That's right, sevusevu. Fijian culture dictates that when visiting a village a gift be handed to the chief, a small thank-you in anticipation of the hospitality you can expect to receive. This cannot be a bunch of flowers or a box of chocolates, in fact there is really only one form of offering deemed acceptable where sevusevu is concerned. It's called kava, known locally as grog, and it's a plant that gets ground into powder, mixed with water and ritually slurped on a daily basis.

Buying sevusevu in Savusavu is not something you do every day of the week and feeling rather like Mork from Ork I took up a hopeful position in the middle of the town's indoor market. "Kava?" I mumbled to somebody rather self consciously, more in hope than expectation, not the faintest idea what to expect. Try and picture an alien wandering into a crowded bar, up to some blokes playing darts in the corner, then muttering in a timid, slightly questioning voice: "Crisps?"

I did feel a bit of a wally, but proudly emerged a few minutes later with a half kilo bag of flour-like powder for an unknown chief and two lovely bananas for me. All I needed to do now was to get on the bus and this mini-adventure would be under way.

The Hibiscus Highway is a lot more Hibiscus than Highway. In fact it's a narrow road and then a bumpy track and it winds around the Fijian coast, linking all the small communities along the way. The windowless vehicle created a welcome breeze and for me, to sit and watch this documentary of Fijian daily life played out in front of me, was a genuinely heart-warming experience. People of all shapes and sizes, mainly large sizes, hauled themselves and their produce in and out of the bus and generally did so with toothy smiles and the enthusiastic help of everybody on board. I noticed that the driver sometimes even waited for elderly customers to get safely up their driveways before pulling away, a true sense of community spirit. Materially these people are very poor, but in so many ways, thought Jenkins The Philospher, they are so very much the richer for it. Would a passenger on the Tube bother to put down his *Daily Telegraph* even if you were bleeding to death next to his briefcase? This really was the opposite side of the world.

The Four-Letter Countries

Buca Bay is pronounced Booda Bay and a group of five other guys also got off there. They were connecting on to the ferry for Taveuni, 'probably' due that afternoon but then again, they seemed to think it might turn up the next morning. A shrug, a smile, Fiji time. But if that was vague then my own plans were even less convincing: "You want to find a boatman to take you to Koia? Who? Why? Why not come with us to Taveuni?" I looked around rather than answer the question, admired the clear water lapping up on a stony beach, my little island in the distance and their very much larger one some considerable way behind it. But there were seemingly no people for miles around, no boats and apparently no more buses until tomorrow. Just how sensible was this plan on a scale of one to ten?

I decided to walk along the road and for reasons I couldn't really fathom my newly-acquired mates opted to do the same. It turned out that they had been taken by the police for a trial in Savusavu, released with a fine for drunken and rowdy behaviour and told to make their own way home. They were young farmers, in their 20s and 30s, eager to get back to work and having seen what the military were doing to people, "would definitely be keeping on the right side of the law."

We walked and talked for over an hour before finally arriving on the edge of a village. The first person we met, a man in his fifties perhaps, emerged from a small house that was surrounded by trees and set back a little way from the road. He was known to one of the lads and seemed a kind, gentle character, rather less imposing than the younger group, and on hearing my ideas he came forth with a very satisfactory plan. He would take me to Koia in his boat for F$30 (£10), we would meet the chief and the villagers there and then come back before dark. I could then stay the night in his house and catch the 7am bus back to Savusavu in the morning. This was, as they say, a result, particularly at a time when a scoreless draw was looming rather large. He went off to get the boat ready and the six of us trickled into the village, sat under the trees, ate fruit, and sheltered from the afternoon sun. It was here that a couple of the lads had a quiet word in my ear: they had no money for the ferry and anything I could do to help would be very much appreciated. I promised to give it some thought.

The sky changed very much for the worse and with it my mood. Torrential rain soon took over, we scurried into an empty house for cover, sat on the wooden veranda and just watched it pour endlessly from the charcoal sky. Then my friendly boatman re-appeared to make the inevitable announcement: our trip to Koia would not be possible on account of the weather, I'd be better staying in this house with the boys until morning. News had arrived via the bush telegraph that their ferry would leave at 07.30, so we were all in the same boat, so to speak. And with that he showed me a small room with a bed and promised to arrange my dinner that evening.

It could have been worse, but it could also have been a bloody sight better. Having my own room was a bonus, those guys did make me a little nervous, but it was as dreary and uncomfortable as hell, not to mention the cocktail of stains on the single grubby sheet. It was 3.30pm, what was I going to do for the next fifteen hours? And who was I going to give my sevusevu to? The boatman? – but he didn't really live in the village. The lads? – but they were just guests too. Nobody? – but what would I do with a bag of powder? I hadn't really seen anybody else, at least not a potential sevusevu recipient.

I decided to give it to the lads, they had after all helped to find me a place to stay. The gift was well received, ten eyes opened widely with delight as I produced the little bag and we all went for a siesta with the promise of a kava session that evening. Perhaps things wouldn't be so bad after all.

We all sat round in a circle watching the kava being prepared. The rain had stopped, it was getting dark now, but the village had no fuel to power its generator. So we sat there in the flicker of the candles and watched as the powder was wrapped in a cloth and submerged into a plastic bowl full of water, the master of ceremonies wringing it out to extract the maximum flavour. He was very happy to pose for my photos and the snapping ceremony gave me every excuse to keep my camera and bag of valuables constantly in sight.

Two of the five lads had gone to another village, but more locals had appeared in their place along with the friendly boatman. The kava was finally ready, everybody sat in perfect silence, and with great expectation the cup was filled and handed to the first person in the circle. He clapped his hands once, drunk it down in one, then clapped three times more. No comment followed, nothing even along the lines of "a bloody good drop of kava is that".

The cup was then refilled, passed to the next person and so it went round. Silence, clapping, drinking, more clapping. Occasional conversation, but only in whispers. And then it was my turn. I clapped hands, looked at the muddy liquid and drained the cup as quickly as possible. It didn't quite make me gag, that's the best I can say about it, but the taste of it was unquestionably muddy liquid-like. In truth it didn't have any effect at all, though I was assured that after a good few bowlfuls of the sludge one's mouth gets numb, speech becomes hard work and sleep finally takes over. All the makings of a really great night out.

Thankfully there was a pause between each round and no pressure on me to partake every time. The guy to my left never missed his turn, I noticed. He was a big man in his twenties with strong features and straighter hair than most people there. His face was new to me and when we got whispering it transpired that he was in fact from Koia, his ancestors were Polynesian and his mother tongue was Tuvaluan. I almost hugged him and punched the air with delight, I might not have made it to the island, but this guy's presence as a fellow kava drinker was enough in my simple mind to render the mission a success after all.

Two hours of hushed conversation and kava was enough for me and when a lady came to offer dinner I jumped at the chance of a change of scene. Everybody else wanted to carry on the session so just Maria and I walked in torchlight, barefoot through ankle-deep mud to her house across the field. Her home was immaculately tidy, a wooden building that reminded me of a large garden shed. The centre of the living room was completely empty, just a rug in the middle, a partition at the far end created the bedrooms and another on the right hand side formed a kitchen area. There was the usual items of furniture around the outside of the room, but no table I noticed. In an armchair sat a man in his late sixties, Maria's father and the chief of the village. We talked as Maria prepared the meal.

He was a pleasant and very polite gentleman, though nothing at all 'chiefly' about him. Did I really expect feathers and a painted face? We chatted about village life and his role and responsibilities as head of the community. "Even the chief has to go out in the fields and dig up his own dinner these days," he commented rather sombrely, obviously referring to former times when his position was greatly revered. Maria then came back in, laid a table cloth on the floor in the centre of the rug and placed my dinner of tinned meat, crackers and breadfruit upon it. They had eaten some hours earlier, she'd been out to buy this for me.

To receive such hospitality from complete strangers is a very humbling experience. Maria and her father were great company and clearly very knowledgeable people – living in a village with no television, telephone and only a limited supply of electricity had certainly not hampered their education. I ate as much of the food as I could to be polite then Maria escorted me back to check my room had been prepared to her liking. Even though, I hasten to add, she wouldn't be staying.

* * * * *

I locked the door behind me and sat on the bed, while the boys next door guzzled bowl after bowl of kava. What a day they'd had, released from custody in the morning, supping kava in a strange village at night. Would this be as unusual for them as it was for me? Did they really have no money? It was hard to know, but I figured that for me to pay their fares home would be a decent gesture. It could wait until morning, but anyway I took out the cash for them, stuffed it in my shorts and packed my little bag ready for the early departure. Then I lay down and waited for morning.

The mattress was no more than three inches thick and the slats beneath created the effect of lying on a ladder. Sleep seemed highly unlikely, so when the lads next door decided to turn the radio on at an outrageous volume I just lay there and grinned to myself and enjoyed the classics of yesteryear brought to us by Fiji Gold. What the hell, tomorrow I'd be back in my comfy four-poster.

I must have fallen asleep eventually because something caused me to wake up suddenly. It was daylight and something in my room had just … moved. Yes, it was the door, my bedroom door, just two metres away. It was closing! Somebody had managed to open it and … Oh no, please no. No, no, no.

Yes. The bag had gone and with it my money, passport, tickets, the lot. I leapt off the bed, only seconds behind whoever had taken it, but there was no sign of any movement. Three of the Tavueni lads were sleeping in a row, were there any other rooms? I ran outside through the swampy grass, my throat dry, a complete state of panic. Maria, lovely Maria, had been on her way over to check all was OK and now she was standing right there in front of me. Her reaction at the news can only be described as one of absolute horror.

Her father was soon at her shoulder and within minutes he and I were walking to the next village to get a lift to the nearest police station. We were there before the officers arrived for work and then had to wait again for them to locate their only vehicle. I wanted things to happen quickly, to get my bag back, though in reality I knew I'd never see it again. And of course, things don't happen quickly in places like Fiji.

Eventually the police took us back to the house in a pick-up truck and then loaded the vehicle with a search party of men from the village. Maria had been told by the Sleeping Three which one of the other two was responsible, that he had wanted to rob me in broad daylight the previous afternoon, but they had talked him out of it. He had come down from the other village at daybreak to do the deed and now he had disappeared into the forest. And as they were now fearful of being implicated, they too would have to make themselves scarce.

Poor Maria was overwhelmed with shock and guilt. Shock because there had never been a crime there in over a hundred years of the life of the village, guilt because she had felt uneasy about the five from Taveuni and had considered telling me to sleep in her own house. "Don't worry," she assured me, "they will find him, beat him, and bring him to justice. You can be sure of that." And with that she went to make some breakfast for me and her father. All we could do now was sit and wait. Her assurances didn't exactly fill me with glee.

The sunny morning had again turned black and all I could do was sit in Maria's house and watch the rain come tumbling down. There was nothing, absolutely nothing I could do but wait. Time dragged, really dragged, but after maybe an hour the police vehicle came back in to view. I tried to imagine what the officers might say to me or what news they would report, and as they got closer I could see they were alone in the cab. No sign of the thief. (Bad. He was still on the run). No search party. (Good, they were still searching!).

Like something out of a silent movie I sat next to the road, watched the vehicle approach from the left, saw the driver wave as he went past, watched the vehicle disappear away to my right and become a blob in the distance. He didn't even stop, but why would he if there was nothing to say? Maria assured me they would be on their way to search the buses and the ferry.

Time dragged even more, one hour, two hours, God knows how many hours. No news at all. Morning became afternoon, the rain got heavier and heavier. Things looked bleak and I was feeling well and truly robbed. What the hell was I going to do? What was I waiting for? What did I really expect to happen? I tried to think clearly, formulate a plan, though my options were so extremely limited it really shouldn't have taken that long.

The Four-Letter Countries

There was a 4pm bus to Savusavu from a village maybe 5kms away and I still had the money in my pocket to pay the lads' ferry fares. (The bastards.) But there was no car or telephone in this village and the rain was so heavy it looked impossible to stand up in, let alone walk for over an hour dressed in a T-shirt. How would I even get as far as the bus? The chief, bless him, wanted to do anything in his power to help, and he had an idea. He would speak to the friendly boatman, borrow his outboard and together we would sail across the bay. All I would have to do was cover the cost of the fuel.

And that's exactly what we did, huddled under umbrellas in the driving rain, we went out to sea and landed at a slipway further up the mainland. The chief could have been forgiven for then turning round and heading straight back home, the sky was as black as night, but he escorted me on to the street and delivered me to a lady's house where I could wait for the bus without getting soaked even further. Then he looked straight at me and I could see this poor old man had tears in his eyes. He embraced me as though I was his own son, mumbled the words "God bless you," planted a gentle kiss on my cheek then turned and walked back out into the torrential rain.

That kind, sweet man made me feel so very much better and reflect that thankfully there is still so much good in the world. My bag of possessions was not, in the grand scheme of things, that important and it was time for me to stop feeling so damned sorry for myself. I was an idiot to have carried valuables and documents unnecessarily, not something that I normally did. So why DID I have all that stuff with me? Even my driving licence for God's sake, for a so-called experienced traveller this was amateurish in the extreme. Embarrassment had now well and truly taken over from self pity, but it didn't help me feel very much better.

And then the journey back. Yes, sitting in wet clothes on a cold bus made me feel very miserable indeed. The world had become one shitty place again and the wry smile I managed when the police boarded the vehicle to search for my stolen bag had long since vanished by the time we pulled into Savusavu. But I was back unharmed, surely that was the main thing? And I had some clean, fresh clothes to look forward to at Beat's place, and I still had a few dollars, and I had the name of the chief's brother in the Savusavu CID. Come on, it could have been a whole lot worse.

Taking a hot shower, changing into warm, dry clothes and sending a series of e-mails had the pleasing effect of regaining an element of control. I even slept surprisingly well that night and by the time the sun came up I was ready to get stuck in to the tedious tasks required of any robbery victim. The first of which was to explain to Beat why I couldn't pay him. I had planned to fly back to Nadi that morning, but the helpful lady at the Air Fiji office got me on to the afternoon flight, let me use her phone to make a few calls and then kindly stored my bag while I went to visit Savusavu CID. I really didn't expect to achieve anything by going to the police station, but couldn't bring myself to leave without one last throw of the dice.

Against all my expectations The Story of The Blue Bag was known to everybody there and Tony, the Chief's brother, was on the case. He assured me that the police in Taveuni would collar the perpetrator if he turned up there, the foreign exchange bureaux would call if he tried to change my US Dollars and his own men in Savusavu were checking out all known contacts. They knew exactly who this man was and he would definitely not get away.

I assured Tony that I'd be phoning in for news and was just about to shake his large hand good-bye when a call came in on his mobile. The raised palm indicated that I should wait, then it became a fist with his fat right thumb sticking up in the air. The thief was here in Savusavu – they were going to nail him right now!

My instructions were to sit in the shade and wait till they got back. Another gentleman was sitting there too and I gleaned from a few minutes' conversation that he was a very senior policeman, Head of

The Four-Letter Countries

Crime for the island, no less. A very distinguished and well-educated man, it transpired that he had been at the heart of the investigations into the earlier coups of 1987 and 2000, and to have his views on the current military intervention was fascinating. The army had effectively just set up their own offices as a parallel service to the police and were making no secret of their brutal treatment of criminals. But it was common knowledge that more and more innocent people were also taking beatings. "You see, Fiji is a small country, everybody is related to one another and with each miscarriage of justice the public support for the army will quickly diminish. At least the police ensure that everybody gets a fair trial."

No sooner had he finished speaking than the police car screeched up the gravel path. My first reaction was to check they had the right man, but within seconds the handcuffed figure, shirt and legs covered in mud, was rolling on the lawn and a uniformed military man was jabbing his large shiny boots repeatedly into the small of his back. This was obviously a joint police and army effort.

I walked over to where this was happening and realised the face was definitely one I'd seen before. Was it really only yesterday? He'd already confessed to stealing the bag and the interrogation process was now supposedly focusing on its whereabouts. The rag doll on the ground was now being systematically stamped on: fingers, ankles, fingers again and each attempt to speak only met with an even more violent response. The swarthy army officer, now bare-chested (but still with beret) and soaked in sweat from his exertions, delivered a volley of abuse with each downward movement of his heel. He snarled and ranted, teeth clenched in rage. This seemed personal to him and he even switched languages from Fijian to English to keep me included: "We are the Interim Government and you will be punished for what you have done". Then more of the shiny boot into ribs, back, ankles, fingers.

I'm all for being tough on criminals, but this was sheer brutality. I stepped in to exercise my right to question the suspect, a little fearful that this intervention might also be deemed the action of an enemy of the state. To the surprise (and did I detect disappointment?) of the military guy, I opted for dialogue instead of blood and this did achieve my two unstated goals: to stop the beating and to find out where my bag was.

The police then formed a circle, questioned the thief, made notes of the answers and gave him the occasional punch on the chin for good measure. He had brought shame on their country and they were going to make absolutely sure he never did it again. My bag, after all that, had been hidden in the trees back up in the village where he'd stolen it.

I was certainly buoyed at the prospect of recovering my stuff, but almost equally deflated by the grotesque spectacle on the lawn of the police station. To think that this show was routine fare for members of the public was a chilling thought and I couldn't help wonder what the little girl with her mother had made of it all as they'd wandered innocently by. It really was the blackest of black comedies and I decided that the three hours I had before my flight to Nadi would best be spent on the terrace of the Bula Ré Café. A little gem of a caff this, with a breeze off the water if you were lucky and a severe mosquito attack if you weren't.

Three hours passed so very quickly as I made notes of all that had happened and ate lunch that I could now probably afford. How life had so very quickly drifted into a fantasy world with time and places distorted out of all proportion like those funny mirrors at the seaside. My watch had been stolen too, just to add to the confusion, and it was only when I asked the waitress the time did I realise that my flight was due to leave in the next fifteen minutes!

Surely, after all this, I wasn't going to miss the only plane with spaces on board. The taxi driver at least seemed to find the whole thing very amusing, thoroughly enjoying his role in the final scene of this cheap action movie. Screeching tyres, passenger running in and out to fetch bags, the challenge of trying to beat the incoming plane to the tarmac. It was a fitting end to a bizarre few days and the sight of a very sweaty man with a mosquito-damaged foot limping across the runway must indeed have been a joy to behold. An end to the chapter and one that certainly made me smile, perhaps even laugh, but only once the plane had been airborne for at least twenty minutes.

* * * * *

Getting back to the main island felt like a fresh start, another trip almost, and for that I was thankful. My mind couldn't wash away everything that had happened, but my feelings towards Fiji and its warm, hospitable people were nothing but positive. The theft of my bag was a freak event, an incident that had to be put into context and left behind. Tony confirmed by phone that the police had found it with all the contents and I could go to pick it up from Nadi airport. I'd been so very lucky to get everything back, a new adventure was soon about to begin and, a little to my surprise, I was really looking forward to my tour round Viti Levu.

I got back into my maps and books and read a great story about Captain Cook. The legendary seafarer had been sailing westwards across the Pacific in 1774 and stopped off in Tonga where he enquired as to the name of the next group of islands. "Viti" came the reply in what must have been a thick Tongan accent (would that be bordering on a lisp?) because Cooky got his consonants badly mixed up. He thought the answer had been "Fiji" and that's the name in English that has been used ever since.

The Suzuki I hired was like a mini jeep with 4WD and all being well would not get stuck on mountains or beaches or lead me into any sort of crisis. Drama-avoidance was the name of the game for a while, so it was an Extra Cautious Old Hector that drove slowly through Nadi town, past the enormous Hindu temple and out along the Queens Road towards the south of the island.

Traffic soon thinned out to nothing and the countryside was as lush as ever. It took little more than an hour to reach Sigatoka, the first major point on the map and, according to my morning copy of the

Fiji

Fiji Times, venue for the Colonial Cup rugby match between Crusaders and Knights. Sure enough I soon spotted the groups of pedestrians heading towards the Lawaqa Park stadium so I parked up, paid my F$5 at the turnstile and found a place to sit on the terraces just as the game kicked off.

The Fijians love their rugby and it was great to see men, women, indeed whole families cheering with such enthusiasm. The atmosphere in the single stand was more like a children's party with laughing spectators and very un-Twickenham like high-pitched screams, everybody having a thoroughly good day out. It was serious sport though, selection for the national side to compete for the World Cup was at stake, and the home side came from behind to win a thrilling match in the dying minutes. From now on, I decided, Crusaders is my team.

The Coral Coast on the south west of the island offers all the natural beauty a tourist could dream of and dawn to dusk sunshine for eight months of the year. In the other four months anything can happen, rain may fall for hours or weeks and sea breezes can turn into hurricane force winds at the drop of a hat. So when the sky was at its blackest and the palm trees struggling to stay upright, I should have known better than to ask the receptionist how long the bad weather was likely to last. "Until April, sir," came the very earnest reply. Not exactly the answer you're looking for in the middle of February.

It's fair to say I didn't see the Coral Coast at its best, though the fierce howling of the wind and the crashing of the waves brought a sort of wild excitement into the emptiness of the hotel. But in truth, rainy days at the seaside are pretty miserable anywhere in the world aren't they, particularly when there's not even the diversion of Mr Punch beating the shit out of Judy. It would soon be time to head into the mountains and, according to my map, this was the ideal place to start out.

Over the next twenty four hours the weather changed from torrential rain to persistent drizzle, the sort of grey, dreary day my Mum and her tireless Mancunian optimism would describe as "quite nice, really". It was certainly improving and spirits were lifted sufficiently to prepare for the next leg with a burst-ette of enthusiasm.

No two maps of Fiji look exactly the same, which is a disappointing effort for a country with very few roads. However, it was reassuring to see that they all show a road from the south of the mainland that cuts north and then loops east and if I were to just keep going along that it would eventually drop down and lead into Suva, the capital of Fiji and the largest metropolis in the South Pacific. That was the plan, anyway.

The little turning off the highway seemed too insignificant to be the road on my map, but it was at least in the right place. It pointed inland towards the cloud-topped mountains and soon became a pot-holed track that rocked the jeep from side to side and made anything above second gear seem positively reckless. Progress was slow, very slow and not at all comfortable. The road passed a couple of villages at the lower levels and traversed precarious bridges over the rivers but as it climbed onwards and upwards between the trees all sign of human life quickly evaporated. The semi-rain continued to pester the windscreen and the potholes were growing larger by the minute – it was all just beginning to feel rather remote. I started to ask myself what I'd do in the event of a mechanical problem (I can't even figure out how to work the radio on my own car) and the only solution that came to mind was to stay put for as long as it took, suck water from leaves and try to snare fat lizards.

Despite the worsening terrain and increasing steepness the little Suzuki didn't let me down. In fact I must have been going for the best part of two hours without seeing another soul when something quite unexpected loomed before me. It was a fork in the road, without a signpost as such, but bizarrely there was a plaque introducing the left-hand track as Wainadiro Road. A simple thing to you, perhaps, but the prospect of finding some life in the mountains definitely got the better of my gut instinct which had been to head the other way. The road was a mess, full of enormous holes, and it started to weave quite steeply downhill. But not for long. A big wide, brown river saw to that. I pulled up, stretched my legs under the drizzly skies and watched the mass of murky water racing from left to right in front of me. It was then that I realised with some excitement there was a village on my left hand side.

The locals were delighted to see me, not because I'm such a great bloke, but because village people, when not waving their arms about singing YMCA, are always pleased when strangers drop in. Within minutes I was sitting in a wooden house with a couple of pregnant ladies, their small army of surprisingly snot-free children and various scythe-carrying men who popped in to have a break from scything. These chaps would all be family members because, when there's only two hundred of you, there is really only one family.

No surprises to learn that this village was Wainadiro and one of three adjacent communities on the river bank. They had their own school and church, as was the norm, an endless supply of fruit and vegetables to pick and dig for a living, fresh fish from the river and the facility of a boat service down to the coast three times a week. What an amazing place to live. No wonder they all seemed so happy.

Apart from intrepid folk that canoe and raft down the river, it's no surprise that few visitors drop in to Wainadiro. Though it did come to light during our conversation that ten minutes away there was an English lady living in a small lodge, only accessible by boat, and yes, they would be happy to take me there. How very curious. "OK, let's go."

Jenny divided her life between the upper reaches of the River Navua and Sutton Coldfield, 24 hours by plane separating the sublime from the utterly ridiculous. The sight of a fellow countryman emerging from the riverbank and even carrying an umbrella was, she confirmed, a rare event indeed, so the tea and Custard Creams were ceremonially introduced to mark the occasion. This had been Jenny's adopted home for a few months of each of the last few years, one of three small self-contained buildings that were now officially a guest-house. The owner came over to join us, a delightful man who had grown up in the area and had just returned from a life on the seas in the Fiji Navy. It was a surreal occasion, tea and biscuits on an isolated stretch of river in the Fijian high-lands with a lady from the West Midlands. Not what I had imagined when I'd set out that morning.

Nor could I have imagined receiving an invitation to lunch. A tradi-tion amongst the villagers of Wainadiro is that every Monday all the members of their community eat together, albeit in several sittings, and I was privileged to be asked to sit down on the floor and join the circle of men. The ladies placed a line of hot dishes in the middle: fish with spinach, cassava, sweet potatoes and all sorts of things I couldn't pronounce or identify, then they retreated into the background. A lovely atmosphere and great fun to talk to the men of each generation, all rugby fanatics, two of the lads professional players based in New Zealand and just home for a family visit. Again I was struck by the worldliness of the young people from what seemed one of the remotest places on the globe, a great credit to the education and discipline that is so evidently a part of their village lives.

When rugby stories finished and we moved on from world politics there came, of course, the cannibal jokes. "So how did you guys actually kill your victims before they went in the pot?" I was curious to know. At which point one of them got up, left the room and returned with a huge smile on his face. "With these," he said proudly, holding up a large chunk of wood that resembled a baseball bat and a short, heavy, nasty-looking instrument with a ball on the end. Poor old Reverend Thomas Baker, he'd only gone to Fiji to lend a hand.

* * * * *

The journey back didn't seem nearly so long. Thanks to the goodfolk of Wainadiro I learned that there was indeed a road to the eastern side of the island, but it was divided into two parts by the enormous river and there had never been a bridge to cross it. A detail that would have been so handy on the map – how many other people, I wondered, had attempted this impossible mountain route? There was only one way to Suva and that was back the way I'd come.

An elderly gentleman of the village took the rare opportunity of a car ride and I dropped him at his son's home in Navua, the first town of any note along the coast. What a joy to drive on flat, paved roads once again. Even the rain had finally stopped, and within two hours of leaving the mountains I was in the capital city.

By Fijian standards, Suva is big. Given that it's home to almost half the country's population and ten times larger than any other town or city, a short visit was pretty much obligatory. And in view of my recent discovery, a circumnavigation of the island was nigh on impossible anyway without passing through Suva at its roughly twenty-past-the-hour location.

A B&B perched on a hill overlooking the city came highly recommended and didn't disappoint. In fact the Suva Homestay was most definitely the best thing about Suva, a lovely old house with wonderful views from the deck that peer down on the peculiar hotchpotch of a city. A couple of hours downtown was really quite enough, little more than a drab collection of third world shops without the chaos or charisma, a scattering of ghastly tower blocks and a couple of unkempt parks. A sort of pre-war Poland with palm trees. To be fair there were a few splendid colonial buildings and the ANZ bank was quite trendy, but that's a scraping of the barrel if ever there was one.

There was no good reason to hang around in Suva, something that the issuing of a temporary passport would have forced upon me, so I followed the signs for the Kings Road and headed north for the top right-hand corner of the island. It soon became a bumpy, untarred surface, the only broken section of the circular highway, but there was plenty of action in terms of small villages and churches and occasionally, in the middle of nowhere, incongruously large, handsome school buildings. And always hundreds of smiling children in impeccable school uniforms, waving frantically and screaming "Bula!" (Welcome!) at the top of their voices.

The Four-Letter Countries

Even a group of road workers at a traffic signal downed tools to wander over for a "Bula!", ask where I was from and wish me a pleasant trip. Warm, genuine, hospitable people.

The countryside then started to change a little, open out into rolling hills and grazing cattle, a tropical Yorkshire Dales. The road was smooth now, the sea had come back into view, once again it was all turning into something pretty spectacular. A pity that the weather was still a little grey and daylight was disappearing fast, but, as always happens with night ... another day soon follows.

* * * * *

The sun was up at 6am and I was exactly where I wanted to be. On the northern-most tip of the mainland, looking out at that gorgeous turquoise water to the string of islands across the bay with the catapult-shaped and delightfully named Nananu-i-Ra taking centre stage. This was the stunning view I'd had from the plane and it must surely be up there as one of the most beautiful places on Earth.

I climbed up into the green hills behind, the sun and wind now really bashing into my face, and soon reached a small cluster of newly-built villas perched on the top of the peak. They were all still unoccupied except for the sales lady waiting for clients, but I guarantee that won't be the case for long. This was state-of-the-art luxury with views that had to be seen to be believed. A true 360 degree experience, raw beauty, nature bringing together almost everything that it has to offer in one little corner of the globe. And to think those gorgeous villas cost roughly the same as a two bedroom terraced house in Peckham!

There were in fact several plots of land for sale almost by the water's edge and if I'd been a wealthy property developer I'd probably have bought them all. If this was anywhere else on the planet surely all the major hotel chains would be there, perhaps a good thing after all that Fiji is thousands of miles away from most of the rest of the world.

The landscape along the north of the island was more of the same rolling hills and jagged peaks in the distance. The highest one in Fiji was just about visible though shrouded in mist at the top – did I have it in me to get a guide and walk for a few hours to the top of Mt Victoria? Mr Positive said it was only 1,323m above sea-level and a chance I might never get again. Mr Negative countered that the heat and humidity was stifling and the views would inevitably be hampered by the swirling mist. I listened carefully and objectively to the arguments presented by both sides and finally reached an informed decision – I couldn't be arsed walking up a mountain.

So I drove up one instead, to a village 20kms inland. It doesn't sound very far does it, but everything in life is relative: if you had to walk barefoot on broken glass for 20kms it would seem a hell of a long way. Ditto the track up to Navala. It was punishing stuff – in the absence of any signs I couldn't even be sure it was the right road – but the scenery was very special and I felt sure the effort would be well worth it. *Lonely Planet* had rated the village of Navala as one of the prettiest in Fiji, a fact that no doubt accounts for the peculiar events which were shortly to follow.

I'd just spotted several rows of thatched huts in the valley ahead when a lady mysteriously appeared at the side of the road and flagged me down. "Are you going in to the village?" she asked in a tone devoid of the usual warmth. "No, I'm going to see the Coliseum, actually," was tempting, but I figured she wouldn't have heard of it anyway. "Then that will be $15". What! Forking out the equivalent of a fiver to look at a village! It just seemed so utterly wrong. But, When in Rome ...

I pulled up at the village gate, more of a field really with orderly rows of thatched huts like a holiday park, and a lady wandered over. Had I paid and had I brought any sevusevu for the chief she wanted to know above all else. A Yes to both got me a token gesture of an escorted tour round the village then she suggested, or rather stipulated, that we should go to drink the kava. "So where is the Chief?" I asked, getting a bit fed up with all this surly stuff. "The Chief? Oh we don't have a chief at the moment. He died about 20 years ago and we didn't replace him". This was not Fijian hospitality at all, it was a tawdry commercialised rip-off, and chieflessness really was the last straw.

It hadn't been a complete waste of time, though. At least I'd enjoyed watching the men build a new 'bure', the traditional Fijian house with walls of bamboo, a thatched roof and an open doorway on three sides that gives them light and ventilation. There are no windows at all and I was pleasantly surprised to find how cool it was inside one when a few of us gathered for the afternoon tipple, another session of clapping hands and ritual pouring of more of that ghastly muddy liquid down our throats.

* * * * *

There was one other village I wanted to get to. Abaca is on the north west of the island in the steeper mountains of the Koroyanitu National Heritage Park and by all accounts only about half an hour of bouncy road. I wouldn't say I was completely at the end of my tether with potholes and lumpy surfaces, but not a great deal of tether remained and I could sense my Suzuki days were drawing to a close.

It proved a very pretty little village trying its best to encourage tourism, but this time in a gentle and pleasing manner. There was a small hut to offer visitors information on local walking trails, and the young lady within, a medical student trying to pay her way through college, couldn't do enough to help. Sadly for all concerned the eco-tourist project she was trying to drive had just suffered a severe blow: the one man taxi service that had ferried tourists up and down the mountain for years had withdrawn his labour and nobody else was eager to take the job on. One look at that road was easy to see why.

Fiji

Her other news was of an incident that had occurred two weeks earlier. A small aircraft piloted by a 21 year old man on his maiden flight had crashed into the mountains above the village and she'd had the gory task of trying to rescue him and the Canadian couple still in the cockpit. Tragically none of the three had survived and most of the recent visitors to Abaca had been TV crews, investigators and journalists looking for a story.

On that sombre note I took a map and followed the trail across the river and up the mountain on the other side of the valley. It was hard going, the path had become seriously overgrown, but the lovely smell of the passion fruit trees and the views across the national park with the bright blue sea beyond more than made up for the soaking shirt and the salty sweat in the eyeballs. The island groups out to the north and west were now clearly in view – the Mamanucas and the Yasawas – and oh, how I dearly wanted to be out there. It was time to feel the coolness of that water, to sample island life, to take it easy for a few days. To do what most normal, sensible people do when they come to Fiji. Relax, have fun. Not sweat their bollocks off half way up a mountain in the heat of the day! And with that thought very firmly in my mind I bounded rather quickly down the slope, jumped aboard the Suzuki and headed once again in the direction of Nadi.

The Yasawa Flyer is a big yellow launch that pulls out of Nadi every morning, delivers people and produce around the delightful chain of islands and returns back to port some nine hours later. It's a bright, comfortable, modern vessel and most of those on board tend to be young backpackers stopping off in Fiji on round-the-world tickets. The waters are calm and the scenery idyllic, the journey not just a means to an end but an experience in itself. An absolutely perfect way to travel except, that is, for the pounding music pumped through speakers, on every deck, for every minute of the voyage. Can you sense a Grumpy Old Man moment coming on?

I tried all parts of all decks, but they had me well and truly cornered. Like it or not my morning cruise was a floating disco and a little spot down in the hold right next to the engines was the only place that offered any sort of refuge. This was the moment I realised that middle-age was setting in. Correction, had well and truly set in. But should we really have to put up with this round-the-world round-the-clock obligation to listen to music on phones and in lifts and shops and telephones and supermarkets and now on boats for God's sake? I pledge I'll do it one day, I'll set up FARTES, Freedom And Right To Enjoy Silence. And no prizes for guessing what the senior members of my organisation will be called.

Where was I? Oh yes. The answer in the end was an iPOD and music of my own choosing (a little classical number) then everything was just fine and dandy. I stood on deck and lapped up the heat of the sun on my face as we chugged through the transparent water and those tiny green islands with white, empty beaches. And behind me the mainland, the mountains of the day before. I thought again about Abaca and the couple from the village who were so grateful for the lift I'd given them on my way back down the mountain. The poor lady had a tooth infection and would have it removed at Lautoka hospital, then they'd take the plastic bag of kava they were carrying to sell in the market to pay for a taxi ride home. And here's me, having a moan about the music on the boat.

The Flyer stops maybe twenty times in each direction and then dinghies from the islands collect and ferry people into shore. Little happens in these places other than tourism, the main difference between one resort and the next is that some promote more of a "party" atmos-phere. You know, drinking, dancing, having sex with strangers, smoking a bit of blow, watching the stars, that sort of thing. So I opted for the Victor Meldrew Island where everybody goes to bed at 9.30 and getting hard means taking on tougher sudoku. It was actually called Naviti, one of the islands in the middle of the Yasawa chain and, according to my book, where a few hundred native Fijians still followed their traditional lifestyles.

The Yasawas was a logical choice. I must admit there had been a minor temptation to fly out to some of the remoter islands heading east towards Tonga, but would I really have seen anything very different for my troubles? This closer group was reputedly more beautiful than all the others, easier to get to, and – a big one this – they were the driest. If you were born in Manchester, you don't go to Fiji in search of rain.

* * * * *

When one is greeted by three men standing on a pontoon in the open sea, each wearing a skirt, a flower behind his ear and playing a musical instrument, there is a sense of having discovered something a little out of the ordinary. It's a tradition that the Botaira resort extends to all arriving guests as they transfer to shore and even I didn't whinge about this little musical interlude.

My new home was one of a dozen or so bures nestled in a row of palm trees on the edge of the beach, a half kilometre strip of unblemished pale yellow sand. Before even going inside I just stood there on the small shaded patio, mesmerised at the sheer beauty and tranquillity of it all. The transparent blue-green sea only twenty paces ahead, the spotlessly clean beach, the white and purple and yellow flowers growing wild amongst the trees and bushes. I couldn't see another person, the only difference between this and a calendar photograph was the soft shoooosshing sound of the sea lapping against the shore. The sun was high and the sky at last a brilliant shade of blue. This was more like it.

There were so many things to do and decisions to make I just didn't know where to start. Would I sit in the deck chair by my door or lie in the hammock strung up between the trees? Or would I go for a snorkel, or even try to find a kayak to explore the bay? That would be pushing the boat out. My thoughts were interrupted by the beating of a drum, as though I hadn't decided quickly enough and my time was up. In fact, this sound could only mean one of four things: Breakfast, Lunch, Afternoon Tea or Dinner.

The Four-Letter Countries

Lunch attracted a handful of other guests, presumably the only other people on this part of the island. A mad flurry of conversation followed where everybody swapped stories, experiences and itineraries and within an hour each had returned to their respective hammocks for a few more hours of isolation. This is the life that everybody dreams of isn't it. But was I going to enjoy it? Might it not get a teeny bit ... boring?

* * * * *

There is an animal under the surface of Fiji's waters that isn't found in many parts of the world. It's spiky and has tentacles with a vicious sting and can rip your body to shreds if you get too close, but the good news is that it won't attack you. It actually looks more like an enormous plant, it comes in a range of peculiar shapes and fantastic vivid colours and it attracts millions of other species of underwater life. It's called coral and it really has to be seen to be believed.

So with mask and snorkel firmly in place (carefully avoiding a repeat of The Oman Fiasco) I headed out to where the water was little more than two metres deep and ducked my head beneath the surface. Thanks to the flippers I was able to glide effortlessly through the clear water, like flying low over a jungle where all the trees are weird shapes and garish colours: incredibly bold blues, browns, purples, and reds. A vicious looking bed of needles was now within touching distance and swimming between them were literally thousands and thousands of fish, species ranging from the size of a finger nail to the length of an arm, some transparent, others seemingly every colour of the rainbow. I tried to follow the movements and behaviour of those sad loners that seemed so content just nibbling away at the coral and in contrast found myself in the middle of dense shoals so great in number that they would take several minutes to pass. And every one of them seemed entirely indifferent to my presence – isn't that absolutely remarkable given the size of a human being relative to such a tiny creature?

I stayed under the water for most of the afternoon, enjoying every second of the spectacle and hearing nothing more than the eerie, exaggerated sound of my own breathing through the snorkel. When I did finally emerge I was shocked by just how close to the beach I was and the realisation that these two worlds literally exist side by side, yet both are invisible to the other. I'd never quite thought of it like that before.

There was a village over the hill from the beach and as always lots of "Bulas!", smiling kids, and an enormous church, living proof that the missionaries did a great job converting Fiji to Christianity. There was a small school too, unfortunately not open the day I was there but the blackboards in the classrooms gave an insight into subjects they were studying.

What exactly is Convection?

What causes the wind to change direction?

What is the lowest level of the atmosphere?

Exactly. Fijians might live a simple existence, but backward they most certainly are not.

I liked the people very much; the Fijians had that special way of making you feel so welcome, and a couple of days later it was my good fortune to be there to share in the lovo. This is their banquet for special occasions, when all kinds of meat and vegetables are wrapped in foil and banana leaves and cooked in the ground for several hours. It was fascinating to watch the process: digging the pit, building the fire, heating the stones up and once the food had been added, leaving it all to smoulder under a huge pile of sand. Such a primitive way to cook, but these guys knew exactly what they were doing and the end result was fantastic.

As was the result the following day. The Fijians can sing, they can perform their scary war dances, they can cook and they can play rugby, all with considerable panache, but I am delighted to report that when it comes to the real game they were found sadly wanting. On my last day before heading home we, the white Europeans, challenged them to proper footie and proudly emerged as 18-2 winners. It was played on grass, but in bare feet and before you ask – no, I wasn't on the scoresheet, but I did play a very important role marshalling the back four.

The Fijians took defeat in their stride and laughed all the way through the afternoon. They are a happy people who live in a beautiful country and it had been my good fortune to be able to share their islands and their wonderful hospitality, albeit for just a few weeks. It was time for me to go, to make the journey to the other side of the world, the daunting prospect of a ten hour flight to LA and then the same again from there.

Was it worth it? I looked up at the jetty to see a trio of large men in skirts, flowers in their hair, smiles and ukuleles at the ready to bid me farewell. There was the answer, and I made myself a promise that one day, touch wood, I'd be coming back to the islands of Fiji.

IRAQ

It was back in 2001 when Ricky Gervais first introduced us to *The Office* and the cringe-inducing antics of the pathetic, eager-to-impress David Brent. A truly original approach to comedy, although at the time very few people realised that the character was actually based on a real life figure who, a few months earlier, had just landed a new job in Washington DC. How the world grinned and gasped in amazement when George W. Bush was declared the winner of the biggest election shambles ever seen outside central Africa.

Within days Tony Blair was over at the ranch to wish George well and to re-assure him that, whatever crackpot ideas he might dream up, the Brits would always be there at his beck and call. Those were the good days for TB, the sleazy antics of his freak-show cabinet had yet to be rumbled and the British taxpayers were still living the dream that one day they would get something back for the billions being sucked from their pockets. George had laid out his international strategy in no uncertain terms: the US would take over the world, starting in the Middle East with the oil-rich countries of Iraq and Iran. All they had to do was wait for an excuse to pounce.

A little further back in history, 1979 had turned out to be a hell of a year. A revolution in Iran resulted in the ruling Shah being booted out and hardline religious leader Ayatollah Khomeini returning from exile to transform the country into a strict Shia Islamic state. And it was in that same year, a few hundred miles further west in Baghdad, that Saddam Hussein, having risen through the ranks of the ruling Baath party and ousted the incumbent Ahmed Hassan al-Bakr, assumed the Presidency of Iraq; an office he was eager to abuse at the earliest possible opportunity.

Knowing that the Americans wouldn't support the Islamic dictatorship next door, Saddam seized his chance just a year into the job. Iraq invaded Iran, a country almost four times its size, and started a war that was to run for eight years with no outright winner and leave 200,000 men dead on both sides of the border. He then attacked the Kurds in the north of his country and the Kuwaitis to the south, finally forcing the US to switch sides and bomb him into submission as their own oil supplies from the latter state were threatened by his continuing rogue incursions. After six weeks of constant shelling, Iraq pulled back its troops and on the last day of February 1991 a ceasefire was agreed. Saddam the madman was down, but unfortunately he most definitely wasn't out.

* * * * *

The Kurds have their own language, their own cuisine, their own very distinctive style of dress, their own music. The only thing they don't have, and never have had, is their own country. It is a sorry tale of as many as 25 million people, half of whom live in the far east of Turkey, with the rest spread over adjacent borders in the mountainous northern regions of Iraq, Iran and Syria. Each group has had to fight its own cause against their respective governments, hence a united struggle to create a single Kurdistan has always been something of a patchy and fragmented effort.

Post-Saddam, one small but fragile achievement has been the (almost) autonomous control of three of Iraq's eighteen states (governerates) in the north of the country. This is known as Iraqi Kurdistan, it is patrolled by a Kurdish army, run by a Kurdish regional government and flies the Kurdish flag with pride. A sensitive situation to say the least, as the Arabs to the south and the Turks to the north resent their very existence and are determined to fight against any suggestion of a fully independent Kurdistan.

Iraq

The blackest moment in the Kurds' long and troubled history came in 1988 when Saddam Hussein and his cousin Chemical Ali plotted the bombardment of Halabje, a small Kurdish town in the shadow of the mountains close to the Iranian border. It was a heinous act even by their gruesome standards. Five thousand innocent people, mostly women and children, were gassed to death on the streets of that town and those that survived were forced to flee their homes and live as refugees for the next three years. A tragic story and one to which, inevitably, we will have to return.

Against the will of the United Nations, and most of the rest of the world, George Bush and Tony Blair took the decision to start bombing Iraq on 20th March 2003. They garnered some support at home with stories of weapons of mass destruction and implications that a failure to invade would be to risk something akin to the eradication of the universe, but it soon transpired that US intelligence had not been so, erm, intelligent after all. In line with expert opinion the weapons simply did not exist and once again the Americans had started a war on a completely bogus pretext.

At least Saddam's nasty regime was quickly toppled and his long reign of terror brought to an end. The Kurds were understandably delighted and the pro-war campaigners in the West quickly moved the goalposts to claim his ultimate capture and arrest as justification for smashing the country to pieces. After a chaotic trial and months of wild ranting from the witness box, Saddam was finally executed, by his own people, on 30th December 2006 for (some of) his crimes against humanity.

Meanwhile Iraq had descended into total mayhem. As many as a million innocent people had lost their lives, Iraqis were killing and kidnapping each other every day of the week and regularly picking off the US and British troops that were stuck in the middle. Bush and Blair, now deeply unpopular figures, insisted that their armies would stay until the job was done, but unfortunately for all concerned nobody seemed to know exactly what the job was, let alone how it would ever be accomplished. It was indeed a sorry mess. This much most people on the planet will know, but, of course, it all had become so much more relevant to me since taking up the Four-Letter Country challenge. I'd now reached the point where I could avoid this deadly part of the Middle East no longer. I had just two countries left to visit: Iraq and Iran.

The daily news bulletins and death counts from Baghdad and Basra had me thinking that going to Iraq had all the makings of a silly idea. Yes, of course it was a Four-Letter Country and yes I did so want to complete this unusual journey, but was it worth getting blown up or held at gunpoint by masked men to plead for my life from the inside of an orange boiler suit? I thought long and hard about this and then, with the help of the internet, came up with a plan.

The good people of Iraqi Kurdistan had put together a website to promote the other face of their tortured country. Theirs was an area free of terrorism, a place that foreigners could safely visit and even think about investing their hard-earned cash. Honest. Normal things like trade shows and exhibitions were happening on a regular basis and business people from all over Europe were taking direct flights into the region. Mmmm ... could this be my chance?

I contacted the Kurdistan Development Corporation (KDC) and registered my interest in paying a visit. If my only route across the border was by dressing up as a business delegate then that's what it would have to be. After all, I did have a suit and a briefcase. The helpful lady assured me that she would keep in touch, she wouldn't forget me as she used to have a friend with the same name as mine. Would it come down to something as tenuous as that? (And what happened to him, I wondered?)

Time moved on, the violence in Iraq got steadily worse, no news from the KDC. It seemed the journey to the Four-Letter Countries could not be completed. Well, unless ... could I just apply for a tourist visa and turn up at the border? Did they have an immigration policy for people who aren't soldiers or journalists? I searched the web for information, sent e-mails to whoever might be able to help, and then something very, very unexpected happened. I found somebody trying to arrange an expedition to Iraq.

His name was Geoff Hann and his idea was to take a group of historians and archaeologists through northern Iraq and across the mountains into Iran. I couldn't believe my eyes, this was too good to be true. OK it would mean dedicating some time to ancient ruins and yes, looking at ancient ruins is about as exciting as listening to fishing on the radio, but what the hell. This was no time to start getting picky. He evidently had decades of experience under his belt, mostly in dodgy places, and would sort out the visas to get us over those tricky borders. Here was my chance: two FLC's for the price of one. I'm in Geoff, I'm in!

The group's first scheduled departure had to be put back, but our second target date looked reasonably promising. Geoff's contact in Iran sponsored our visas in return for a princely sum and the Kurds assured us they would let us over the Iraqi border even if Baghdad didn't agree to stamp our passports ahead of departure. I met Geoff in London to talk through the plan and once the money was handed over I realised, with more than a little trepidation, that there was no turning back. The next time we would meet would be in Diyarbakir, a place I'd never heard of in the far east of Turkey. All I needed now was to book myself on to some flights.

* * * * *

The cab picked me up at 04.30 on a crisp, clear Wednesday morning. A hint of daylight, even at that hour, a sure sign that summer was well on its way and the early gang were already at work building the stalls for the St Albans midweek market. 'An ordinary day in the safe world of a comfortable middle-class British town,' I couldn't help thinking, as I moved a step closer to Luton airport, Turkey, Iraq and Iran.

The Four-Letter Countries

Five hours later I was in Asia. An Easy Jet had flown the diagonal path across Europe to a small airport just east of Istanbul, the stunning city where the bridges over the Bosphorous join two so very different continents together. I hadn't been there for many years, that world of minarets and bazaars and sweet tea and carpets, and I'd actually forgotten what an enchanting place it is. A waterscape to rival that of Sydney, but with magnificent historical and religious buildings at every turn and that endless cobbly maze of shops and restaurants, each with a grinning man at the door and a story to lure you inside. I walked a lot, soaked up the warm spring sunshine and the next evening took the two hour flight from one side of Turkey to the other.

Diyarbakir is a long way from Istanbul in every sense. From a modern, thriving city on the edge of first world status, I found myself walking along pathways of rubble and looking into shops that were no more than market stalls in windowless alcoves. To be fair there were signs that they were trying to move forward, but there was little within those dark old walls that encase the city to inspire any visitor to hang around. It felt pretty sad and miserable to be honest, scruffy people looking bored, drinking tea, smoking a lot. The banter of the Bosphorous had been well and truly left behind; in toilet terms this was very much hole-in-the-floor territory. If Turkey ever joins the EEC, I couldn't help thinking, 'this backward outpost of Europe is the mighty challenge that lies ahead.'

The saving grace of the city was an elevated spot on its outer rim looking out at the surprisingly green countryside in all directions. From here I could see the Tigris, at this point just a small river setting out on its 1,100 mile journey southwards towards Baghdad and Basra, eventually to join its big brother the Euphrates and flow out into the Gulf. Exciting stuff, Tigris and Euphrates. Unmistakable geographical landmarks that have been there for thousands of years, the lifeblood of the ancient civilisations of Mesopotamia. They did great names in those days didn't they? Did you know Mesopotamia actually means The Land

Iraq

Between Two Rivers? (I didn't.) It was easy to get lost in all this romance, but once my feet were firmly back on the ground it all became a scary reminder of the direction that I too was about to follow. It's OK for rivers, what have they got to lose?

I met Geoff as agreed in the reception of a dour little hotel and introduced myself to a group of very English-looking people scattered around the threadbare chairs that constituted the lobby. I had wondered what sort of characters would choose to spend their precious holidays in Iraq and mentally prepared for the worst, but on first impressions at least they seemed quite normal, pleasant individuals. There were inevitably a few 'socks and sandals', but nothing in the way of folk-club beards, clip-boards or particularly embarrassing garments for which Brits of a certain ilk have become internationally renowned.

Over the kebabs, there had been plenty to talk about with my new friends, all of whom were completely up to speed with the story of the 800-kilo bomb that had exploded in Erbil the day before. What? Bomb? What fucking bomb? Erbil? Capital of ultra-safe customer-friendly never-a-problem Iraqi Kurdistan? The place we are heading towards tomorrow? Surely this had to be somebody's idea of a joke. But nobody had smiled or grinned or suddenly burst out laughing.

Geoff had seemed unruffled at the news, but did give us a very serious briefing to outline the difficulties that we might face, what to do in certain circumstances and how we should react and respond in the face of questioning. It was all starting to sound rather daunting and as we talked tactics I suddenly had the peculiar thought that this is what it must be like to plan a bank robbery.

It took us a little more than three hours to reach the Iraqi border, a pleasant journey through rolling green countryside, passing the sign for the city of Batman away to the left. In a minibus full of mature grown-up people I suppose I was the only one secretly hoping we might have a reason to go there, if only to see if it was twinned with a place some-where in the world called Robin. But it wasn't to be. We kept straight ahead, very straight indeed, eventually running parallel to a high mesh fence on the right side of the road and passing a watchtower on stilts every kilometre or so. This was, I eventually realised, the eastern-most end of Turkey's border with Syria, the point at which the three countries all come together.

* * * * *

The sign across the border reads 'Welcome to Iraqi Kurdistan' and the Turks don't like it one little bit. To them Kurdishness is synonymous with terrorism – as Britons used to view the republicans of Northern Ireland – and they simply refuse to acknowledge Kurdistan's existence. To them Iraq is Iraq, end of story, and if their own Kurds think that a grain of Turkish soil will ever be yielded to create a similar enclave then they have another think coming.

We'd been told to expect a grumpy departure from Turkish immigration (why do you want to go over *there*?) and a warm welcome from the Iraqi Kurds and yes, it all went pretty much as predicted. The Iraqis offered us smiles and cups of tea as they applied visas to our passports and then warm handshakes from the Minister for Tourism (Kurdish states) who had come personally to the border post to receive us. He would escort us to the city of Dohuk, but not before a visit to the immigration VIP lounge with icy air-con, leather sofas, outrageous chandeliers and, this time, very ornate cups for yet another round of tea.

I sat there in disbelief, staring at my new visa while passing the fancy sugar bowl to my neighbour on the sofa. I'd actually done it, whatever happened now I'd made it to Iraq, the cradle of civilisation and now FLC number 9. This was it, the country in which the first human settlements were built over 5,000 years ago, the home of the king with the most fantastic name of all time. Nebuchadnezzar. I swear if I ever have a son or a dog or even a budgie then that is what I'll call him. This stamp in my passport would allow travel anywhere inside the

Iraq

Kurdish-controlled area, essentially the north and north-east of the country; the English equivalent of arriving south across the border at Gretna Green with permission to travel in Cumbria, Northumberland and down as far as say North Yorkshire, with the added similarity that this is also Iraq's coolest, wettest and reputedly most picturesque region.

Our host delighted in telling stories of the economic successes of the Kurdish states, talking us through the swathe of new commercial buildings alongside the smart dual carriageway. The investment was certainly there for all to see. As was the huge American barracks where, he explained proudly, the troops could safely take refuge after weeks of duty in the dangerous Arab regions to the south. Iraqi Kurdistan, he assured us, was a beautiful place where people lived well and tourists could savour the magnificent scenery, enjoy warm Kurdish hospitality and walk the streets without fear. Not one of us had the heart to ask about the 800-kilo bomb.

We joined up with Highway 2, then hung a left for Dohuk rather than carrying straight on to Mosul (1.5hrs, probable death) or Baghdad (6 hrs, certain death). An orderly little town it was too, sitting in a pleasant green valley and exuding an air of cleanliness and tidiness that had been so absent in Turkey's east. We checked into what seemed like a brand new hotel on the outskirts of town then split into smaller groups. A few of us changed Dollars for Dinars from a shop where banknotes were stacked up in the window (what else do you put in the window if money is all you sell?) and then scoffed a kebab in an impeccably clean little caff. So this was it. Daily life in Iraq. And it all felt … well, normal, I suppose. Everyday-looking people wearing every day looking clothes doing every day sort of things. But what had I expected?

By the time we got back to the hotel the sky had turned dark and thunderclouds were gathering ominously. Geoff's briefing further darkened the mood. Tomorrow we would attempt to reach a Yezidi shrine (Yezidis being a minority branch of the Kurds, whose specific religious beliefs define their ethnicity), but we should be warned that some roads in the region might now be too dangerous to use and owing to recent developments there was also additional tension surrounding this particular ethnic group. A Yezidi girl had just been stoned to death for marrying a Muslim, so the husband had gunned down 12 Yezidis in a minibus by way of revenge. The Yezidis were now threatening a mass slaughter to set the record straight.

I lay on my bed and wondered – if you'll pardon the expression – what the fuck I was doing there. No, not the bed, a country where people blow each other up and stone each other to death and inflict all sorts of miseries upon one another in the name of religion and power and pride and tradition and heaven knows what else. Was I going to be snuffed out in pursuit of a sodding shrine owned by a group of people I'd never even heard of and – between you and I – couldn't really give a toss about? This was lunacy, absolute bloody madness.

Cheer up, get a grip, where's that radio? It was 7.15pm Saturday evening and when you are three hours ahead of UK that means the BBC World Service listener will shortly be welcomed to Radio 5Live's Premiership commentary. And would you believe I actually enjoyed listening to Sheffield United versus Wigan Athletic, the last-day-of-the-season drama that would see Neil Warnock's boys tumble to the Championship. It was such a welcome respite, forty five minutes without talking bombs, security or death. And then came the International News.

I can't remember exactly how they worded it, but the second bomb to hit Iraqi Kurdistan in four days made one of the three main headlines on the BBC. There had been many deaths and countless injuries in Makhmour ... a town just outside Erbil ... the capital ... the city to which a group of British retards are heading after their Day Out To A Yezidi Shrine.

When I turned the radio off, the room seemed strangely still and quiet except for the sound of the rain outside. I looked around at the white walls, the fridge, the air-conditioner. All the appliances seemed to be made by the same manufacturer, the owner, obviously a wealthy man who knew how to succeed in that part of the world. The name of the company? Arcelik! My thanks to you Mr Arcelik for that much needed smile.

The thunder still rumbled, lightning flashed away over the mountains and then suddenly all the power in the hotel went off. It didn't feel such a normal place any more as I lay there staring at the ceiling, quietly grinning and thinking about Laurel and Hardy, debating with myself the vital question: which one of them was it that used to say: "another fine mess you've got me in to"?

* * * * *

The Yezidi temple is to the north-east of the dangerous and violent city of Mosul. Neither our minibus driver nor our 19 year old translator seemed convinced of the reasons for seeking it out, but felt that they could get us there in one piece provided we kept to roads that they knew to be safe. It didn't sound terribly encouraging, but I wasn't as tired as the night before and the sun was now shining, two key factors in my simple little world of positive thinking.

The journey itself to the small Yezidi town was interesting, though a constant reminder that this was a country at war. Worse still, a country at war that had just been on the wrong end of two very large bombs. Checkpoints were frequent, groups of very worried-looking men in combat jackets were stopping vehicles at all major junctions, darting around with rifles in one hand and usually mobile phones in the other. We quickly got used to the routine of the serious soldier boarding the bus, scouring passports and matching the faces, then breaking into a broad smile and finishing off with a "Welcome to Kurdistan."

But how could we be sure that these heavily-armed men were going to be friendly? How did we even know they were Kurdish? What was to stop a maniac holding up the bus, climbing on board and pumping us all

251

with bullets? Surely anybody could get hold of a combat jacket and set up their own road block? These were questions to which there would never be satisfactory answers, so I decided to focus my attention on something else, like Yezidis.

I read quite a lot about them, even re-read some sections of one book, but at the end of it found myself totally baffled. All I could decipher is that their favourite amongst God's seven angels is called Melek Taus, they have established a reputation as devil worshippers, their religious script is known as The Black Book, they don't wear blue clothes and they don't eat fish. Anything more you really need to know?

We sat in a small group to take tea with one of their top sheikhs, but, despite the efforts of our translator, the experience offered little further insight into their mysterious world. Happily for the rest of the group we were led up a hillside to photograph a Yezidi graveyard and then ushered into a dark cave which housed the tomb of Sheikh Adi, the reincarnation of the aforementioned Melek Taus.

It had been a day out with a difference and once again it brought home to me the extent to which our world is divided into so many millions of tribes, sects, languages, and, perhaps most significantly, religious beliefs. Iraq itself is a particularly confusing part of this jigsaw. Arabs make up perhaps three quarters of the 27 million population, Kurds form the largest minority and the 2 million Turcomans rarely seem to get a mention. They all speak different languages, Arabic, Kurdish and Turkish, but at least share a common religion in Islam. Don't they? Well no, not really. In fact that's where the problems really start, because 60% are Shia Muslims and 40% are Sunnis.

Saddam was a Sunni and during his days in charge so was everybody else in any position of power. This irked the Shia majority – it's only in Iraq and Iran that Shias do constitute majorities – and so it comes as no surprise that they saw Saddam's downfall as their big opportunity. The rest, as they say, is history. The two sides are desecrating religious sites and slaughtering each other on a daily basis while allied troops trying to prevent all-out civil war are a constant target. Meantime the Kurds and the Christians and the Jews and the Yezidis just try to keep their heads down and hope that one day the chaos will all come to an end. What a place to live! And for that matter, what a place to come for a holiday.

The plan was to keep on the move as much as possible and never to tell anybody where we were going next. So the next morning, after the now familiar breakfast of bread, tomatoes, cheese and olives, we slipped quietly into the minibus and headed in a south-easterly direction for Erbil.

Erbil is sometimes called Arbil, or Hawler or even Howler and it's the largest city in Iraqi Kurdistan. Getting there had proved to be pleasingly uneventful as we used a series of smaller roads to cut a big corner and avoid joining Highway 2 until we were safely to the east of Mosul. There were numerous checkpoints along the way, but the passport inspections and the sight of gun barrels poking through sandbags was, to my amazement, already starting to become a way of life.

First impressions of the city were that of a grey, sprawling ugly mass brightened only by the red, white and green of the Kurdish flags. It wasn't a pretty sight, though the ancient walls of the citadel, perched on a hillock in the centre of the city, did add a certain charm and the bazaar just beneath it made for a good old wander. This definitely felt more Kurdish now, quite a few of the men dressed in their traditional outfits that look like boiler-suits with a very low crotch, cummerbunds at their middle and flattish turbans that reminded me of Danish pastries. Some of the women chose the chador, the black full length outfit worn throughout the Muslim world, though there weren't that many and certainly none had their faces covered. All in all, Kurdistan didn't feel very Islamic, more an extension of Turkey than the start of the Middle East proper, and that I suppose is exactly what it is.

Looking back at history, the Ottoman Empire ruled much of Europe, north Africa and the Middle East for six centuries and almost the last three hundred years of this included Iraq. Up to the time of the First

The Four-Letter Countries

World War the country was governed from Constantinople, as Istanbul was then known, until you-know-who came along to sort things out. Yes, it was the good old Brits who invaded and defeated the Turks, capturing Baghdad in 1917 and then running the country under a 'British Mandate' for the next fifteen years. It wasn't until 1932 that Iraq was granted full independence.

As often seems to happen in places that were colonised or 'administered', things went badly wrong soon afterwards. The British had installed an unpopular monarchy in Iraq which struggled along until 1958, but then it all came to a predictably nasty end – King Faisal and Nuri Said, a leading politician, were killed in a violent revolution with poor Nuri's body being driven over in the street by buses. Another ten years of coups and counter-coups followed that and then the Baath party assumed control. Funny how the million dollar question in 1932 is the same as the million dollar question 75 years later. "Would it have been better for the British to stay longer or should we never have been there in the first place?"

So, where was I? Wandering around the bazaar, looking at the people and wondering to myself whether I might be allowed to take a few pictures. Memories of Chad will haunt me for the rest of my days and, because of that experience, rarely do I remove the camera from its pouch without written approval in triplicate and signatures from everybody present. OK, I exaggerate, but photography is a sensitive business and caution now very much the name of my game. I had nothing to worry about here, however. Everybody I approached seemed honoured and amused at the prospect of appearing on film and a simple shot invariably resulted in requests from passers-by eager to get in on the act. It also lead to numerous handshakes and attempts at conversation that would never otherwise have happened, just a pity that the language was such an obstinate barrier.

Back at the hotel we talked plans and tactics over a glass of cold Efes, a tasty Turkish beer that is widely available in Kurdistan. (I love that approach to Islam, the moderate view that says the odd pint or a glass of wine never did anybody any harm). Geoff's forward plan was an excursion to Mar Matti the next day, an ancient monastery and a famous landmark in the world of eastern Christianity. It was back towards Mosul, on the fringe of the Arab/Kurdish border, but hopefully the roads would be OK.

I thought about it. If an ancient monastery was unearthed at the end of my street then I would probably make a point of sauntering down there and having a look at it on a day there was nothing on telly or the newsagent had forgotten to deliver my paper. But was I really prepared to gamble against being hijacked or executed or bombed into small pieces to have a butcher's at Mar Matti? Risking life and limb for a Yezidi shrine was one thing, ancient Christian monasteries quite another matter.

I decided to pass on Mar Matti and instead walked the streets of Erbil. There was no real sense of danger, only a scattering of military here and there, and to all intents and purposes people were going about their business in the usual way. It was almost easy to forget that just a week earlier a huge explosion had – quite literally – shaken the city, until a taxi took me to the place where it had happened. The Ministry of the Interior was located about a mile from the centre, surrounded by other large office buildings, an area that in appearance could just as easily have been a trading estate in Biggleswade. At 8am the previous Wednesday morning (5am BST, while I was sitting at Luton airport waiting for my flight) a suicide bomber had parked a truck full of explosives in front of the building. The blast ripped it apart. And not only that building, every building I could see in all directions for hundreds of metres. If you recall the devastation the small rucksack bombs caused in London, imagine what the equivalent of forty suitcases packed with explosives can do.

It was an eerie sensation. Every building had been abandoned, the only sign of life was a handful of soldiers guarding what remained and the sad, pathetic sight of the Kurdish flag flying over the stricken ruins.

The Four-Letter Countries

Incredibly only fourteen lives had been lost, an hour later in the day and it would have been a very different story. I stood there in the absolute silence, took a few photos with the permission of the soldiers and climbed back into the taxi. This was as near to death as I wanted to be.

It hadn't been the most uplifting afternoon and I got back to the hotel feeling as most people must when they go to visit places like Auschwitz. Meeting up with the rest of the team cheered me up, even though they themselves weren't in the best of spirits – the trip to the monastery had had to be aborted as the area was deemed too unsafe to enter. Apparently they wouldn't have had a problem to get there, but they were told that insurgents could have cut off the road and intercepted them on the way back. And then it would have been up to me to hatch a plan and move in single-handedly, under cover of darkness, to snatch them away to safety.

* * * * *

Unless I tell you otherwise, dinner in Iraq involves some sort of a kebab with bread and salad. So the last night in Erbil was a special treat when we headed out to the fancy, bomb-protected compound of the former Sheraton hotel and had fresh fish scooped from a pond and barbecued before our very eyes. It felt very strange to be in a Western style restaurant and a bottle of smooth Lebanese red wine worked wonders for the spirits, not to mention raising the body temperature against the fierce air-conditioning. Ooops, I can feel a little rant coming on. One of my many hobby horses goes like this: when the outside air temperature is absolutely glorious, why, oh why, oh why, do swanky restaurants feel compelled to go down another twenty degrees and freeze the nuts off their supposedly valued customers? I hate it, loathe it and despise it with a passion and one day might even set up my own terrorist organisation to target restaurants that subject innocent diners to this offensive, mortuary-slab experience. Singapore, you have been warned.

Iraq

It didn't take long from the big city to find ourselves up in the lush green meadows and surrounded by the sort of craggy peaks you'd expect to find in Derbyshire. We were heading east now towards Lake Dokan, the overcast skies of the previous few days had turned to sunshine and suddenly I had the bizarre sensation of being on holiday. Soldiers and guns were nowhere to be seen, just wild flowers and a gorgeous landscape and far away in the distance the snowy tops of the Zagros Mountains.

The reason for the scenic route was to cut out Kirkuk in the same way that we'd by-passed Mosul earlier in the week. Kirkuk has been a particularly sensitive city since oil was discovered there in the 1920s and so, not surprisingly, one for which both the Kurds and the Arabs are fighting to take control. I was more than happy to forgo its main tourist attraction, the Tomb of Daniel, to reach the next destination with my head still firmly on its shoulders.

From the holiday town of Dokan – understandably a favourite with the troops from Baghdad – we left the lake behind and dropped into the city of Sulaimaniya, another one that can be spelt pretty much any way that takes your fancy. The Ashti Hotel turned out to be a gem and its spacious bar, coffee shop and internet café the place for the well-to-do and educated locals to hang out. A local journalist joined me for a chat (I soon found out he spends all day and most evenings sitting there joining people for chats) and talked me through the hopelessness of living in a country with no real future and the inevitability that its educated people would leave families behind to seek opportunities elsewhere. A story that, sadly, I have heard so many times before.

It was such a pleasant hotel, and as it turned out, such a very pleasant town. Wide boulevards and tidy parks soon became narrow, sloping streets and with that mountain backdrop and the colourful open market the place had the warm, homely feel of a Hovis advert. The highlight of my afternoon was watching the men in their baggy Kurdish pants, charging into the streets wheeling stalls piled high with all sorts of produce and the angry faces of the taxi drivers suddenly stranded in a sea of total chaos. A scene of absolute mayhem, but it was a happy, fun, colourful mayhem. At least for those of us who didn't have to drive anywhere.

*   *   *   *   *

16th March 1988 will go down as one of the bleakest days in the history of mankind. It was on that Wednesday afternoon that the 75,000 or so residents of Halabje, an Iraqi town close to the border with Iran, first heard the sound of low-flying aircraft heading towards them. They knew what was coming. The Kurds who lived there had long been a thorn in the side of Saddam Hussein and their collusion with Iran, the country with whom the Iraqis had been at war for eight years, had been the final straw in the eyes of the mad dictator and his cousin Ali Hasan al-Majid, the aforementioned Chemical Ali.

The planes dropped chemical bombs onto the town and even chased the people that were sprinting across the fields in a desperate bid to escape. Blue and green poisonous gases filled the air and within a few hours 5,000 innocent people had choked to death, many of them women trying to protect their children. Those that survived gathered their possessions and fled across the border leaving behind the smell of death and soon all that was left of Halabje was an eerie yellow mist hovering over the town. It wasn't Chemical Ali's first such attack – his Anfal campaign had been systematically targeting other Kurdish communities for the two years prior to that – but this was by far the most devastating and the one that made all the headlines.

It took us a little under two hours to reach Halabje from Sulaimaniya where the large memorial at the entrance to the town was impossible to miss. We stopped and stared for some minutes at the strange-looking building and tried to work out what had happened. Here was a sort of concrete tent-shaped creation with angled digits like a closed hand protruding from its peak, but half of it seemed to have been damaged by fire. Was it supposed to look like this? The manager of the site came out to meet us, invited us to take tea in his office, and explained all.

Those who had survived the 1988 attack returned to the town after three years and, with the promise of help from the Kurdish regional government, set about rebuilding their community. But precious little assistance materialised other than the memorial site itself and in 2006, after years of protest had failed to produce tangible help, local students ran riot and desecrated the memorial building. So now they needed money to repair it as well as everything else that needed doing!

The Kurds of Halabje are understandably determined that Saddam's atrocity against their people never be forgotten. Thus our cup of tea came with a slide show, one gruesome shot after the other of the corpses piled in the streets, huddled in doorways, spreadeagled in the fields. Then two English-speaking guides, whose own families had been decimated by the attack, were assigned to show us around the site, the seemingly endless list of names of the people who perished and even the bombs that were still there two decades later. Everybody in the town had lost family or friends and without even the consolation of knowing where loved ones were buried, the memorial site was the only place for most people to mourn their losses.

What is known for sure is that up on the hillside to the east of the town there is a field where hundreds or even thousands of bodies were interred in mass graves. A rectangular wall marks the spot and an iron gate in the shape of two bombs tells the rest of the story. I stood there in the sad, overgrown field, but there were no gravestones and no flowers except for those growing wild amongst the weeds and long grasses. Nobody knows exactly whose bodies lie in those enormous pits and hence I suppose this unvisited, uncared-for cemetery is a place most people would prefer to forget.

As though a day out to Halabje wasn't enough to contend with, some desperate soul put forward the suggestion that a visit to a disused prison could be incorporated into the return journey. He'd read that this was now a museum depicting the squalid conditions and displaying instruments of torture to which inmates had been subjected during the Saddam regime. Luvly jubbly.

And so we went for a stroll around the dungeons, a grim reminder that there is always a far worse option than death. This was one of many places where people were brought to be suspended by their arms, or have the soles of their feet beaten, or their anuses prodded with long, pointed sticks. I picked up the anus-prodder still lying across the table, wondering if anybody in the world had ever done anything so heinous to deserve to be on the receiving end of such a ghastly instrument. And then I thought about the person who invented those little plastic sachets for sauce, mustard and mayonnaise.

More than likely those that were brought here wouldn't even be criminals, probably just ordinary blokes who stood up for what they believed in, or voiced their opinions, or wrote a poem that somebody didn't like. Poor buggers that were just unlucky enough to be in the wrong place at the wrong time. It was, I have to concede, fascinating to see how these scenarios had been so vividly portrayed and if you ever find yourself with an hour to kill in Sulaimaniya I strongly recommend you check out the old nick. But that was more than enough for me for one day, I'd had my fill of death and bombs and bodies and torture. It was time to change tack, head back, take a long hot shower followed by a long cold hard-earned glass of that beautiful sparkling amber liquid. In fact, better make that two.

* * * * *

There are three border crossing points in the Zagros Mountains between Iraqi Kurdistan and the enormous country that is Iran, my tenth and final Four-Letter Country. Geoff's research had found two of them to be in areas considered dangerous and so had requested that our sponsors in

Iraq

Tehran seek government approval for us to cross at Haj Omran, the most northerly of the three. Thankfully for us they had confirmed that this would be in order and on the agreed day a vehicle would be sent to collect us on the Iranian side. All we had to do was get there. This was a long way north, back up to Lake Dokan and well beyond, high up in the mountains close to the town of Rawanduz. It would take the best part of a day, so we would try to find a place to sleep somewhere close to the border and then early the following morning set out for the actual crossing point.

In a way it was a pity to have to head north when there was so much of Iraq we still hadn't seen. But staying alive always needs to be a big priority and to move any closer to Baghdad would simply have been a risk too far. I would particularly have liked to get to "the marshlands", a swamp the size of Lincolnshire where the Tigris and Euphrates form a V in the south-east of the country just before Basra. The Marsh Arabs have been living there for the last 5,000 years and, although Sadaam tried to force them out by damming and draining the area, it seems that of late they have managed to stage something of a comeback. Maybe next time I'm in Iraq the world will be a safer place. Dream on.

The journey up the eastern border turned out to be a pleasant day trip in the country and by late afternoon we'd travelled as far as we could risk going whilst still retaining the hope of finding a hotel. Local knowledge steered us to the town of Diana, but it seemed such a scruffy desolate place and fitting that its only hotel had quite recently been abandoned. One look at it was easy to see why and we breathed a collective sigh of relief when it was categorically ruled out as a possible venue. A strange reaction perhaps considering that we were high up in the mountains and had nowhere else to go.

We continued east and climbed even higher. Scruffy towns were now no more than just scruffy villages. Where on earth were we going to sleep? The drivers wound down windows to seek advice of tea-drinkers on the streets, old men who smiled and waved their arms and pointed.

The Four-Letter Countries

But what sort of accommodation could they be pointing towards when even the houses looked little more than glorified stables? The road had started to zigzag now and we climbed higher still.

Up, round a long bend, up, round another long bend, up, round... what the...? I do not believe this! I must be losing it, imagining things. It had to be a mirage, a trick of the mind. Surely. Surely I could not be looking at several neat rows of luxury chalets, a sprawling complex of modern brick and shiny glass and red tiled, sloping roofs cut into the side of the mountain with a restaurant at its centre, a restaurant in all but name identical to ... wait for it ... a Little Chef! Somebody had very kindly transported a brand new holiday park all the way from Anglesey or Conway or Betys-y-bloody-coed and plonked it on a remote hillside in a destitute area of eastern Iraq.

How or why it came to be there is a mystery that will forever remain unsolved. Very few of the bungalows showed any sign of habitation and the estate manager – for want of a better title – was only too pleased to swap a couple of sets of keys for a juicy wad of fresh greenbacks. Within minutes grown people were behaving like children that had never known the pleasure of a lounge with satellite TV, a kitchen, two bedrooms and a bathroom with a real toilet. We even had bunk beds, now how exciting is that?

A brief stroll around our estate and a few cursory photos of the wonderful scenery delayed the visit to the Little Chef for as much as twenty five minutes. The welcome desk and cash register just inside the front door came as no surprise at all, the place was just as Cheffy on the inside as it appeared from a distance, though this one served beer and the obligatory kebabs. In fact the only disappointment was the absence of a laminated menu and a ketchup-stained *Daily Mail*.

The beer and the surprisingly good Lebanese red wine flowed, this was after all our last night in the country and it was turning out to be so different from what we'd expected. To add to the occasion a local gent on an adjacent table sent a bottle of wine over as a gesture of hospitality and then stood up to formally welcome us to his country. What a nice touch. He then took his leave with the rest of his group and went off to start a party of his own.

Half an hour later we were heading back along Acacia Avenue when he called us over to join the merry throng on his patio, to listen to Kurdish music and drink some whisky. It was actually more of an instruction than an invitation, this was clearly a man not used to taking no for an answer. Tumblers of scotch duly appeared accompanied by a huge plate of lamb chops and another rousing speech-cum-rant from our obviously well-oiled host. The gist was that it was great to have visitors to Kurdistan, his people were up there with the best in the world and all Turks and Arabs were absolute bastards. Oh, and he was very rich – "Would anybody like to use my phone to call anywhere in the world? Be my guest."

Being his guest was indeed an entertaining experience, a view held by all except a lady in our group who only drank water and wasn't big on humour. She just didn't see the funny side of it when we relocated her to a seat alongside the drooling Mr Rich who was now quite evidently determined to add her to his impressive portfolio. It made for fascinating viewing: how would he get that podgy right arm around his new neighbour when his hands were already occupied with a huge glassful of neat alcohol, a fat cigar and a mobile phone? Some of us were secretly willing him to move in tongue-first with a fresh mouthful of smoke and bits of meat on his chin, but sadly it wasn't to be. Another plate of sizzling chops arrived to confuse him even further and our lady smartly seized the moment of hesitation to bid him goodnight and effectively bring the party to a close.

* * * * *

Five hours later the sun was up and looking rather brighter than we were. There was no breakfast to eat or bags to pack, so by 7am the bus was chugging out of our mountain paradise and once again leading us up those hairpin bends towards the snowy peaks. The anticipation of the border crossing and the adventure of a brand new country ahead seemed to stifle the hangovers and by the time we finally got to the immigration post some three hours later everybody was pretty chirpy and in good form.

And what a wonderfully remote and primitive place it felt. The snow was now almost touchable, albeit just dirty patches hidden from the sun, and the drop in temperature demanded that crumpled fleeces made debut appearances from the bottom of everybody's bags. The bus pulled to one side on the muddy road, now little more than a track cutting through the lush green mountains and we were all drawn to the action in the distance away to our right: an enormous gathering of men, hundreds of them on horseback like something straight from a cowboy movie, presumably some sort of unofficial cross-border market.

As it turned out, we had plenty of time to watch them. The tactic was for Geoff, in his capacity as leader, to deliver his official documents to the senior immigration officer and we would follow with passports as soon as the nod was given. The problem on this particular morning was that Geoff didn't come back and there was nobody to do any nodding. What could have happened? Was there some sort of problem? Where on earth was he? We went to find out.

He was safe and sound, but agitated as hell. Somebody in the confusion of foreign tongues had indicated that the Iraqi Kurds were not allowed to let foreigners leave through that crossing and only a phone call from somebody more senior could permit the rule to be waived. Geoff looked a broken man, he knew that to turn back could mean a detour of hundreds and hundreds of miles. And so he sat there in a tatty armchair in the tatty office staring at the shoulder-shrugging man behind the desk, willing him to change his mind. To make it worse, the immigration boss seemed to speak little or no English – you never could be sure – but at least he gestured that a phone call might possibly be forthcoming. And then he got on with his crossword.

Iraq

Two hours passed. We were hungry and there wasn't any food. We were thirsty and there wasn't even any water. We were bored and the novelty of the horse traders had long since worn off. It was starting to feel cold and just a teeny bit hopeless. What a bloody cock-up. If there was going to be a problem surely it would be getting into a country, not getting out of one?

The phone call did eventually come from somewhere and to everybody's great relief our departure through the border had been approved. Even the immigration bloke seemed to share our moment of joy as he gathered together the passports and personally escorted our vehicle a few hundred metres up the track. He just needed to be sure, before stamping us out, that the Iranians were definitely going to let us in.

So we'd done it. We'd travelled across Iraq from one side to the other and were still alive to tell the tale! Iran by comparison should be like a trip to Disneyland, we even had the luxury of visas in our passports and the knowledge that our sponsors had been given approval for us to enter through that border. If all went to plan there would be a driver waiting to collect us on the other side.

A huge gate across the road, photographs of two Ayatollahs and different (though similar) flags with the green bit at the top told us that the other side was indeed Iran. Like prisoners on the day of release, we walked up to the metal barrier where people were standing expectantly on either side, some of them showing papers and passing through a small pedestrian section that opened independently of its mighty cousin. And then we saw him, the waving man, our new driver all the way from Tehran brandishing a little identity sign. We were almost there and it was a very relieved Geoff that produced his first smile of the morning and poked his right arm through the bars for the handshake that had never looked like happening.

Formalities still had to be completed, so once the bags had been unloaded we were ushered into a large shed next to the big gate and asked to sit and wait. Again. We were seriously hungry now, it was lunchtime and we'd been on the go for six hours without anything at all since our lamb chops and whisky from the small wee hours. Please can we just get on our way? Our Kurdish mate went to speak with his Iranian counterparts and between them they would get the pile of passports stamped.

We just had to be patient. Some watched the TV in a language they couldn't follow, some tried to read, some of us wandered outside to see what if anything was going on. There seemed to be quite a few people involved, looking at our passports, talking animatedly, waving arms. And even, could it be, shaking their heads? There was some disagreement, but why, what? Then an Iranian chap, dressed smartly in shirt and trousers and exuding the authority of a person in charge, came over to address the weary shedfolk. The gist of his message was quite simply this. We would not be allowed to enter Iran.

The news was received by a very loud team groan and a lot of mumbled obscenities. Only the authorities in Tehran could allow us to cross there and this matter was way beyond his control, he assured us unhelpfully. At which point, the normally calm and diplomatic Geoffrey, completely lost it. But we have been given authorisation by Tehran because our very important travel company fixed it and the bus is there and if you speak to The High Up Government Person in the capital they will tell you in no uncertain terms that we can and must and will use this very border crossing, came the words of the red-faced one. More shrugs, more mumbles, more conversations in languages we couldn't start to follow was the immediate response. Then at least a shred of hope. He would try to speak with Tehran.

And so we were back to the 'waiting for the phone call' routine. The decision maker, if such a person really existed, would inevitably be too important to speak to immediately. It could take an hour, or half a day, or we could still be sitting there a week on Tuesday. We were fed up and even worse, we were very very hungry. How long were we prepared to sit this out? What were our alternatives?

Then a bad situation started to get even worse. Without approval from somebody on high it appeared that no crossing points from Iraq would be available to us, the only route into Iran would be via Turkey. Via Turkey! That would mean going right back across Iraq to where we'd started, heading north across the border then turning right and crossing the mountains again. A ludicrous scenario equal to driving from Bristol to Cardiff via Inverness and Aberystwyth. Nobody in their right minds could seriously expect us to do that.

We waited an hour, two hours, three hours. I looked around at the silent people and wondered at what point it would be acceptable to contemplate eating the flesh of a colleague. Who would I go for first? How would I explain to their loved ones back home the circumstances that had driven me to such a desperate act? Then somebody had an idea, a very smart plan that in hindsight could have been hatched many hours earlier. Our Iraqi drivers were still sitting outside, somebody could go back to the last village we'd passed through and return with the entire contents of a supermarket or restaurant or preferably both. It was the best news we'd had all day and I was more than happy to volunteer my services.

Half an hour later I was swigging water and stuffing my face with dry bread as the stubbly man and his assistant threaded bits of chicken on to sticks and laid them over burning coals. It was as spit-and-sawdusty a place as you would imagine finding in a mountain border village, but the speed and efficiency with which they performed, de-skewering the cooked meat into huge circular pieces of fresh flat bread, adding salad and pickles, and then rolling the big Iraqi sarnies into lunchboxes, was an example of fast food catering at its very finest. How the faces of my fellow sheddies were going to light up when Meals on Wheels finally turned up at the border.

Before we'd even reached the big metal gate I could see there was activity ahead. It was our guys, and yes, they were dragging bags and cases from the shed and preparing for departure. Whoopee, we were off, on our way, and we had a delicious meal to look forward to. That's travel for you, one minute everything is doom and gloom, the next minute all those miseries are forgotten and the adrenaline of adventure pumps you forward once again. Iran here we come!

Being very careful not to drop the neatly stacked boxes, I stepped down from the bus and walked the walk of a happy man, trying to decide the most appropriate venue for the long-awaited feast.

"We're going back."

I can't remember who said it and at first the words didn't really register. Then I looked at the faces.

"We're going back. Tehran says we can't cross. We have to go to Turkey."

It could have been a wind-up, a little wheeze they'd plotted in the hour I'd been gone, but I could see they were really loading bags onto our Meals on Wheels bus. It was 5pm, we'd been there all bloody day and now we had to turn round and retrace our steps. What a complete waste of time. Shit. Bollocks. Bastards. There's three to be going on with.

We would get to Erbil by 10pm, sleep in our usual hotel until five the next morning and then head in a north-westerly direction back towards Dohuk and the Turkish border. With a following wind we'd be out of Iraq by the middle of the next day and then we'd work out what to do next. That was the best poor old Geoff could come up. He'd been given a bum steer by the Iranians, all his carefully laid plans were now sadly in tatters, it hadn't been a good day. So I handed him a lunchbox, assured him it wasn't his fault and insisted he enjoy every mouthful of his chicken kebab.

The journey in the dark back to Erbil was our first taste of road-blocks by torchlight, but, in the main, those hours passed without incident and notably very little conversation. It was a relief in a perverse sort of way to be on the move to somewhere and the smiles of the hotel staff who welcomed us back set us up nicely for a fresh and positive start the next day.

Iraq

A few hours' kip and the early morning sunshine did the trick as it always does. The laughter and the banter was back, the roads were free of traffic and even the checkpoints seemed particularly good humoured that morning. By lunchtime we were stepping from the bus for the very last time, saying a final farewell to our drivers and transferring into the taxis that escort pedestrians through the border formalities.

No waiting, no sitting around. Not this time. The only minor hassle came from Turkish immigration who insisted on a thorough search of all the bags and the confiscation of any items bearing the name, the map or the flag of Kurdistan. A routine procedure apparently whereby all offending material is removed, stared at for a couple of minutes, torn into small pieces and tossed into a skip strategically positioned for this very purpose. And each such action comes with exactly the same three words of explanation: "Kurds are terrorists".

* * * * *

And so we'd crossed Iraq from west to east and then again from east to west. Not exactly according to plan, but, in a country that is falling apart at the seams, very little does go according to plan. From my own perspective there had only ever been one important objective. That was to be luckier than the 4,000 or so American and British and other poor soldiers from around the world who had arrived there as able-bodied young men and who had left in wooden boxes with the flags of their countries draped over the top.

It would have been good to leave with the thought that next time round the country will be safe, stable, even thriving. But how can that ever be? The Kurds despise the Arabs and the Turks and the feeling is mutual. The Sunnis hate the Shias and vice versa, the Arabs loathe the Jews and the Americans for supporting them. And, as though that isn't bad enough, the militant factions within each group kill each other or

The Four-Letter Countries

brutalise their own people for not being militant enough. For the sake of the innocent majority who have to live in the Middle East, I do hope that one day it gets sorted out but, in my heart of hearts, I can't help but feel that the end of the world might well come first.

IRAN

"Welcome to Iran".

He said it proudly and with a warm smile that somehow conveyed the impression that he really meant it. Little did he know that we'd been sitting on a minibus for eighteen hours a day, living on a diet of Coca Cola and Pringles and forced to listen to Turkish music, just to hear those magic words. After all the shenanigans up in the mountains we'd simply walked up to immigration, handed over our passports and collected the rubber stamps. Three minutes. All done. Welcome to Iran.

And little did he know that – most importantly – this was FLC number 10, that his country marked the beginning of the end of one man's wacky journey to the more obscure parts of the globe. It felt good, really wonderful, and I smiled a lot inside as I sat there admiring the pages in my passport.

It had been a hell of a long journey, not purely in terms of distance, but the geography and the politics that had stood in our way. Turkey's bottom right hand corner had turned out to be a beautiful green and mountainous place, but with the slowest of roads and a higher level of security than anything we'd encountered in Iraq. Passports were checked and details recorded with tedious regularity, though, mystifyingly, nobody showed the slightest interest in the contents of our bags or the inside of the vehicle. In fact if we'd been carrying guns or bombs or anything dangerous none of the eight checkpoints that held us for three quarters of an hour at a time would have been any the wiser. Are you reading this, Mr Kurdish Insurgent?

The Four-Letter Countries

Our driver was sitting patiently in the car park, the same poor bloke that had spent a whole day fruitlessly waiting for us at the Iraqi border, and we dived into the bus like a man on fire might approach a swimming pool. It was as though we had to get away before somebody in the immigration department came running out to say there had been a terrible mistake or they needed to wait for a phone call before we could leave.

We shot off down the road past photographs of Ayatollahs and, once well out of sight of official buildings, pulled into a small shopping mall to stock up on food and cash. I recklessly traded $200 for 1.8 million Riyals – a neat fold of green bills for a sackful of blue ones – and then savoured the delights of a hot baked potato with fresh coriander.

It was time for a grin. FLC number 10 already felt so different from number 9, even just standing in a big car park. It was hotter for a start and it just felt so much more ... advanced? Could I put my finger on it? There would be plenty of time to think about that.

This was the north west of Iran, further north than we'd originally planned to enter, top left of a gigantic sloping square. And how it gives me untold pleasure to inform you that Iran is the largest of all the FLCs. Yes, even bigger than those monsters we visited in the Sahara all that time ago. A diagonal line from here to the Pakistan border and the Gulf wouldn't be much less than the distance of my original flight from London to Istanbul, I can't think of any better way than that to try to impress you.

The plan for the first day was an ambitious one and – looking at those incredible distances – would take many hours to accomplish. We would travel in a southerly direction, down the west side of Lake Orumiyeh and then a few hundred kilometres further, still parallel with the Iraqi border, to the town of Sanandaj. A logistical challenge in itself, but with a major diversion thrown in – we would cut east into the countryside to visit The Throne of Solomon, one of the country's many historical sites. I was just happy to be there, to go with the flow and, anyway, this was to be my final day with the group. The plan all along had been to go my own way once into Iran. Tomorrow things would be very different.

The view from the bus revealed a much more developed country than I had imagined. The roads and motorways looked just like those of Europe, beautifully paved with large green signs and modern lighting, and everything written in English script as well as Arabic. And such gorgeous scenery: an attractive lake, lush green fields, wild flowers, a snowy mountain backdrop. This was real culture shock, a totally unexpected leap back into civilisation, a sort of Switzerland with squiggly writing and blazing sunshine. I could start to get to like this.

It was almost dark by the time we pulled up, not good news to those eager for photos of Solomon's Throne. Thus my fellow travellers positioned cameras in front of their anxious faces and hurled themselves from the bus, running and snapping at anything and everything the hillside had to offer. I stood alone in silence to admire the stunning scenery, a 360 degree landscape made even more dramatic as the colours of the daytime became black and grey images of the night, and then I jogged up the hill in pursuit of my mates. I soon found myself standing alongside a volcanic lake amidst the remnants of ancient walls, a site, all told, perhaps the size of the new Wembley Stadium. Whoever had created this, whatever it was, had certainly chosen a beautiful place and once the clicking of shutters had started to abate I timidly posed a few questions.

It was Geoff who explained that this had been a place of worship for the Zoroastrians, a shrine thought to have been built around the time of Cyrus and Darius (The Greats) and later, during the Sassanian period, a royal palace. It then lay abandoned for several hundred years before the Mongols came along to restore and further enlarge it. The names rolled off his tongue with baffling speed and fluency and I have to admit that I wasn't just out of my depth, I was gulping water and watching my life pass before me. This was Iran, a country full of history, and I would have to make the effort to understand a little more.

The Four-Letter Countries

Trying not to expose my total ignorance I grappled for dates, tried to sort them into some kind of order and then went in for a bit more detail. I won't bore you with it all just yet, but can tell you that Cyrus and Darius ruled the region around 500BC, the Sassanian period was a thousand years later and the Mongols arrived between 1220 and 1340. So people had been coming to this place on and off for at least two and a half thousand years and, looking out at that dramatic horizon, it was easy to understand why.

It was dark now, but still beautifully warm, all that was left was the shimmer of the lake and the eerie shapes of the walls and the mountains way out in the distance. After several days of sitting in a bus, this hour of serenity was the ultimate therapy, the detour had been well and truly justified and the prospect of another five hours travelling to reach Sanandaj just slightly less daunting.

Andrew and Nigel were the youngest members of our little group, two very funny, easy-going guys who shared (with each other) a strange fascination for anything that involved combat, war, death or torture. They too intended to leave the next day and very kindly invited me to join them on their planned excursion, which, true to form, was to an area known as the Valley of the Assassins. A car would collect them for the six hour drive east to Qazvin and then the following day would continue on to Tehran. Thanks lads, please count me in, and on the way there you can tell me what it's all about ...

We finally arrived at Sanandaj at two in the morning and, after saying our farewells to Geoff and the team, the three of us young(er) lads set off to travel from west to east five hours later. Another adventure was about to begin, but now we were in charge of our own destiny and with the added luxury of a private car.

I think you'll like the story of The Assassins. It goes back to a strange cult that existed in the 11th and 12th centuries, a group of Ismailis that protected their trade routes by infiltrating powerful circles, often in disguise, and discreetly murdering any individuals they deemed to be a threat. Their leaders lived in castles up in the mountains and amongst the most feared and famous was Hassan-Al-Sabbah, based high above the valley of the Alamut river. It was up there on the peak of the mountain that he would drug and indoctrinate future members of his group, and it was these users of hashish, the 'hashashin', that would ultimately give the term assassin as a cold-blooded killer to the rest of the world.

Now it made sense why Andrew and Nigel were getting so excited. The plan was for us to stay the night in the town of Qazvin then, early the next morning, head up to Alamut Castle, a couple of hours drive further east and only a short distance away from the shores of the Caspian Sea. The sea that is, in fact, a lake, the largest lake in the world, though the Romans who first arrived there and found the water to be salty couldn't have been expected to know that. Its area is around 371,000 square kilometres, which means you could fit the whole of Germany inside the Caspian Sea. Now there's a thought.

Qazvin was full of modern cars and flashy shops and restaurants and fast food bars and smartly dressed people and traffic and bright lights and the whole experience was absolutely overbloodywhelming. I felt like Crocodile Dundee, a redneck from the dusty outback who'd woken up one morning to find himself surrounded by the streets of Hong Kong or the skyscrapers of Manhattan. This was a long, long way from Iraq and, for that matter, a long way from any picture of Iran that my mind had created.

I waited until late afternoon to head out of the coolness of the hotel then with the help of reception took a taxi to the 'coffee net', as internet cafés were apparently known. Again, it all seemed light years ahead, a spotless room full of new computers and a pleasant young guy in charge who spoke a little English. It was a comfortable place to spend a couple of hours, incoming mail was all quite positive and everything seemed to be slotting nicely into place. I handed over the equivalent of fifty pence – could it really be that cheap? – and headed for the door.

The Four-Letter Countries

"Please – you have card?" A smiling man I hadn't noticed before.

What did he mean? A business card I supposed, a chance to make a pen-friend?

"Sorry, no," I smiled back as politely as I knew how.

"Please – come." He looked at me directly between the eyes, stood very close, smiled and then placed his hand on my upper arm. He didn't seem to speak any other words of English.

What the hell was going on? He opened the door on to the street, gestured for me to pass through it and, still with a grip on my arm, nodded towards a small car parked at the kerb. The back door of it was wide open and a man holding a walkie-talkie was standing alongside.

"Police – Come."

Police! These were policemen in plain-clothes? Telling me to get into a vehicle. There had to be some sort of mistake. We all stared at one another, waiting for something to happen. Walkie-talkie man looked at me sternly, and nodded.

My legs turned into blancmange, my mouth dried up, and a nasty bubbly sensation churned the lower stomach, an inner trembling I hadn't known for a very long time. Not since Chad, in fact. I tried to reason, to ask questions, but it got me nowhere at all. He didn't understand, just kept repeating the instruction.

"Police – Come."

How was I going to get out of this one? Climbing into the back of that car was not an option, neither was running away. The only way forward was, in fact, backwards, so I turned gently back into the café muttering and smiling as I moved. The grip on my arm did not let go, but thankfully, nor did it tighten. And thus the odd couple returned to the manager's desk.

The reaction from the young lad in charge, who seemed to under-stand what was happening, was, I suppose, mildly reassuring. As though we were old comrades against a common enemy, he waited for the policeman to look away then raised his hands palms outwards and winked as if to say: "Just hang in there mate, this will be OK". At least that's what I hoped he was saying. Did I have my passport?

Hotels in Iran are obliged to hold the passports of foreign guests at all times and so no, I didn't have my passport. But come to think of it, I did have the card of the hotel. Was this the card he'd been asking for all along? Why hadn't I thought of that before? I handed the precious piece of cardboard over to the policeman, if that's what he really was, and in taking it from me he finally let go of my arm. And then he used his free hand to telephone the hotel.

The conversation that followed seemed to go on for quite some time, but as I don't speak a word of Farsi (Persian) I had no idea what was being discussed. A Farsical situation, I might have reflected in a lighter mood. Was he telling them they wouldn't ever need to worry about making my bed? That I was an enemy of the state and about to be dealt with accordingly? I looked again towards my internet buddy, the only person in the world to know where I was, and tried to glean my fate from the expression on his young face. But at that very moment the phone was returned to its cradle and the caller turned round to face me, the judge about to pass sentence.

"It's OK," was all he said, though he did offer a lame handshake and that false watery smile as he returned the card of the hotel. I presumed, wrongly, that he would then turn and leave, but instead he waited for me to make the first move, to walk out into the street towards walkie-talkie and the car. It could have been a trap, I will never know, but the true coward inside me suggested a long drawn-out fiddling around inside my bag to delay the exit as long as possible. Thankfully the tactic exhausted his patience. He headed back upstairs, and, after a further ten minutes, like a small rodent emerging from a hole in the ground, I poked my head onto the street and scampered very quickly along the busy pavement.

* * * * *

The Four-Letter Countries

We weren't long out of Qazvin before the road started to climb into the Alborz, a range of mountains that starts up near the border with Armenia and works its way around the shores of the Caspian to sit behind the city of Tehran. We were all well rested at last and in good spirits, the sun was shining and the boys delighted with my tale of the run-in with the secret police and close shave with the inside of an Iranian gaol. Bring on the Valley of the Assassins!

It took us about two hours in the car and ten minutes up a steep track on foot to reach the castle, the former home of Hassan-al-Sabbah. There isn't a great deal left of it other than the foundations, but that really isn't the point. As any estate agent will tell you it's all about location, location, location. And this was some location. We sat on top of the mountain, where the chief assassin had spent his days, and gazed out in amazement at the countryside below and beyond. Rolling meadows as bright green as a billiard table, wild flowers in reds and yellows and purples, tiny villages on the hillsides, enormous peaks covered in snow. This scenery was as good it gets, up there with Switzerland and the Austrian Tyrol. Whoever would look at this picture and think ... Iran?

It was the sort of place you could sit all day and not get bored, that peak amongst peaks, a sort of Machu Picchu of the Middle East. We stayed longer than planned, chatting to some local teachers about the Liverpool v Milan Champions League final scheduled for that evening, and then, as one, reluctantly made our way back down the side of the mountain. No question about it, if you were running an assassination operation there could be no better place to set up your head office.

Iran was turning out to be more than a big surprise. I hadn't realised just how high it is – there are mountain ranges to the north, south, east and west – and two thirds of the country sees snow during the winter months. And when you think its area is three times the size of France, that is two Frances' worth full of snow!

Iran

The journey back was the route we had come, but it offered another perspective of the beautiful valley. It seemed so much quicker to get back to Qazvin, as is often the case with return journeys, but we were more than ready for our hard-earned lunch. The driver took us to a traditional restaurant obviously frequented by the more affluent and here the kebabs came in different qualities of meat, choices of rice, complementary side salads and very sour yogurts. And the drinks trolley: Coca Cola, 7Up, and non-alcoholic beer, perhaps the most pointless invention known to man.

The motorway from Qazvin to Tehran is a multi-laned affair that makes extremely light work of the 148 kilometres that separate the two cities. A pleasant ride it was too, despite the Iranian kamikaze driving, though the sky did noticeably move from bright blue to murky grey as the metropolis loomed ever closer. It was fiercely hot in the afternoon sunshine, but even in late May the snow was still there on the peaks towering above the capital, an impressive backdrop to the city, despite the haze.

Arriving in Tehran felt little different from the suburbs of any first world city. The traffic lived up to its reputation, but everything felt very orderly, even down to the signals with large digital indicators counting down the seconds to the lights changing colour. This was a city full of life, modern and vibrant. Somehow it didn't feel as though it belonged in the Middle East. It didn't even feel Islamic, I could see very few mosques and most of the women were wearing jeans rather than black chadors. On the face of it, it didn't look so very different from driving around London.

There were however two constant features to remind us that this was indeed the Islamic Republic of Iran – the ubiquitous photographs of the bearded Ayatollahs, the late Khomeini and his successor of almost the same name, Mr Khameini. They always appeared side by side and, like Ant and Dec, with the same one permanently on the left. The first of these had led the Islamic Revolution in 1979 (Khomeini, not Ant) and in the last ten years of his life transformed the country, for better or for worse, into what it is today.

So a visit to Khomeini's shrine seemed a fitting place to start and, after checking into the smart little Hotel Mashad, I took a cab back along the motorway to his final place of rest. It wasn't at all what I'd expected. I can only describe it as an enormous out-of-town hypermosque, a hideous complex resembling an airport terminal surrounded by a car park the size of the Ukraine and a shabby, failed attempt at some gardens. Oh, and a little shopping mall on either side of the mausoleum selling cheap souvenirs.

I removed my shoes, stepped in through the men's entrance and handed them over the counter in return for a disc. Surely it couldn't possibly be as bad on the inside as the exterior would have us believe? Not for AK, or rather Imam Khomeini since his upgrade, the most revered person in the history of the country and now the name of the international airport.

The large marbled hall with its many pillars still had the unnerving suspicion of a converted warehouse, but it did offer a certain air of dignity and splendour. The Imam's coffin and that of his son lie side by side in an enclosed area to the left with everywhere else covered in carpets for those wishing to pray or read the Koran. Or, as I noticed in many cases, send texts and chat on the mobile.

It was pleasantly cool and calming and what better place to do a little reading up on the man himself and his place in Iranian history. The revolution of 1979 was the big turning point, the year that the Shah was finally forced into exile after more than half a century of his family's despotic rule. It had become a nasty dictatorship, political and religious beliefs had effectively been banned and the normally tolerant Iranians had taken to the streets in what turned out to be violent and bloody protests. Khomeini had long held the belief that the country should be ruled by Islamic law and, reminiscent of Castro in Cuba twenty years earlier, the people welcomed the bearded one back from exile to lead the Revolution.

Iran

And exactly as Fidel Castro had done, he was quick to implement the most drastic of changes. Whereas Cubans (perhaps unknowingly) had embraced communism, so Iranians would henceforth be ruled by Sharia law – all aspects of every day life would be governed according to the Ayatollahs' interpretations of the Koran. Music was banned except for military marches or religious chanting, while women were obliged to wear headscarves and loose fitting garments hiding all but their hands and faces. Males and females over seven years old, unless related, could not mix, would be segregated in schools and public buildings and obliged to turn in opposite directions even on entering a bus. Alcohol was strictly forbidden and those breaking the rules could expect to face the lash.

As I headed back into town and then sauntered through Tehran's affluent northern suburbs, past the chic furniture stores, art galleries and Mercedes showrooms, it was hard to comprehend that this was in fact the same country. Teenage lads looked the same as they do the world over with trendy T-shirts, spiky hair full of gel and mobile phones to their ears while women walked around freely in tight-fitting tunics, Levi jeans and high heeled shoes, smartly made up with lipstick and mascara and all the usual female potions. It seemed to me their only concession to Islam was the wearing of the headscarf and at times even that was a half-hearted gesture. So is Iran changing?

No question that, since the days of Khomeini, at least some of the rules have been relaxed, but word on the street is that there are moves to tighten this up. I read that females were being arrested and reprimanded for 'lowering moral standards' and that even the breasts of mannequins in shop windows were being amputated to create a less arousing alternative. The clothes shops of Tehran, for now at least, certainly look much the same as those in the western world with endless boutiques offering women the usual range of sexy underwear, skimpy tops and tight fitting skirts. The girls only have to look demure in public remember; they change into regular clothes at home or when visiting friends.

The Four-Letter Countries

It was quickly becoming apparent to me that there are two very different Irans. There's the one that the visitor sees, a modern country full of kind, friendly, hospitable people desperate to join the rest of the world. And then the one that we hear about, religious extremists determined to follow the path of Islam and the bearded folk from rent-a-mob who turn up for flag-burning ceremonies when the western TV crews are in town. The division within the political parties is similarly clear-cut, the liberals who would prefer that people interpret and follow Islam according to personal choice and the conservatives who rule the roost and insist that all aspects of life be imposed by legislation.

I'd been told by previous visitors to expect a very warm welcome in Iran and assured that the only danger would come from trying to cross the street. True to form everybody had so far treated me very courteously (even the guy who'd tried to arrest me!) and looking around now at the horrendous traffic, it was easy to understand where they were coming from. Any city of 12 million people that sells petrol at 6p a litre is inevitably going to have a lot of vehicles on the road, yet strangely the fuel situation in Iran is a major bone of contention – they haven't got enough. Is this some sort of joke? Apparently not. Iran has endless supplies of oil, but does not have the capacity to refine it and so, according to my copy of the *Tehran Times*, a system of rationing would shortly be introduced. A crazy old world isn't it?

* * * * *

There are times in a man's life when he needs to take a rest from culture, education and the endless quest for self betterment and instead do a little bit of what comes most natural to him. To myself and most of my fellow countrymen this usually involves little more than a few pints of freshly pulled ale and a game of footy on the telly and it was with that sentiment at the forefront of our minds that we gathered around the bed of Room 15, Hotel Mashad, Tehran on our first Wednesday evening in the city. We'd already tuned in to channel 3 in readiness for the Champions League Final and it just didn't seem appropriate or respectful to be drinking iced water as we watched Steven Gerrard lead the Scousers out to face the boys from Milan, hell bent on revenge following Liverpool's incredible win in the 2005 final in Istanbul.

Match commentary in Farsi didn't exactly add to the atmosphere. It all seemed a bit flat for our lads' night in, the much anticipated diversion from our usual evening entertainment of Coca-Cola and kebabs and then ... a rare brainwave from yours truly. Turn the TV down and get the BBC World Service on! I twirled the knobs through a myriad of mysterious languages and irritating crackles and finally, that familiar voice, and the crowd in the background, we were there ... "It's Riise with the corner for Liverpool..."

We looked up at the TV in excitement only to realise that the ball hadn't yet gone out for the corner. The sound was well ahead of the pictures, like answers coming before the questions, an even worse scenario than a Persian commentary. It was all a bit of a disappointment, as was Liverpool's feeble effort. The Italians lifted their cup, Andrew and I slugged a couple more bottles of water and Nigel, well, he had long since fallen asleep.

The lads flew back to Britain and insisted that my priority should be to visit their favourite attraction before leaving Tehran. The Martyr's Museum is one of many in the city, but as I walked around that silent building it was easy to see why those sick, gory bounders from Guildford had loved it so much. Each exhibit depicted a photograph of somebody whose life had been lost in the name of Islam, a detailed description of how and where they'd been killed and more importantly, in the case of the real heroes, how many infidels they had eliminated en route to Paradise. One area was dedicated entirely to suicide bombers of the Middle East, their photos taking pride of place and mounted on the wall above funeral pictures and the coffins of those Jews that they'd slaughtered. Oh yes, I could see why Andrew and Nigel had felt the need to come here twice.

The Four-Letter Countries

The horror of death and the hatred of war and the sheer madness and futility of it all left me feeling drained and sickened. It was time for a cleansing outdoor pursuit, a visit to somewhere happy and smiling, back to the other Iran.

The chair lift goes from the northern suburb of Darband and takes sightseers and walkers up the side of the mountain to a platform high above the city. A lovely thing to do as an escape from traffic, noise or photographs of young people blowing each other up into millions of small pieces. It was busy up there and I was amazed to see how Iranians have embraced mountain walking with such vigour, even men and women together, suited and booted and getting stuck into it in a serious way. Then, on reflection, I suppose it's easy to understand their enthusiasm. Opportunities for any sort of social interaction are very limited in Iran and almost all sports are off limits for women because the no-flesh rule makes no allowances for sportswear. Have you ever seen a pole-vaulter wearing a chador?

Skiing in Iran is popular for the same reason. Khomeini banned it shortly after the revolution, but the slopes were re-opened in the mid-1980s with separate pistes for men and women. That has now been relaxed, though women have to queue separately for lifts and there are signs dotted around to remind men that their eyes mustn't wander!

The views from the peak were well worth the ride, though it would have been so much better without the haze. Mt Damavand is Iran's highest mountain and apparently on a clear day it's possible to see the top of it from Tehran, but clear days don't happen very often in such polluted cities. Still, all of this wonderful scenery really was a bonus to me and I felt an urge to seek out a bit more before moving on to explore the rest of the country.

Tehran was an interesting city in which to spend a few days and with its rich diversity would be a dream long weekend destination for (tee-total) lovers of galleries and museums. I would be sorry to leave in a way, but there was so much to see in this enormous country and it was time to head off to another region. But before I did ... I just couldn't resist it.

For less than twenty quid a driver would take me the 60kms to Mt Damavand, wait there for a few hours and then bring me back to the hotel. It would be a pleasant day out in the country if nothing else and on a Friday, the day for prayers, the roads would hopefully be very much quieter.

At 5,671 metres Mt Damavand is 800 metres higher than Mont Blanc, the queen of the Alps and the highest mountain western Europe has to offer. It had to be worth a quick gander and sure enough it wasn't long before we saw its elegant snowy peak poking out in the distance. Two hours after leaving the capital, I found myself sitting amongst the wild purple flowers on the lower slopes of the mountain, the only person seemingly for miles around. I sat for a long time with just the sound of the warm breeze and gazed up at this almost perfect triangle, similar in appearance to the much photographed Mt Fuji and at this time of year its upper third perfectly coated in what looked from a distance like fresh virgin snow. There is something very calming about mountains.

As lunchtime approached, we headed back for Tehran passing families heading the opposite way for their picnic in the country. The scenery was as lovely as ever, it was such a colourful journey and even the roofs of the houses added another dimension, the clusters of bright green and red and yellow shining out across the valley like something from a children's story book. We stopped for posh kebabs in the town of Rudehen and, not for the first time since I'd arrived in Iran, the driver tried to persuade me to let him pay for lunch. A very typical gesture of these warm, hospitable people.

* * * * *

The name Shiraz will be instantly familiar to anybody who enjoys a glass of red wine. It has now become one of the most popular varieties, a flavoursome and full-bodied drop produced from a deep purple grape, but, of all ironies, it originates in a country that no longer permits the sale or consumption of alcohol. That's right, the city of Shiraz is in the south of Iran.

The famous grapes were transported to France back in the 12th century and would ultimately be cultivated in all the main wine producing regions of the world. Today those grown in Shiraz are officially only used to make juice, but as one Iranian gentleman told me with a huge grin on his face: "Who is to know what you do in the privacy of your own home?" Hopefully nobody, thought I, with the going rate for a crafty tipple said to be somewhere in the region of eighty lashes.

Stepping from the plane into the wide bowl of craggy, dusty mountains around the airport of Shiraz, felt like another world from the golf-fairway greenness of the landscape I'd started to get used to. The ninety minutes in the air, a distance of 900kms due south, meant the tip of Oman was now closer than the city I'd just left and as I looked around at this new destination I saw in my mind those harsh grey mountains of the Musandam Peninsula. It was the first time I'd thought about it, but I'd now almost completed a circle, around the world from the first FLC to the last and nearly back to the first again. And then, a few minutes later, the crowning glory. I saw a road sign pointing the way to Bandar-i-Abbas, the home of the smugglers in the speedboats who zip across the Straits of Hormuz. Wow, that all seems such a long time ago doesn't it?

Shiraz is known as the city of roses and nightingales and I loved the serenity of its parks, the ornate mosques with such distinctive bright blue tiling and the spectacular shrines where its famous poets are laid to rest. They really were something else, particularly the tomb of a 14th century gent name of Hafiz which was completely surrounded by walls of mirrored glass and set in the most delightful of gardens. Such a far cry from Khomeini's burial place back in Tehran, this man had apparently gained cult status for his poems of love and the fact that he had memorised the entire Koran. Not bad going when you consider it has 114 chapters and chapter two alone contains 286 verses.

There are over 2 million students in Iran, many of whom attend the famous University of Shiraz. It gives the city an air of youthfulness and I was interested to hear that the classes aren't gender-segregated as they are in schools, although all the girls do have to sit together within the classroom. There are, in fact, more females than males at university across the country, the boys who fail the entrance exams are ushered into the army whilst the girls revise at home and take them again. Given all that I'd read about female repression in some parts of the Muslim world this came as a pleasant surprise. With 70% of Iran's population under the age of 30, should we expect to see a lot of changes in the years ahead?

It was time to start the long journey north and, whether I liked it or not, the ancient site of Persepolis was one that had to be ticked off. It's an important place in the historical world, an enormous complex dating back to the pomp of the Persian Empire, more than five hundred years before the birth of Christ. In those days of Cyrus the Great and his son Cambyses II, the Persians had not only ruled the Middle East, but spread their influence as far west as Egypt, Sudan and even into Libya. The empire gained even further in strength under the leadership of Darius the Great and it was he who ordered the construction of Persepolis. I should mention incidentally that Darius was not elected for the position of leader, but was one of a group of men who agreed to take over if his horse was the first to neigh at dawn on one particular morning in 515 BC. How much more interesting life could have been in the United Kingdom of the 21st century if only Blair and Brown's Labour party had adopted a similar selection procedure.

There were only a handful of other tourists amidst the huge expanse of ancient walls and pillars, a sad reflection of the state of Iran's once-booming tourist trade. Well presented and translated signs explained the stories of the former palaces and the vaults that housed all the treasures and how Alexander the Great had come along a couple of hundred years after Darius, razed it all to the ground and run off with the booty with the help of his 10,000 mules and 5,000 camels.

The inscriptions in the stone walls held my attention longer than anything else, carvings that represented the peoples of the twenty three nations ruled by the empire. Great names like the Cappadocians and Bactrians and Parthians and Elamites, ancient civilisations that stretched from the shores of the Mediterranean right across to China in the east. And this was the place to which all their leaders had come 2,500 years ago, right here where I was standing, a massive annual gathering of the great and the good, the powerful and the wealthy. The Royal Ascot of the Persian Empire; although presumably without Ladies' Day.

The view of the ruins from the top of the adjacent mountain had been rather more impressive than it had at ground level. I sat up there for quite some time, just me and a few nomads who were herding their sheep and goats to the higher ground, their annual migration away from the heat of the coastal plains. At one time apparently a quarter of Iran's population had moved around the country to live off the land, but, as with the tribes of Africa, their way of life has gradually been forced to change. It's sad to see these traditions go by the wayside, so, pre-descent, I made a rather silly noise and departed the scene with my heartiest nomad-friendly wave.

A quick pee before getting back on the road brought something of great interest to my attention. Not an anatomical issue I hasten to add, but something that had been lurking in the sub-conscience throughout my Iranian toileting experiences and only now had crystallised as an indisputable fact. You see, a gentleman's toilet in the Islamic Republic of Iran is no different from that of its female counterpart. We are talking a line of traps with holes in the ground and never, under any circumstances, is there a single urinal in sight. Don't ask me why, nobody seems to have the answer, but the poor old Iranian blokes just do not have a pot to piss in.

Iran

* * * * *

Whilst mountains dominate the landscape of Iran's enormous perimeter, the middle of the country is a very different story. And if you look at the map you will see that Yazd is as middle as you can possibly get. It took most of a day to get there, a bus ride across miles of flat plains of wheat, barley, and rice fields, even the bright yellow rape seed we see in the south of England, and then scraggy bush, ultimately giving way to a harsh sandy desert. There was little of interest on the roadside other than small shops with samples of their wares stacked in front though we did pass a couple of abandoned caravanserai, large-walled paddocks in the desert built as overnight stopping places for travellers and their camels.

Yazd looked different. Old. Hot. Deserty. And for the first time, very Islamic. Almost all the ladies were dressed in black, the mosques were now more prevalent and many of the sandy buildings had strange rectangular towers poking from their roofs. An ancient cooling system I later discovered, wind towers designed to grab any passing breeze and circulate it throughout the lower part of the buildings. This was the middle of the desert, fiercely hot by day, freezing cold at night, and with little by way of protection, often uncomfortably windy.

Within a couple of hours of my arriving in Yazd, so had a sandstorm. The blue sky turned a strange shade of brown, palm trees started rocking wildly and an invisible swirling dust forced cowering pedestrians to cover their faces. Luckily for me, I was about to enter a Zoroastrian Fire Temple.

Despite its outwardly Islamic appearance, roughly 10% of the people of Yazd are Zoroastrians, followers of the world's longest running religion. (Did you know the late Freddie Mercury was a Zoroastrian?). As with most faiths, it seems a mighty complicated business and the more I read about it the less I understand, but there are a couple of aspects I sort of grasp. The first is that they worship fire and direct their five daily prayers towards a flame, or failing that, a nice bright lightbulb. Hence the fire temple, an ever-burning torch behind a glass screen, one of eighteen in the city and surrounding villages. The second, and even more fascinating, is their belief that the bodies of the dead should not pollute the soils of the earth. So what do they do with them, I hear you ask?

I went to see the Towers of Silence just as dusk was falling. This was the edge of the town and the start of the desert, but the sandstorm had abated. It was calm; seemingly no sound or movement for miles around. Two hills like enormous dunes dominated the landscape and on top of each, where a fort or a castle might have been expected, was a circular wall of stone. It took perhaps twenty minutes to climb up the path to the one on the right, up to those grey walls almost twice my own height, and thence into an arena that looked for all the world like a disused bullring. But this was no sporting venue, this was where the Zoroastrians had buried their dead.

Prior to 1971 the priests had carried the deceased into the towers, laid their bodies on the ground and waited for the vultures to swoop down and do what vultures do best. It wouldn't take long for the greedy birds to carry away the flesh, all that would remain was a pile of bones for the priests to wash in acid and inter in the pit, a mass grave in the centre of the tower. An efficient eco-friendly system you might think, but not so, according to the residents of Yazd. They got really fed up with bits of corpses descending from high into their back gardens and rather churlishly told the Zoros that they would need to come up with an alternative, more conventional system. So now they are rather boringly coated in concrete and lined up in a graveyard while the majestic Towers just sit there in the desert enjoying the Silence.

* * * * *

Iran boasts a wealth of modern, pleasant hotels and payment by credit card was never a problem. So with only food and transport to pay for, it did make it extremely hard work to get through the bag of cash. A taxi rarely cost more than the equivalent of $2 and the best meal money could buy, might, if I really pushed the boat out, stretch to $5. Even when I got the zeros mixed up and excitedly dished out ten times too much, an annoying bundle of the stuff would always be thrust back into my palm. The wad of notes just would not go down no matter how much I tried, surely I wouldn't be compelled to go shopping. It wasn't even Christmas!

The food situation had picked up quite a bit. Since leaving Tehran I'd pledged to seek out non-kebab options and found myself eating girlie food like chicken with plums and pomegranates or rice with veal and raisins. A very distinctive feature of Persian cuisine is the addition of fruit and sweet sauces to their meat dishes, similar I suppose to the way we eat apple sauce with pork or Del Monte pineapple rings with gammon. Quite nice in a peculiar sort of way, though I could never quite get used to the fact that the barley soup, served ahead of every meal, tasted as though it was mixed with some sort of cheap perfume.

The dining highlight for me was at the disused public baths in Yazd. In the days when few houses boasted their own bathing facilities the people of the town, and every other town in the country, would make a regular visit to the public amenities. The hammams became a focal point of the community and some would offer luxurious facilities to cleanse, relax, enjoy a massage or simply catch up on the local gossip. Today most have closed down, or re-opened as museums or, in the case of my find in Yazd, converted into a restaurant.

It wasn't just the ornate tiling and the cleverly converted pool area that impressed. A cold yoghurt soup with walnut and cucumber made such a great change from Scotch Broth With Brut and then came my first opportunity to sample a Dizi. A bowl of lamb, beans and potatoes arrived with a pestle, an empty soup bowl and a plate of bread and, after a short but intense period of staring and wondering, I happily mashed and dunked my way through the early afternoon. Lancashire hot pot just like mi' Ma used to make.

The Four-Letter Countries

Walking through the narrow alleyways and arches in the old part of Yazd was a taste of the Middle East in the Middle Ages. It was unbearably hot and the old houses looked like igloos of sand in various states of ruin, some still lived-in, others abandoned, though it wasn't easy to tell which was which. It was a fascinating stroll back through time and I was particularly intrigued by the two large but not identical knockers on every door (now don't be rude). Why two? Can't you guess? One for male visitors and one for female, each with a slightly different sound, so the person beyond the door can be sure to dress appropriately before opening.

I resisted touching anybody's knockers and departed Yazd in the welcome coolness of an air-conditioned bus. The plan from here was to make for the city of Isfahan, a further 300 kms to the north and west, and from there fly back to Tehran and on to London. "And on to London," I mumbled to myself, realising for the very first time that the next stop would effectively be my last. This was, I reflected rather morosely, the beginning of the end.

The final few hours on the road passed without event (except for overtaking a group of fanatics jogging the 650kms to Tehran to mourn the anniversary of Khomeini's death) and, if spirits were sagging a little, arriving into the city of Isfahan was exactly what was needed. My first impression was that of the greenest city I'd ever seen, full of parks and flowers and a lovely river and elegant wide boulevards with tall trees forming long straight lines along the pavements. Once again, Iran had served up a big surprise.

* * * * *

President Ahmadinejad took office in August 2005 and wasted no time at all in making himself deeply unpopular. His arrogance and talk of 'wiping Israel off the map' brought nothing but embarrassment and unnecessary hardship to the decent, hospitable people of Iran, not to mention the destabilising effect it had on the rest of the world. And what of the country's tourist industry? Do the people in power really want it to prosper or would they prefer to forgo the dollars and, as used to happen in the communist countries, keep their citizens apart from the rest of the world? Who knows the answer to that one?

I read the *Iran Daily* at every opportunity and watched snatches of local TV when surfing the channels. Neither seemed geared towards entertainment, but instead focused endless coverage on the war of two decades earlier, lest anybody forget that Iran were the victims and that the evil aggressors in The West had supported Saddam Hussein.

This was the other Iran, the only Iran that most people get to see or hear about. The not very pleasant Iran, the Iran that arrests our seamen and women and makes them talk gibberish in front of the cameras. The Iran that nobody really trusts.

The President also decided on assuming office that he would take an aggressive attitude towards Daylight Saving – in fact he would wipe it off the map. The clocks would no longer be moved forward in the spring, so darkness at 7pm and daylight at 5am could help everybody take a more Islamic approach to life. So that's why we'd moved backwards in time from Iraq when convention dictates that travelling east winds the clocks the other way.

All of which meant that it was dark by the time I checked in to the hotel. It had the feel of a well-run establishment and there was even an information desk manned by an English speaker, an opportunity not to be missed. So I made enquiries about the local wrestling.

The last time I'd seen wrestling or even thought about it was as a kid when Dickie Davies brought it to our screens before the footie scores on a Saturday afternoon. Even at that tender age I was smart enough to recognise a load of crap when I saw it (I did spend alternate week-ends watching Man City) and never imagined the time would come when I would actively seek out an evening at ringside. But this wasn't any old wrestling, this was Iranian wrestling, or more accurately, as it was explained to me, the gym where the wrestlers go through their routines. A driver would take me there after dinner, it would be open until 10pm.

The taxi driver spoke little English except to say with a toothy smile: "Iran people and England people very friend". How just a few words can go such a long way. The gym was obviously new territory for him as well, so once we'd been directed through the back streets to the innocuous little entrance he decided to park up and join in the fun.

The room looked more like a small dance hall than a gym, octagonal in shape, with a sunken area in the middle, and a line of chairs around its outer walls creating the image of a balcony. Sitting atop a podium on one side was a large sweaty man beating a drum and it was at his behest that we took a seat in the (empty) viewing gallery within touching distance of the men who were performing in the pit. There were ten young chaps dressed in what looked like football shirts and three-quarter leggings and they seemed to be engaging in some sort of a Morris dance without bells or hankies.

All the time the drum was beating and the fat man was shouting out what I guessed to be lines from the Koran to which the gyrating Morris men (and soon even my taxi driver) responded in unison. Then one of them would move to the middle of the circle, perform an energetic set of twirls and reel off a series of solo mantras in response to the Fat One and his wild, aggressive pounding.

I looked around the 'gym' for any sort of connection with sport and there on the far wall was a reassuringly fine display of photographs of the great Iranian wrestlers of yesteryear. The challenge for me now was to try to link the activities of those big brawlers with these lithe young fellows chanting to the drummer and for that I would simply have to wait and see what happened next.

I watched and I waited, but to my confusion and disappointment it was just more of the same - even the taxi driver was starting to look bored and he could at least understand what was going on. There was no point in sitting through any more and so I dropped a few Riyals into the fat man's hastily produced tin and returned to the hotel in search of an explanation.

Which went something like this. The chanting is in the name of Ali, son-in-law of the prophet Mohammed, and the training is aimed at attaining a level of physical and mental agility equal to that of the great Muslim warriors. The entire performance is a symbolic gesture and a manifestation of their pride in Islam. And wrestling? Nobody seemed very sure, but the consensus was that these chaps probably don't get involved in the physical stuff. Try explaining that one to Dickie Davies and Giant Haystacks.

* * * * *

Fridays are the odd day out in the Muslim world, the day when most things close and even the less religious pay their respects to Mohammed. All sense of life seems to evaporate and it always reminds me of those dreary Sunday afternoons in England in the grey days when it seemed the recorded football highlights was the only permitted form of enjoyment. No better day than this to have a walk by the river and then go and find out what the Shaking Minarets are all about.

The River Zayandehrud is not the best for storing in the memory or rolling off the tongue, but the residents of Isfahan, Iran's third largest city (Mashhad is number two, since you ask) are understandably very fond of it. Particularly on a Friday, as I was to find out, when they come in the thousands to hire out a flotilla of pedalos, drink tea under the lovely arched bridge and picnic on the grass at the side of the water. This is the only Iranian city to be blessed with a river running through it and when you think about it, if you want to be taken seriously as a Beautiful City of The World, which Isfahan most definitely is, a river, a lake, or an ocean is an absolute must.

And so to the Shaking Minarets. No, not a pop group, but a little mausoleum on the outskirts of town housing the tomb of a local mystic.

The Four-Letter Countries

The name of the deceased is really of little significance here because his main claim to fame are the two minarets that point up to the sky on either side of the building. (Perhaps you remember Monty Python's Arthur Two-Sheds Jackson?) At 1 o'clock every day, in front of a gathering crowd, the caretaker shins up on to the roof, clambers into the right hand minaret and rather crudely sets about thrusting his body back and forth to the delight of the cheering onlookers. By the time he's worked himself up into a lustful frenzy the tower is rocking scarily from side to side, the bell is clanging away and all hell is being let loose. And then comes the pièce de résistance. Our hero points across to the other corner of the building where, to everybody's delight and astonishment, the other minaret is also swaying like billio. We wonder how it can be, we cheer in a controlled Islamic sort of way and then we all go away as happy as Larry.

For the first and only time during my stay in Iran, the sky then turned grey and it rained persistently for the whole afternoon. Now it really felt like a 1980s British Sunday and, by the time evening arrived, I had a throbbing headache and was convinced that Larry, the smartarse, was once again much happier than I was. What could I do to cheer myself up?

Watch BBC World on the telly? Raid the fridge and drink all the bottles of water, one after another, until not a single drop remained. Go and get a paper and read the *Iran Daily's* latest on the uranium enrichment programme? I lay back on my bed, cursed the uncomfortable Iranian pillows that were always like sacks of cement and wondered whether in fact I'd been in the country for quite long enough.

To everybody's great relief, Mr Grumpy died peacefully in his sleep and in his place Mr Happy woke up eight hours later to a clear head, an even clearer sky and the hustle and bustle of a Saturday morning in Isfahan. This was it, the last day of a long and, at times, bizarre journey around the world, and I was determined to enjoy every minute.

According to the proverb: "Isfahan is half the world" and a few hours spent relaxing in its greenery and gawping at the bewildering architecture was enough to understand why. I didn't think I had it in me to visit yet another mosque – a few weeks of squinting at squinches and pawing at parapets had seriously taken its toll – but there was something compelling about those elegant domes, the stunning blue tiles and the intricate mosaics.

I managed just one more.

All the beauty of Iran seemed to be captured in Isfahan's enormous square, the Maydan Imam, said to be three times larger than St Mark's in Venice. I sat there in the sunshine and squeezed out the last few drops of this amazing country: the domes and the minarets, the fountains and the flowers, and, as ever, the mountains in the background. It was a happy place, packed with families enjoying the pleasant surroundings, so different from the picture of Iran that has been painted for the rest of the world. Almost as if to read my mind, a voice from behind broke the silence: "Hey Mister, welcome to Iran, where you from?"

I told him and as these kind people always do, he smiled graciously. And he chuckled...

"Tell your friends to come. Tell them we are normal people. We promise not to kill them. Honest!"

* * * * *

Two hours to go before leaving for the airport and just hanging around would have made for a disappointing anti-climax. So I gave it a few minutes' thought, listed the options in my mind, narrowed it to a short list and decided on my final two missions. One of them you might be able to guess; the other, you have no chance.

It took me longer than expected to track down the first one. He was just finishing off his existing client, adding the final touches, but I only had to wait a few minutes before he gestured me into the chair. For me there is always an extra buzz of excitement attached to a haircut in a foreign country, a bit of a story guaranteed and at least the excuse of cultural difference when you go home looking like a knob, or a German.

It started a little scarily when I detected a very strong, (once) familiar smell of alcohol and saw the old chap brandishing a cut-throat razor. A man who despised the infidels, had got secretly tanked up at lunchtime and now, on what had seemed a regular Saturday afternoon, had been presented with the moment of his dreams. A westerner in his chair, no resistance, throat exposed. Dead meat.

I then saw the bottle of alcohol that he used to clean his tools and in no time at all he was scraping hair very carefully from the back of my neck. He carefully worked through what looked like the whole set of his gleaming but antiquated equipment to get the back of my head to a satisfactory Iranian standard, whatever that might be. He was toiling away behind me for what seemed an eternity and I started to get a little edgy, partly because I couldn't see what he was up to and partly because I now seriously feared what he had in mind for the rest of my barnet.

As it turned out, I need not have worried. Once he'd got the back to a military length, out came the mirror, my white cape was unclipped and stripped away and a distinguished bow confirmed that, as far as he was concerned, the job was complete. Upon payment of five dollars I was free to leave, the rest of the haircut would just have to wait until some-time next week! At least I still had an hour, enough time to get where I wanted to be.

There are three interesting bridges that cross the river in Isfahan. I asked the taxi to drop me at the one where the water flows through the arches and luckily found a vacant table on the pontoon in the corner that serves as a floating café. It was late in the afternoon, getting a little cool-er now, but the sky was still a rich shade of blue. Perfect. I collected a silver tray with teapot and glass from the small vending booth under-neath the bridge and chose the seat that faced west along the river towards the setting sun. Not a famous river, nor a particularly long one, but the beauty of water isn't measured in sizes or shapes. This journey

Iran

around the world had taught me many things, introduced different cultures, religions, food, clothing, the subtle variations from one country to the next, but, I now realised, had also encouraged me to appreciate that which is constant. Only at that moment did it occur to me that water had been an ever-present theme of this epic adventure: the mighty rivers of the Mekong and the Niger and the Tigris and those lesser-known ones in the semi-desert of Chad and the jungles of Peru. The lake in Togo and the sparkling pale green oceans of Cuba and Fiji, and, a long time ago, back at the very beginning, the incredible fjörds of northern Oman.

And now this, an unknown river in an unknown city and, in so many ways, an unknown country. My final memory would be a line of ladies sitting on the river wall, all dressed in black, the crystal clear water flowing through the arches, the sun dipping down on the Zagros mountains away in the distance. It was The Four-Letter Countries that had brought me here, nothing else, and for this, and all those other unexpected treasures, I would be forever in their debt.

The Four-Letter Countries

ALPHABET TRAVELLING:
THE RECIPE FOR A PERFECT
HOLIDAY

Ingredients: 1 bag Scrabble letters
2 dice
1 atlas

Method: Pick a tile from the bag, throw the dice, then locate a country with that initial and the corresponding number of letters. This is your destination.

If you pick an X or throw a 2, stay at home, paint the house, and try again next year.

Maybe see you in Azerbaijan.

ABOUT THE AUTHOR

David Jenkins was born where the City of Manchester Stadium stands today. Educated at Stockport Grammar, he hitchhiked to France the day he left school and has trotted the globe ever since. He has waited tables in Switzerland, sprayed crops in Israel, crewed yachts around the Pacific and his – "greatest sporting achievement" – cleaned the urinals at the prestigious Sydney Cricket Ground.

He gave it all up to become a professor in Japan and then run a business school in Rio de Janeiro before setting up his own company to deliver newspapers across Africa.

His interests include Rod Stewart, crocodiles and Manchester City. This is his first book.